THE COLD WAR

A Re-appraisal

THE
COLD WAR
A Re-appraisal

Edited by

EVAN LUARD

FREDERICK A. PRAEGER, Publishers
NEW YORK · WASHINGTON

BOOKS THAT MATTER

Published in the United States of America in 1964
by Frederick A. Praeger, Inc., Publishers
111 Fourth Avenue, New York 3, N.Y.
All rights reserved
© Thames and Hudson 1964
Library of Congress Catalog Card Number: 64-25786
Printed in Great Britain by
The Camelot Press Ltd. London and Southampton

CONTENTS

Introduction   7

Chronology 1945-1963   19

1   The Partition of Europe   45
    WILFRID KNAPP

2   The Rise of Communist Power in the Far East   62
    GEOFFREY HUDSON

3   Germany   84
    DONALD WATT

4   Berlin   120
    PHILIP WINDSOR

5   The Middle East   140
    ELIZABETH MONROE

6   South-East Asia   163
    BRIAN CROZIER

5

7 Africa   191

    MARY HOLDSWORTH

8 Latin America   220

    RAYMOND CARR

9 The Polarisation of the Communist World   243

    EDWARD CRANKSHAW

10 Polycentrism in the West   263

    MAX BELOFF

11 The Conditions of Coexistence   281

    EVAN LUARD

12 The Cold War and the Future   307

    SIR WILLIAM HAYTER

Notes   329

Index   337

INTRODUCTION

The object of this book is to survey the history of the cold war up to the present; and to consider the ways in which it may evolve in the future.

This is in many ways a favourable moment to re-examine the cold war. For that struggle has clearly arrived at a turning-point. Some indeed would claim it is already over. Others assert that it has been affected only in its inessentials, and that in its fundamental aspects it remains unmodified.

Differences on such points hinge partly on semantics. For a term so perpetually called into use, the phrase 'cold war' is remarkable for its lack of accurate definition. It could perhaps be defined as a state of intensive competition, political, economic and ideological, which yet falls below the threshold of armed conflict between states. The term could presumably be applied to any such intensive conflict within the international community. But normal usage presupposes that the two parties consist of 'Western' powers and political parties on the one hand, and 'Communist' powers and parties on the other.

'West' in this sense is a technical term which, by extension, includes those powers, in Latin America, Asia, Africa and elsewhere, which identify themselves with the purposes and principles of the Atlantic world. 'Communist' could presumably include either, or any, kind of communism currently professed. Cold war might thus in theory include some form of struggle on two fronts, between Western forces on the one hand, and two conflicting versions of the Marxist faith on the other. Equally it might be applied to a contest between the West and one only of those forces, while the other remained neutral. If, on the other hand, one protagonist of the Communist creed became in time more and more identified with the Western powers, and increasingly involved in altercation with the other, this would bring about such a transformation of the existing struggle that it could scarcely meaningfully continue to be known under the same name. One of the problems, indeed, that this volume has to consider is how far the assumptions that have gathered around a contest in which Russian communism was the main antagonist remain applicable at a time when a new version of the faith, bearing the same brand-name, has arrived to contest hegemony within the Communist world itself.

Other difficulties of definition arise. One concerns the temperature denoted. At certain times over the last fifteen years, for example in Korea in 1950-53, the cold war has not been notable for its frigidity despite the fact that at that time one of the major protagonists was still not formally engaged. In certain parts of the world even today, fighting continues between pro-Communist and anti-Communist forces. At what time do such relative alterations in temperature bring about a qualitative change to a different variety of war? Is any situation short of global conflict 'cold war'? Or do we experience periods of cold war punctuated by shorter intervals of some hotter version? Conversely, at what point does the temperature of cold war drop to that of cold peace? And can the situation even today be held to fall under the same category as during the period when the term first came into use; a period that included the absorption of the East European nations into the Communist orbit, the blockade of Berlin, the Truman doctrine, the Marshall plan and German rearmament, civil war in China, Greece, Malaya, Indo-China and elsewhere, as well as the Korean War? Finally, are the differences that remain today, over Berlin, the division of Germany, the off-shore islands, Formosa and others sufficiently different in kind from those that have existed between similar alliances in peacetime in the past to earn the designation 'war'?

Some would maintain that the feature that distinguishes the present struggle from those of the past is its ideological content. It is probably true that the identification of the two great blocs of the contemporary world with specific political doctrines is closer than any that has existed in the case of similar alliances in the past. Yet there are certain difficulties in the way of regarding the contest as primarily an ideological one. Any attempt to arrive at satisfactory definitions of the ideological positions held by the two sides must remain arbitrary and inaccurate. It could perhaps be maintained that the *minimum* content of the ideology of the Atlantic world includes a belief in the principle that governments should be chosen through a system of free elections, under a multi-party system and universal franchise, at regular intervals; in freedom of association and discussion; in freedom of the press; and in the independence of the judiciary and the rule of law (though it might be questioned how far some of these are *essential*, as opposed to concomitant, elements of the Western faith). The minimum content of the Communist creed is perhaps a belief in common ownership of the means of production, distribution and exchange; the enjoyment of dominant, usually exclusive, political power by the Communist party, as vanguard of the proletariat, including control of all communications media; and a system in which economic decisions are taken primarily, though not exclusively, through the decisions of centralised bodies, rather than of dispersed managements. But as has often been noted, a proportion of the nations that owe allegiance to the Western cause, profess and practice at home political doctrines that diverge considerably from the norm professed within that alliance. Conversely, there exist considerable differences among Communist states concerning the way in which their own political principles should be interpreted.

In addition, the attitudes and strategies of the alliances have been conditioned undeniably often by factors other than ideological conviction. It is indeed arguable that the contest has at all times been at root a power struggle between dominant nations, for which ideological explanations have merely provided a convenient, and morally appealing, rationalisation. It has derived above all from apprehensions, of both leading powers and their allies on each side, concerning their own security, believed to be threatened by the actions of the other. Certainly, a large number of the most important issues and initiatives within that struggle can be understood more easily in terms of those ambitions and apprehensions than of the ideological predilections of the two parties involved. And it would appear mainly because such apprehensions are to-day, on both sides, somewhat less acute than fifteen years ago, at least in Europe, rather than because of any shift in ideological viewpoints, that the mood of the contest appears now so different from what it was then.

This does not mean that there are not indeed senses in which the present division differs from the confrontation between rival alliances in previous ages. The fact that the struggle is world-wide does not in itself represent a fundamental difference. Even the power struggles of nineteenth-century Europe were fought out in every corner of the globe. But the association of political alliances with political principles and philosophies has certainly in some measure transformed the nature of the struggle. For one of its effects is that each side is able to enjoy the support of a fairly substantial number of adherents within the territory of the other; a situation almost never encountered until today. Appeals for the support of outside powers may be made as much in terms of political principle as of national advantage. Relationships based on purely national self-interests thus become intertwined, in a complex interaction, with other factors of a less material nature.

But if the basis of the struggle is not primarily ideological, what are its root causes? Does the cold war derive directly from specific issues, East Europe, Germany, Berlin, Indo-China and Formosa? If so, how is it that, though not a single one among these is significantly nearer solution than ten years ago, the entire character of the cold war is so indisputably different from what it was then? Or are the conflicts that have emerged over these only the symptoms of more deep-rooted causes? And if ideology is only a rationalisation, what are those deeper causes? Are the *moods* of alliances an independent factor whose relation to specific issues and ideological concepts is only marginal and haphazard? Do they, in this case, derive partly from vague suspicions and dim tribal memories, inherited from thirty years earlier, or even from the previous century? How far can the changes that have occurred in them today be attributed to the rising standard of living in the Soviet Union; to the increasing power of China; to improved communication; to strategic immunity; or other factors?

Perhaps there are no simple answers to such questions. But certainly there are a number of developments since the period when the cold war first broke out which have transformed the relationships within the two blocs, and have posed some of the problems raised by the account presented in this volume.

First, the strategic balance has been transformed. *Between* the alliances, the development on either side of an inter-continental nuclear capacity, already, or very shortly to be, invulnerable, has meant that in many ways the balance has become more stable than in earlier times. The previous situation, in which a preponderance of nuclear power was faced by a preponderance of conventional forces, each arousing apprehension that it might be employed to exploit the advantage possessed in its own field, has been replaced by one in which each side has sought to become equipped to reply in kind to any threat of whatever nature. On the one hand, the leading powers of each alliance have attempted to increase the scope of deterrence by declaring they would meet even a conventional attack with a nuclear rejoinder. On the other, the dangers the so-called stalemate could represent in encouraging action on a smaller scale has had the effect that there are increasing attempts to arrive at equilibrium even in the conventional field alone.

Equally, *within* the two alliances, a totally different balance of interest has arisen. The European and Chinese partners, neither of whom can yet match the invulnerable striking-power of their leaders, have become anxious to redress this situation. Yet paradoxically, despite their nuclear vulnerability, because they are anxious to preserve the deterrent capacity of the nuclear weapons their alliance disposes of, and because they remain today somewhat more militant in mood than their major partners, they are even more anxious than these that the strategies of their alliances should be uninhibited in reliance on a policy of nuclear deterrence. Each has sought to develop the basis of an independent nuclear power. And each is less than at any former time ready to accept a position of subordination or dependence over strategic policy. As a result there is an increasing division of strategic interest among the *partners* of each alliance; and increasingly a common interest among their invulnerable leaders. One of the problems that arises, therefore, is how far this situation may affect the future development of relations between the blocs as a whole.

Secondly, in Europe at least, the arena where the conflict originally was mainly concentrated, there exists today a stability that was never known in the years immediately after the war. This is partly the result merely of habituation. But the consequence is that, except perhaps among one or two of the most deeply interested parties, there is now little inclination to overturn the *status quo* on either side. In the early years of the conflict (as Mr Knapp, Mr Windsor and Mr Watt show in their contributions below) the Soviet Union appears to have hoped that, as some of their holy books foretold, the catalyst of war, or of economic crisis, might be the stimulus of revolution in certain countries of the West, above all Germany. Conversely, the West continued to hope, and to demand, until well into the fifties that the régimes absorbed under Communist rule in Eastern Europe might be displaced there. For long both wished to bring about the reversal of the policies followed by the other within their own halves of Germany. And it is the occasional revival of threats to the *status quo*, for example in Berlin, that in recent years has principally served to revive the acrimonies of earlier years. But today the hopes of change have been frustrated so long that they no longer possess any great dynamic power within the body politic of Europe. There is increasing readiness to coexist with the *status quo*. And the accomplishment of this stability in the most sensitive frontier area of the cold war has contributed, perhaps more than any other factor, to its reduced intensity today. How far, therefore, is that increased stability a permanent factor, and how far, even if it subsists, may it be replaced by new instabilities outside Europe?

Thirdly, there are the changes that have resulted, partly as a result, from the loosening cohesion within the two alliances. Less acute dangers demand less rigid discipline. Europe, increasingly united by cultural and institutional links, and increasingly conscious of its growing economic power has become (as Professor Beloff shows in his account) more and more conscious that its interests are not always identical with those of the United States and (even apart from its more extreme manifestations in the policies of General de Gaulle) has come to demand a role of greater independence in the coalition of the Western powers. In the East, (as Mr Crankshaw demonstrates) China similarly challenges the hegemony of the Soviet Union within the Communist world; and equally feels that the Soviet Union may sometimes neglect its own interests in dealing with the West. In both cases economic integration of some partners, within the Community and Comecon, tends to harden the barriers between those allies enclosed and those without. In both cases, strategic differences accentuate political. In both cases, the leaders of each group are increasingly apprehensive about the spread of nuclear and political power to lesser, and perhaps less responsible, allies. Will this mean that each alliance will find increasing difficulty in formulating united and coherent strategies in relation to the other?

Fourthly, there are the changes arising from the decline in ideological fervour within each group. In the late forties and early fifties, whether or not as a result of purely national differences, ideological enthusiasm on both sides was raised to an intensity that it is difficult now to recall. Each tended to assume that the political complexion of the post-war world it had battled to create would largely mirror its own political predilections. While the United States, though ready and anxious to withdraw to its own frontiers once more, none the less tended to assume that the past struggle would have been largely in vain if the world had not been once more made safe for democracy in the process; the Soviet Union apparently believed that large parts of Europe might quickly become ready for the Communist millennium. From the mid-fifties there has been a steady deflation of evangelistic passion. The dissolution of the Comintern in 1956 roughly coincided with the recognition by the United States administration that the liberation of East Europe was not an enforceable policy. But this trend has not taken place in equal proportions in all sections of each alliance. While in the earlier period it was the leaders of each group which were the most militant and uncompromising in their attitudes to the other, sometimes having to be restrained by apprehensive allies (as in the flight of Mr Attlee to Washington in 1951, or the journey of Chou En-lai to Europe in 1957), today it is, on the contrary, the leaders who are the most anxious to reach mutual, and sometimes private, accommodations; while it is their allies who represent the most conservative forces, anxious to restrain the enthusiasm of their less inhibited leaders for reconciliation (so that Mr Khrushchev has sometimes been held back by fears of encouraging support for Chinese views, and Mr Kennedy, through fear of encouraging support in Germany for French attitudes). West Germany has denounced 'the spirit of Geneva'.

China has denounced 'the spirit of Camp David'. While East Germany has a vital interest in encouraging a tough Soviet line on Berlin, West Germany has the same in relation to Western attitudes. Is it possible, therefore, that in the future the main protagonists of the cold war hitherto, now, increasingly, ideologically indifferent, geographically remote and strategically secure, will be more and more ready to retreat again within their own borders, while the intensity of the struggle will be sustained more and more by those who have hitherto been the junior partners?

Next, there is the change which has come about through the rise of new nations all over the world, and the consequent shift in the political centre of gravity of the world. At the time when the cold war opened, there were only just over fifty members of the United Nations. Today there are over 110. While in its first fifteen years the contest was overwhelmingly centred on European problems, especially that of Germany, today it is increasingly centred in Asia, Africa and Latin America. Yet the inhabitants of those areas themselves have shown themselves (as the contributions of Mr Crozier and Miss Monroe, Mrs Holdsworth and Mr Carr demonstrate) largely indifferent to the rivalries of the Euratlantic world; they have shown hostility towards attempts to implicate them in that struggle. While at first contested, even denounced by Western and Communist leaders alike, this attitude is today increasingly accepted by both the main protagonists. But the emergent countries have today become immersed in new (or old) rivalries of their own, sometimes involving armed conflict, which are only marginally related to ideological issues. Many of these, the conflict between India and Pakistan, Israel and the Arabs, Egypt and Saudi Arabia, Algeria and Morocco, Indonesia and Malaysia, Somalia and Ethiopia, and the innumerable petty disputes of Latin America, have retained much of their original intensity, even while that of the cold war has faded. At the same time new ideological struggles have arisen within those regions – revolutionary nationalist republicanism against revolutionary traditionalist monarchy in the Middle East, radical revolutionary *Fidelismo* against conservative middle-class constitutionalism (or militarism) in Latin America, cautious Francophile negritude against radical Anglophone multi-racialism in Africa – that appear to them far more important than the ideological dichotomies of the Atlantic world. These may contain the seeds of new cold wars of their own, employing concepts wholly different from those of the old one. Yet while the power struggles of Europe and North America may remain of little interest to such countries, those countries may themselves remain of importance, strategically or politically, to the super-powers of the north. What, therefore, will be the shape of the political and ideological alignments that emerge within the new world arising beyond the borders of traditional great power supremacy; and can these remain unrelated to the political doctrines and influence of the dominant world powers?

Finally, there is the most fundamental of all the developments of the modern world: the rapidly increasing economic division between the more and the less developed regions of the world. This is made more dangerous in that it tends to coincide with another division of the world, under the pressures of inevitable economic and technological forces, into large-scale continental or sub-continental groups. This increasingly affects not only the political organisation but the loyalties of the members of each group; and may therefore in time, if new factors do not supervene, lead to the development of an intense regional competition, a continentalism, as powerful and as divisive as the nationalism it succeeds. It is possible that certain of the ideological faiths within the existing world, for example that variety of the Communist creed proclaimed by China, may, and may increasingly, make a deliberate appeal to such divisions. One problem to be considered, therefore, is the effect of such a development on the existing cold war. Will the Soviet Union increasingly come to be regarded as a

have-power, confronted with ever-growing demands on its bene-
ficence by those less fortunate? Will Communist and anti-
Communist creeds increasingly compete above all as generous
benefactors or rival practitioners of rapid development? Will the
world once more become divided, as thirty years ago, between
status quo and anti-*status quo* forces? Finally, is there a danger of the
emergence of a new cold war, more profoundly divisive than any
that has so far existed, in which the divisions of ideology corres-
pond, as they have never done before, with the economic class
interests of the nations who uphold them, and may perhaps
divide the world not only by continent, but by race, and even
colour too?

All these trends must inevitably exercise a profound influence
on the existing cold war. And the most fundamental problem of
all those that arise therefore is how far, in these circumstances, the
cold war in the future will resemble that of the past. The main
object of this book is rather to recount the past than speculate
about the future. But sometimes a consideration of the past may
serve also to help confront the future. It may, for example, help
us to determine how far the assumptions that have prevailed in
previous decades will continue to hold good in the future.

Although arranged largely on a regional basis, because of the
regular migration of the cold war to new areas as these have become politically important, the book none the less follows a fairly
consistent chronological progression. The first chapter therefore
describes the emergence of the struggle in the immediate post-war
period, and the gradual hardening of the division between the two
blocs. The greater part of the book consists of an examination of
specific issues and areas that have become the subject of dispute,
undertaken by acknowledged experts in these fields. Each is
designed to outline the main course of events in the area concerned since 1945, to describe the principal issues that remain, to
consider the basic interests involved for either side, and to consider the way the situation may evolve in the future. The next

chapters describe the factors that have emerged to alter the distribution of power in both Eastern and Western blocs during the course of the last few years, and to consider the impact of these developments on the future of the cold war. A final chapter presents a general survey of the possible future course of the conflict.

A number of the chapters are based on papers delivered to a seminar in international relations at St Antony's College, Oxford. All have been rewritten for the purposes of this book. And the entire volume is designed to be read as a self-contained history of the cold war to date, considered with special relation to its possible course of evolution in the future.

EVAN LUARD

St Antony's College
Oxford.

CHRONOLOGY OF THE COLD WAR 1945-1963

1945   5 JANUARY   Lublin Committee recognised by Soviet Union as provisional Government of Poland. US and Britain continue to recognise the Polish Government in London.

11 FEBRUARY   Yalta Agreement. Soviet entry into the Japanese war, Allied Control Council for Germany, Reparations Commission, more broadly based Polish Government, and Council of Foreign Ministers agreed. Disagreement on future régimes in East Europe, and extent of reparations from Germany. Agreement reached between Greek Government and ELAS-EAM for end of Greek Civil War.

MARCH   Soviet Government demands revision of Treaty with Turkey on régime in Turkish Straits. Turkey refuses. Soviet Government denounces Treaty.

APRIL   Treaty of mutual assistance between Soviet Union and Lublin Government. President Roosevelt dies; succeeded by Vice-President Truman. Argentine Government of Peron accepted as member of UN against strong protests from Soviet Union.

6 MAY   Allied victory in Europe.

8 MAY   Cancellation of Lend Lease by US Government. On strong protest by Soviet Union, decision reversed.

26 MAY   Mr Harry Hopkins flies to Moscow to plead for broadening of Polish Government.

JUNE–SEPTEMBER   Soviet requests for the Dodecanese and Trusteeship over Libya rejected by Western powers.

29 JUNE   Polish Provisional Government of national unity recognised by Soviet Union, US and UK.

15 JULY–2 AUGUST   Potsdam Conference. Agreement on many subjects, but deadlock on elections in East Europe, disposal of Italian colonies and increased Soviet rights in Turkish states.

AUGUST   Soviet Union joins war against Japan. Occupies Korea north of 38th Parallel. Communist administration in North Korea established.

6–9 AUGUST   First atomic bombs dropped on Japan. Japan surrenders.

16 AUGUST   Mr Churchill denounces 'police governments' established in East Europe and declares that 'a tragedy on a prodigious scale is unfolding itself behind the iron curtain which divides Europe in twain'.

20 AUGUST   Lend Lease again cancelled. Soviet Union protests.

OCTOBER–DECEMBER   Chinese Nationalist Government protests against Soviet failure to evacuate Manchuria. Sporadic fighting between Nationalists and Communists in North China and Manchuria.

2 OCTOBER   Breakdown of Council of Foreign Ministers meeting in London on European peace treaties.

2 NOVEMBER   Provisional Government in Hungary recognised by US and UK.

10 NOVEMBER   Albanian Government recognised by Soviet Union, US and UK.

DECEMBER   Soviet Union announces she will evacuate Manchuria by May.

16–26 DECEMBER   Council of Foreign Ministers agrees on preparation of peace treaties in Europe, Far East Commission and Allied Control Council for Japan, policies for China and Korea, and broadening of Rumanian and Bulgarian Governments. Slight broadening of Rumanian Government results.

1946   19 JANUARY   Iran complains to Security Council concerning failure of Soviet Union to evacuate Azerbaidjan. Supported by US and Britain. Soviet Union brings counter-charges against presence of British and French troops in Syria and Lebanon, and British troops in Greece and Indonesia. Later uses veto and walks out of Security Council.

5 FEBRUARY   US and Britain recognise reconstituted Rumanian Government. Remain dissatisfied over Bulgarian Government.

MARCH   Mr Churchill at Fulton denounces 'police governments of East Europe' and Communist Fifth Column which represents 'growing challenge and peril to civilisation', and calls for alliance of English-speaking peoples to meet this danger.

24 MARCH   Soviet Union agrees to evacuate Azerbaidjan by 6 May.

31 MARCH   Greek elections supervised by Western powers. Soviet Union refuses to participate. Victory for Populist (Royalist) party.

APRIL   US offers four-power treaty, including demilitarisation of Germany and her exclusion from all alliances. Soviet Union refuses.

21 APRIL   Socialist Unity Party (SED) established in Soviet zone of Germany.

MAY   Pro-Communist Government in Kurdistan established.

3 MAY   General Clay announces delivery of reparations from US zone to Soviet Union to be halted.

JUNE   Treaty of alliance between Soviet Union and Nationalist China implementing Yalta provisions.

21

11 JULY US offers to merge her zone with other zones. Accepted by Britain, 30 July.

SEPTEMBER Serious fighting between Greek Government forces and Communist guerrillas in North Greece breaks out.

SEPTEMBER–OCTOBER Greece complains to Security Council about support by Yugoslavia, Albania and Bulgaria for guerrilla activity on her northern borders. UN commission set up to investigate.

OCTOBER Elections in Bulgaria lead to absolute majority for Communist party. Declared unfair by US and Britain.

NOVEMBER Elections in Rumania, denounced by opposition parties and US and British Governments as unfair; lead to return of National Democratic Front Government, including Communists. Later Communist and Social Democrat parties fuse and take over government.

NOVEMBER–DECEMBER Council of Foreign Ministers reaches large measure of agreement on European peace treaties. Deputies asked to prepare treaty with Germany.

1947 JANUARY US withdraws from truce organisation in China. Deadlock in talks between Nationalists and Communists.

1 JANUARY Bizonia, an economic union of US and British Zones in Germany set up.

19 JANUARY Communist-organised elections in Poland bring about defeat of Peasant Party. Mikolajczyk flees to West. Western Governments accuse Soviet Union of breach of Yalta Agreement.

FEBRUARY Nationalists order Communist delegation to leave Nanking. Resumption of fighting between Communists and Nationalists.

MARCH President Truman announces that US will take over British commitments for economic and defence assistance to

Greece and Turkey (Truman Doctrine). UK complaint against Albania over mining of British warship in Corfu Channel. Defeated by Soviet veto in Security Council.

MARCH–APRIL Foreign Ministers' talks on reparations and establishment of united German Government break down.

MAY Communists expelled from government in France and Italy.

JUNE Marshall Plan announced. Rejected by Soviet Union. Czechoslovakia accepts, but later, after Soviet pressure, declines to join.

JULY Article by George Kennan on 'containment' of Soviet Union in *Foreign Affairs*.

AUGUST Elections in Hungary bring about defeat of Smallholders Party. Coalition of Communists and Social Democrats formed.

SEPTEMBER Cominform (Communist Information Bureau) established.

OCTOBER Bulgaria, Yugoslavia and Albania condemned in UN for action on northern borders of Greece. UN Special Commission for the Balkans established. Communist Government set up in mountains of North Greece.

NOVEMBER–DECEMBER Further meeting of foreign ministers on Greece and Austria. Soviet Union proposes withdrawal of foreign troops from Germany. Western powers reaffirm need for military support of West Germany.

30 DECEMBER King Michael of Rumania abdicates.

1948 FEBRUARY Discussions between Western powers on future of Germany and international authority for Ruhr.

FEBRUARY–MARCH Government crisis in Czechoslovakia. Soviet Deputy Foreign Minister visits Prague. Coalition government replaced by Communist government. Jan Masaryk dies.

23

MARCH Brussels Treaty between Britain, France, Belgium and the Netherlands.

MARCH–JUNE Chinese Communists win important victories in North China.

20 MARCH Soviet Union withdraws from Allied Control Council in protest against Western discussions on Germany.

APRIL South-East Asian youth conference at Calcutta, followed later by armed uprisings in Malaya, Philippines, Burma and Indonesia, and parts of India.

7–20 JUNE Western powers at London conference announce joint policy for Western zones; establishment of Constituent Assembly to prepare federal constitution and currency reforms in Western zones and West Berlin.

23 JUNE Conference of Foreign Ministers of Soviet Union and East European Governments declare London conference a violation of Potsdam Agreement, demand four-power action to establish all-German government, and ensure demilitarisation, joint control of Ruhr, and continuation of reparations. All rail traffic between Berlin and Western zones cut off.

JUNE Yugoslavia expelled from Cominform.

I JULY Soviet representative withdraws from Berlin Kommandatura.

END JULY Counter-blockade of Soviet Zone by Western powers. Soviet authorities stop all road and water traffic to Berlin. Supplies maintained by air.

AUGUST World Peace Movement started. Final breakdown of talks of UN Military Staff Committee for creation of Security Council force.

1949 14 JANUARY US State Department announce support for a North Atlantic Pact.

28 JANUARY Soviet Foreign Minister denounces Treaty of

Brussels, Marshall Aid and proposal for North Atlantic treaty as anti-Soviet, and a violation of UN charter.

4 APRIL   North Atlantic treaty signed.

8 APRIL   Occupation Statute granting large measures of self-government to the Western zones promulgated.

28 APRIL   Comecon established to promote economic integration between Soviet Union and East European countries.

MAY–JUNE   Foreign Ministers again fail to reach agreement over unification of Germany and régime in Berlin.

5 MAY   Four-Power agreement on raising of Berlin blockade and counter-blockade.

12 MAY   Basic Law, establishing federal constitution in Germany, approved by Western military governors.

JULY   Soviet Union explodes atomic bomb. Military government of Japan abolished by US.

AUGUST   Elections in West Germany and establishment of West German Government under Chancellor Adenauer.

1 OCTOBER   People's Republic of China established.

7 OCTOBER   German Democratic Republic established in East Germany.

1949–1951   Series of purges in East Europe including execution or dismissal of Communist leaders in almost every state of the region, accompanied by attacks on the Church and imprisonment of prelates in those countries.

1950   JANUARY   Soviet Union leaves Security Council and other UN organs in protest against refusal to award China seat to Communist China.

MAY   West Germany invited to become associate member of Council of Europe. Schuman Plan for coal and steel pool in West Europe announced.

24–25 JUNE Invasion of South Korea by North Korean troops. Security Council call on members to 'furnish such assistance to the republic of Korea as may be necessary to repel armed attack and to restore international peace and security in the area'. US troops despatched from Japan.

1 AUGUST Soviet representative returns to Security Council and, as Chairman for the month, prevents effective discussion of Korean problem.

SEPTEMBER Western powers agree to end state of war with Germany and announce they will study means for the 'participation of the German Federal Republic in the common defence of Europe'.

END SEPTEMBER UN troops arrive at 38th parallel in Korea.

OCTOBER Pleven plan for establishment of European Defence Community put forward. Uniting for Peace resolution circumventing veto in Security Council passed by UN General Assembly.

1 OCTOBER China warns that she will not 'stand idly by' if UN troops cross 38th parallel.

5 OCTOBER Assembly resolution authorises UN troops to cross 38th parallel to 'ensure conditions of stability throughout Korea'. China repeats threat that she will not remain indifferent if UN forces advance towards Yalu River.

NOVEMBER–DECEMBER Soviet Union denounces plan for rearmament of Germany as 'breach of Potsdam Agreement and British and French Treaties with Soviet Union'. Proposes four-power conference for demilitarisation of Germany.

8 NOVEMBER General MacArthur confirms that Chinese troops are engaged in Korea.

NOVEMBER Chinese representative received at UN. Refuses cease-fire unless US forces withdraw from Korea, Formosa and elsewhere in Far East.

14 DECEMBER General Assembly appoints cease-fire committee, which puts forward new proposals.

19 DECEMBER NATO Council approves West German participation in integrated European armed forces under NATO supreme commander.

31 DECEMBER China launches new offensive across 38th Parallel.

1951 17 JANUARY China rejects UN proposals, but later suggests cease-fire followed by negotiations for withdrawal of all foreign troops, US withdrawal from Formosa and other Far East problems.

31 JANUARY China condemned as an aggressor in UN Assembly.

1 MARCH-JUNE Meeting of Foreign Ministers' deputies fails to agree agenda for meeting of Foreign Ministers.

MAY US conducts successful experiments in hydrogen weapons.

JUNE Mr Malik in broadcast in New York proposes cease-fire in Korea.

JULY Japanese Government permitted to establish national police reserve of 75,000.

SEPTEMBER Japanese Peace Treaty signed at San Francisco. Soviet Union attends the conference, but refuses to sign the treaty. No representative of China invited.

3 SEPTEMBER Western Foreign Ministers announce readiness to amend occupation statute to enable Germany to participate in EDC.

17 OCTOBER Greece and Turkey join NATO.

26 OCTOBER US embargoes shipment of strategic materials to any nation threatening US security.

1952 JANUARY Western powers propose comprehensive conventional disarmament, subject to adequate inspection. Forces of US, Soviet Union and China to be limited to 1½ million, UK and France to 7–800,000. Soviet Union demands flat-rate cut by one-third.

MARCH–AUGUST Soviet Union proposes four-power discussions on formation of all-German government, withdrawal of foreign forces within a year. Germany to be permitted armed forces necessary for her defence, but not to join alliance against a power which took part in the war against her. Western powers demand free elections throughout country as condition for signing peace treaty and establishment of all-German government.

27 MAY EDC agreed subject to ratification.

1953 5 MARCH Death of Stalin. Mr Malenkov becomes Soviet Premier.

11 MAY Mr Churchill calls for 'conference at highest level . . . between the leading powers'.

17 JUNE Rising in East Berlin and East Germany. Korean Armistice signed.

15 JULY Western powers propose meeting of Foreign Ministers to discuss reunification of Germany and Austrian treaty.

AUGUST–SEPTEMBER Western governments demand free elections in all Germany. Soviet Union proposes provisional German Government composed of representatives of West and East German Governments and four-power conference on Germany, and conference with China to discuss reduction of tension.

20 AUGUST Soviet Union explodes hydrogen bomb.

NOVEMBER Soviet note attacks Western powers for uniting against her at Foreign Ministers' meeting, for refusal to agree to five-power conference, for rearming West Germany, and planting bases all over Europe and Middle East.

DECEMBER   Agreement to hold conference on Berlin, German reunification and Austrian Treaty the following year.

1954 JANUARY   Berlin Conference. No agreement on future of Germany, Austria and European security. Agreement to hold conference at Geneva to settle Korean question and discuss Indo-China. Disarmament to be discussed by five-power sub-committee of nuclear powers.

JANUARY–MARCH   Vietminh forces win series of successes in Indo-China. Garrison of Dien Bien Phu threatened.

29 MARCH   Mr Dulles declares that the imposition of the Communist system on South-East Asia 'should be met by united action'.

EARLY APRIL   Mr Dulles proposes joint warning to China to cease supplying aid to Indo-China under threat of naval and air action against Chinese coast. Later flies to London and Paris. British Government refuse to join in military intervention or joint warning.

1 MAY   Soviet inter-continental bomber on display in Moscow.

APRIL–JULY   Geneva Conference. No agreement on Korea. US refuses direct contact with Chinese representatives. Armistice agreements for Laos, Cambodia and Vietnam pending elections in 1956. Withdrawal of Communists from Cambodia and from all except two north-east provinces in Laos.

24 JULY   Soviet Union denounces EDC and calls for conference to discuss system of collective security.

9 AUGUST   Balkan pact between Greece, Turkey and Yugoslavia.

30 AUGUST   French Assembly rejects EDC.

SEPTEMBER   Manila Treaty for Seato signed by US, UK, France, Australia, New Zealand, Pakistan, Philippines and Thailand.

SEPTEMBER–DECEMBER Chinese attacks on off-shore islands. Tachen Island evacuated by Nationalists.

3 OCTOBER Paris agreement for Western European Union, as alternative to EDC. West German rearmament agreed subject to renunciation of certain types of weapons.

23 OCTOBER Occupation of West Germany ended. Occupying powers reserve rights over Berlin and German reunification.

DECEMBER Soviet Union threatens denunciation of treaties with Britain and France if Paris agreements are ratified. NATO accepts in principle adoption of tactical atomic weapons in Europe.

1955 JANUARY US Senate authorises use of US troops where necessary to secure Formosa, the Pescadores, and 'related positions'.

8 FEBRUARY Mr Malenkov succeeded by Mr Bulganin.

24 FEBRUARY Baghdad pact between Turkey and Iraq.

APRIL Britain joins Baghdad Pact.

15 APRIL Austrian Government after discussi... ‧ ‧ ‧ promises to refrain from joining military alliance, or granting military bases on its territory.

18 APRIL Bandung Conference. Chou En-lai offers to discuss ways of reducing tension in Far East with US representatives.

5 MAY WEU established.

7 MAY Soviet Union denounces treaties with Britain and France.

9 MAY West Germany admitted to NATO.

10 MAY New Soviet disarmament proposal, accepting many points of Western proposals, accepting simultaneous reductions and controls, and offering observation posts on airfields

and communication centres to guard against surprise attack.

14 MAY   Warsaw treaty signed.

15 MAY   Austrian State treaty signed, providing for Austrian neutrality and withdrawal of foreign troops.

27 MAY   Soviet leaders visit Belgrade. Normalisation of inter-state relations between Soviet Union and Yugoslavia agreed.

JULY   Political discussions open between US and Chinese representatives. Have continued intermittently ever since in Geneva and Warsaw.

18–21 JULY   Summit Conference at Geneva. President Eisenhower proposes 'open skies'. Mr Eden proposes demilitarised zone on East-West border. Mr Bulganin proposes collective security treaty.

SEPTEMBER   Chancellor Adenauer visits Moscow. Diplomatic relations between Soviet Union and West Germany established. Pakistan joins Baghdad pact.

27 SEPTEMBER   President Nasser announces agreement to purchase arms from Czechoslovakia.

OCTOBER–NOVEMBER   Meeting of Foreign Ministers fails to reach agreement on measures to implement summit directive. Soviet Union demands collective security treaty. West demand German reunification on basis of free elections, as first step.

NOVEMBER   Persia joins Baghdad pact.

DECEMBER   Mr Bulganin and Mr Khrushchev visit India, Burma and Afghanistan and deliver anti-Western speeches there.

1956   JANUARY   East German forces accepted within Warsaw Pact.

JANUARY–MARCH   Mr Bulganin, in correspondence with

President Eisenhower, insists on right to participate in Middle East settlement.

13 FEBRUARY   Soviet Foreign Minister warns that despatch of US and British troops to Middle East could represent 'gross violation of the UN charter' and create a threat to the peace.

14 FEBRUARY   Mr Khrushchev makes secret speech denouncing Stalin.

18 APRIL   Cominform dissolved.

18–27 APRIL   Soviet leaders visit UK. Interest in Middle East declared on both sides. Agreement to increase cultural exchanges.

14 MAY   Soviet Union announces reduction of conventional forces by 1·2 million men within a year.

15–20 MAY   French Prime Minister and Foreign Minister visit Moscow. Agreement to increase cultural exchanges.

20 JUNE   Normalisation of inter-Party relations between Soviet Union and Yugoslavia, with each 'free to determine its own road to socialism'.

28 JUNE   Poznan riots in Poland. Mr Gomulka readmitted to Polish United Workers' (Communist) Party.

18 JULY   Rakosi removed as First Secretary of Communist party in Hungary.

19 JULY   US and Britain cancel Aswan Dam loans because of Czech arms deal.

26 JULY   Nationalisation of Suez Canal.

SEPTEMBER–OCTOBER   Exchange of notes between Soviet Union and British and French Governments on Middle East situation.

23 SEPTEMBER   In Security Council Soviet Union vetoes 18-Power proposal for joint operation of Suez Canal.

20 OCTOBER Mr Gomulka re-elected Secretary General of Polish United Workers' Party in presence of Soviet leaders. Marshal Rokossovsky dismissed as Minister of Defence.

20–22 OCTOBER Demonstrations in Budapest.

24 OCTOBER Mr Nagy, previously expelled from Communist Party, reappointed Prime Minister of Hungary.

28 OCTOBER Mr Nagy promises general amnesty and negotiations for withdrawal of Soviet troops, but rejects UN intervention. Movement of Soviet troops reported. Western powers propose resolution accusing Soviet Union of violently repressing rights of Hungarian people.

29 OCTOBER–NOVEMBER 1 Suez expedition by Israeli, French and British forces. Soviet Union demands new Bandung Conference to bring about withdrawal.

30 OCTOBER Budapest radio reports withdrawal of Soviet troops. Soviet Government announces readiness to discuss problem of stationing troops in all East European countries.

1 NOVEMBER Nagy Government renounces Warsaw Pact and declares Hungary's neutrality. Soviet troops invade Budapest in force.

2 NOVEMBER Mr Nagy appeals to UN. Soviet Union vetoes Security Council resolution by US, Britain and France.

3–5 NOVEMBER Soviet Union threatens use of rockets to 'crush aggression in the Middle East'. Proposes to US joint action to counter Anglo-French aggression in Egypt.

4 NOVEMBER Mr Nagy overthrown as Prime Minister. New Government under Kadar formed.

5 NOVEMBER Britain and France agree to withdraw from Egypt.

17 DECEMBER Agreement between Soviet Union and Poland, reaffirming Polish-Soviet alliance on basis of 'non-interference

in internal affairs' but confirming 'temporary stationing of Soviet military units in Polish territory' by mutual agreement.

1957   5 JANUARY   Eisenhower doctrine announced. Confirms US readiness to secure Middle Eastern countries against 'armed aggression from any nation controlled by international communism'.

FEBRUARY   Soviet Foreign Minister suggests joint four-power declaration on Middle East including renunciation of arms shipments, of foreign bases, and foreign intervention. Rejected by Western powers.

MARCH–MAY   Correspondence between Eisenhower and Bulganin on measures against surprise attack. Britain proposes test ban.

21–24 MARCH   At Bermuda Conference between Eisenhower and Macmillan, US agrees to participate in military committee of Baghdad Pact.

25 MARCH   Treaty of Rome establishing European Economic Community signed.

APRIL   Crisis in Jordan. US 7th Fleet despatched to Beirut. Soviet Union protests at 'open military demonstration against countries of the Arab East'.

20 APRIL   Soviet Note suggests four-power declaration on Middle East, and stresses the danger of stationing nuclear weapons in West Europe or allowing them to West Germany.

JUNE–JULY   Soviet Union proposes two- or three-year moratorium on nuclear tests under supervision of international commission, discussions on Eden plan for demilitarised zone in Central Europe and talks on general European security plan.

JULY   Syria accuses Turkey of planning counter-revolution in Syria. Soviet Union proposes Summit Meeting.

JULY–DECEMBER   Introduction of tactical atomic weapons in Europe.

1 OCTOBER   First Soviet sputnik launched.

2 OCTOBER   Rapacki plan for nuclear-free zone in Germany, Poland and Czechoslovakia.

DECEMBER   NATO adopts US plan for supply of intermediate range missiles to member states.

1958   JANUARY   Bulganin proposes new Summit Meeting to discuss world problems. Western powers announce they will join only if there is adequate preparation by Foreign Ministers.

12 JANUARY   President Eisenhower proposes that Soviet Union and US should renounce veto in Security Council, agree on use of space for peaceful purposes only and seek reunification of Germany through all-German elections.

27 JANUARY   US-Soviet Union cultural agreement providing for exchange of broadcasts, films, theatre-groups, orchestras, scientific missions, sports teams and students signed in Moscow. Renewed at 2-year intervals ever since.

27 MARCH   Mr Khrushchev replaces Mr Bulganin as Prime Minister.

31 MARCH   Soviet Union announces unilateral suspension of nuclear tests for six months.

MAY   Civil war in Lebanon. Army *coup* in Algeria brings General de Gaulle to power in France.

JULY   Revolution in Iraq. US troops sent to Lebanon, British troops to Jordan. Mr Khrushchev suggests Summit Meeting to consider Middle East crisis.

JULY–AUGUST   Conference of East-West experts in Geneva produces plan for world-wide control of nuclear tests through control posts all over the world, including Soviet Union and US.

2 JULY   US Atomic Energy Act amended to make possible supply of nuclear knowledge to countries which have already

made 'substantial progress' in the development of nuclear weapons.

31 JULY   Mr Khrushchev unexpectedly visits Peking to discuss differences over Middle East crisis, off-shore islands and Communist policy.

AUGUST   Intensive bombardment of off-shore islands from Chinese mainland. US naval forces convoy nationalist reinforcements to the islands and Mr Dulles announces US forces might intervene in the defence of the islands in case of attack. Mr Khrushchev declares 'an attack on the Chinese People's Republic would be an attack on the Soviet Union'.

31 OCTOBER   Parallel negotiations begin in Geneva for test ban agreement, and measures against surprise attack.

10 NOVEMBER   Mr Khrushchev announces Soviet Union will hand over her functions in Berlin to East German Government.

27 NOVEMBER   Soviet Union repeats this declaration in Notes to Western powers, declaring that the situation in West Berlin can no longer be tolerated. Offers to negotiate either on demilitarised free city of West Berlin, or German Peace Treaty. No move will be made for six months.

14 DECEMBER   Three Western powers announce they intend to stay in West Berlin. Declare they will not negotiate under threat, but offer to discuss questions of Germany and European security.

1959   10 JANUARY   Soviet Union addresses invitation to all nations who took part in war with Germany to peace conference. Attach draft peace treaty incorporating proposals for free city of West Berlin, withdrawal of foreign troops from Germany within a year and exclusion of West and East Germany from any military pact.

15 JANUARY   Franco-Soviet cultural agreement.

FEBRUARY   Western powers propose four-power conference.

21 FEBRUARY–3 MARCH Mr Macmillan visits Soviet Union. Communiqué suggests possibility of controlled zone in Central Europe.

7 MARCH France announces she is withdrawing her fleet from NATO command.

15 APRIL Mr Dulles replaced as US Secretary of State by Mr Herter.

MAY–AUGUST Foreign Ministers' Conference in Geneva, with representatives of West and East Germany. Western powers offer to limit forces in West Berlin in return for guarantee of free access. No agreement.

7 MAY General de Gaulle declares he will not allow NATO nuclear weapons on French territory unless France shares in their control. Later US fighters and fighter bombers from France are deployed in Britain and West Germany.

JUNE–JULY Visits by Mr Kozlov to US and Mr Nixon to Soviet Union.

15–27 SEPTEMBER Mr Khrushchev visits US. Has informal discussions with President Eisenhower at Camp David. At UN proposes 'general and complete disarmament' within four years.

END SEPTEMBER Mr Khrushchev visits Peking. Publicly urges moderation on China in external policies.

NOVEMBER–DECEMBER Treaty for demilitarisation of Antarctic agreed and signed.

20 NOVEMBER Agreement establishing EFTA signed.

21–24 NOVEMBER New agreements between US and Soviet Union on cultural exchanges providing for exchanges of scientific delegations, musical and theatrical tours, and exchanges of students and for co-operation in research on peaceful uses of atomic energy followed by similar agreements with Britain and France.

3–19 DECEMBER President Eisenhower tours Asia and Africa.

19–21 DECEMBER Western powers agree to Summit Meeting in 1960. Reject any unilateral change in Western rights in Berlin.

1960 JANUARY–FEBRUARY Mr Macmillan speaks of 'wind of change' in tour of Africa.

14 JANUARY Mr Khrushchev announces further cut of 1·2 million in Soviet forces.

19 JANUARY US and Japan sign new treaty of mutual co-operation and security.

26 JANUARY Mr Ulbricht declares that East Germany will ask Soviet Union for nuclear weapons if West Germany receives them from US.

FEBRUARY Mr Khrushchev visits India, Burma and Indonesia. Visit ignored by China.

3 FEBRUARY Soviet jamming of BBC broadcasts ceases.

MARCH Mr Khrushchev visits France.

APRIL Chinese press opens bitter ideological attack on current Soviet policy of peaceful co-existence.

5 MAY US U2 plane shot down over Soviet territory.

17 MAY At Summit Meeting in Paris, President Eisenhower takes personal responsibility for U2 incident and refuses to apologise. Conference breaks down.

26 MAY Large demonstrations in Japan against security treaty with US.

27 MAY US ends aid to Cuba.

JUNE Soviet delegate leaves ten-power disarmament talks at Geneva. Later Soviet Union announces reversal of unilateral disarmament previously announced. President Eisenhower asked to postpone visit to Japan as his safety could not be assured.

6–15 JULY Mutiny breaks out in Force Publique in Congo. Katanga declares its independence. UN force despatched.

20 JULY   Polaris missile successfully fired from submarine.

AUGUST–SEPTEMBER   *Coup* by neutralist forces in Laos establishes neutralist government under Souvanna Phouma. Followed by counter-*coup* by right-wing forces. US and Soviet Union become involved in support of right-wing and neutralist and Communist forces respectively.

1 AUGUST   Malayan emergency comes to an end.

SEPTEMBER   Soviet Union demands establishment of troika system in UN organisation.

5 SEPTEMBER   Mr Kasavubu, Congo President, dismisses Prime Minister Lumumba, who refuses to accept dismissal. Rival delegations sent to UN. Reports that Soviet Union is sending equipment to support Lumumba forces.

14 SEPTEMBER   Army *coup* in the Congo led by General Mobutu. Mr Lumumba appeals for UN protection. Arrested by military forces, 2 December. Lumumbist administration under Mr Gizenga established at Stanleyville.

19 OCTOBER   US embargoes almost all trade with Cuba.

25 OCTOBER   Cuban Government announces nationalisation of all US firms.

NOVEMBER   Moscow conference of Communist Parties reaches compromise agreement on Communist aims, incorporating both Soviet and Chinese views.

1 NOVEMBER   Announcement that Polaris submarine base is to be established at Holy Loch.

22 NOVEMBER   UN agrees to seat Kasavubu delegates against strong Soviet protest.

6 DECEMBER   French Government passes Bill for the establishment of an independent nuclear force.

1961   3 JANUARY   Communist-led 'National Front for the liberation of South Vietnam' set up in South Vietnam. US breaks off relations with Cuba.

13 FEBRUARY   Mr Lumumba murdered in Congo.

14 FEBRUARY   Soviet Union calls for dismissal of Mr Hammarskjoeld.

23 MARCH   Censorship of press despatches from Moscow ended.

17 APRIL   Unsuccessful invasion of Cuba by anti-Castro forces from US supported by US naval forces.

1 MAY   Castro declares the 'socialist' character of the Cuban revolution in outspoken terms. Further nationalisation measures.

8 MAY   International control commission re-established in Laos.

16 MAY   International conference on Laos opens in Geneva.

3 JUNE   Meeting between Mr Khrushchev and Mr Kennedy in Vienna. Agree to seek peaceful settlement in Laos.

6 JUNE   Renewed fighting in Laos.

JULY–AUGUST   Flood of refugees from East Germany to West Berlin reaches 10,000 a week.

AUGUST   Castro spokesman announces formation of united party of the Revolution on 'Marxist-Leninist' lines.

10 AUGUST   Britain applies for membership of Common Market.

13 AUGUST   East Germany builds wall to divide East and West Berlin.

20 AUGUST   US reinforcements move to Berlin. Plans for increasing US military strength in Germany.

15 AUGUST   Mr Adoula's government recognised by UN as only legitimate government of Congo.

SEPTEMBER   UN breaks off relations with Katanga. UN troops seek to win control of the province, but suffer heavy losses.

1 SEPTEMBER   Soviet Union resumes testing of nuclear

weapons in the atmosphere, for the first time by either side since 1958. Conference of non-aligned states opens in Belgrade.

18 SEPTEMBER Mr Hammarskjoeld killed in air crash in Northern Rhodesia.

20 SEPTEMBER US and Soviet Union issue statement of agreed principles of disarmament, but reach no agreement on principle of verification of retained weapons.

17 OCTOBER Mr Khrushchev says timing of German peace treaty not important.

31 OCTOBER Stalin's body removed from the Lenin Mausoleum, and place-names bearing his name changed.

NOVEMBER 1961–JUNE 1962 Intensified war between Communist guerrillas and Government forces in South Vietnam. Increased US assistance to Government, including participation of military mission with over 10,000 men.

19 NOVEMBER East Germany reinforces Berlin Wall.

I DECEMBER Dr O'Brien, UN representative in Katanga, resigns. Later, UN forces win control of most of Katanga. Fidel Castro declares, 'I am a Marxist-Leninist, and I will be one until the last day of my life'.

9 DECEMBER Soviet Union breaks off diplomatic relations with Albania. Agreement on neutralisation of Laos: talks begin for formation of Coalition Government under Souvanna Phouma.

20 DECEMBER Katanga accepts authority of central Congo Government

1962 29 JANUARY Conference on suspension of tests breaks down after three years of negotiations.

31 JANUARY OAS votes to expel Cuba from organisation.

II FEBRUARY Exchange of U2 pilot, Captain Powers, for Soviet spy imprisoned in US.

MARCH–APRIL US and Britain resume atmospheric nuclear tests.

14 MARCH Eighteen-nation disarmament talks begin in Geneva.

23 JUNE–23 JULY Laos Cabinet agrees to cease-fire. Laos neutrality agreement signed by fourteen nations.

5 AUGUST Soviet Union starts new series of atmospheric tests.

19 AUGUST Destalinisation of Hungarian Communist Party.

22 AUGUST Soviet Union abolishes office of Berlin Kommandant.

3 SEPTEMBER Katanga accepts U Thant's plan for reintegration of the Congo. Cease-fire signed and new federal constitution inaugurated.

9 SEPTEMBER Chinese nationalist U2 aircraft shot down over China.

20 SEPTEMBER Border fighting between India and China intensified.

20 OCTOBER–20 NOVEMBER Chinese attack in strength on India's North-East Frontier and the Ladakh area. Invade large area of North-East Frontier territory.

22 OCTOBER President Kennedy reveals building of missile site by Soviet Union in Cuba. Orders partial blockade and searching of Soviet ships on the high seas.

29 OCTOBER Mr Khrushchev agrees to dismantle missile sites in return for US undertaking not to invade Cuba.

29–31 OCTOBER Destalinisation in Bulgaria. India accepts military assistance from US and Britain. Mr Menon resigns.

20 NOVEMBER Soviet Union agrees to withdraw Soviet bombers from Cuba. Blockade ended.

21 NOVEMBER China orders cease-fire and withdrawal of $12\frac{1}{2}$ miles behind the lines of actual control on 7 November 1959.

5 DECEMBER US and Soviet Union reach agreement on co-operation in peaceful uses of outer space.

17 DECEMBER Six Colombo powers put forward plan for settlement of Sino-Indian border dispute.

21 DECEMBER Nassau agreement between US and Britain. Polaris missiles to be supplied for British nuclear submarines. These to be integrated, with British V-bombers, in joint NATO multilateral force, except when supreme national interests are at stake.

28 DECEMBER UN troops again engaged in heavy fighting against President Tshombe in Katanga. President Tshombe flees to Salisbury, Southern Rhodesia.

1963 JANUARY Announced that US Jupiter missiles to be withdrawn from Turkey and Italy. US plans for multilateral nuclear force of surface ships with mixed crews discussed with NATO countries. UN forces re-establish Central Government control in Katanga. Mr Tshombe accepts new UN plan for integration of Katanga.

14 JANUARY General de Gaulle makes clear his opposition to British entry to EEC and refuses offer of Polaris missiles under Nassau agreement.

22 JANUARY Franco-German treaty of co-operation signed.

FEBRUARY Archbishop of Lvov released in Russia after eighteen years imprisonment. Revolution in Iraq. General Kassim executed. General Arif becomes President. Severe measures against Communists arouse Soviet protests.

6 FEBRUARY US places further restrictions on ships trading with Cuba.

19 FEBRUARY Soviet Union agrees to withdraw all troops except training missions in Cuba.

21 MARCH Hungarian Government announces amnesty for those taking part in 1956 revolution.

APRIL–MAY Dr Castro visits Soviet Union for a month.

22 MAY African Summit Conference. Organisation for African Unity established at Addis Ababa on lines proposed by moderate elements there.

20 JUNE   Agreement on 'hot line' between White House and Kremlin signed in Geneva.

25 JUNE   Mr Tshombe dismissed as President of Katanga.

JUNE–JULY   First Secretary of Rumanian Communist Party fails to attend meeting of Communist leaders in Berlin. Rumania, anxious for greater economic independence, increasingly dissociates from Soviet line in Sino-Soviet dispute.

JULY–SEPTEMBER   Sino-Soviet ideological dispute carried on in more bitter terms than ever. Soviet Union accuses China of violating her sovereignty. China accuses Soviet Union of encouraging revolution in Central Asia.

6–20 JULY   Soviet-Chinese ideological talks in Moscow. No agreement, but decision to reopen talks later.

5 AUGUST   Nuclear test ban treaty covering all except underground tests signed in Moscow. China and France refuse to sign.

SEPTEMBER   Destalinisation in Czechoslovakia. Mr Siroky, the Prime Minister, replaced.

4 OCTOBER   Archbishop Beran of Prague released.

NOVEMBER   US and Soviet Union join in supporting unanimous UN resolution banning the placing of nuclear weapons in orbit. President Diem of South Vietnam overthrown. Army régime established in his place. Greek Government begins to release Communists imprisoned during Greek Civil War.

22 NOVEMBER   President Kennedy assassinated in Dallas. Vice-President Johnson becomes president. Soviet Union expresses horror at assassination. Chinese press indifferent.

12 DECEMBER   US announce cuts in military spending and closing of thirty-three bases at home and abroad.

16 DECEMBER   Soviet Union announces reduction in defence expenditure.

17 DECEMBER   Agreement allowing visits from West Berlin to East Berlin over the Christmas period.

1 THE PARTITION OF EUROPE

Wilfrid Knapp

It was scarcely possible for the best of political prophets to foresee in 1945 the shape which the world would have taken five years later. The line that had come to be drawn down the centre of the Continent; the division of Germany; the onset of the cold war – which was neither war nor peace – all this was beyond the prediction of both statesmen and commentators as the war drew to its close. The momentum of change over this quinquennium, and the fact that the new world was so far outside the expectation, and even more the intention, of statesmen pose in an unusually clear form one of the recurrent problems involved in interpreting political change. Should not the events of these five years be seen as the outcome of forces over which men could not hope to exercise any real control? Did individual decisions make any serious practical difference to the course of events; did they not rather merely alter developments at the margin? Do not the changes which came about over these five years form a pattern similar to other observable patterns in the past, and therefore predictable not indeed from the hopes, intentions, ambitions or character of the statesmen who happened to be in office at the time, but from the fact that with such and such a conjunction of forces in the world, only a single outcome was possible?

This grand view of international politics obviously has its attractions. Take, for example, the problem of Germany. For seventy years since the unification of Germany, European politics had been dominated by the existence in the centre of Europe of a power which by its industrial potential and geographical position, by the hard work of its people, and even more by their national-ism, would have a natural tendency towards the domination of the Continent. Throughout the war – the second world war to be fought precisely because no pacific solution had been found to the problem of Germany – the statesmen of the 'Grand Alliance' had been preoccupied with the question of security against Germany, and their preoccupations had only diminished, without disappearing, as their own rivalries with each other began to emerge.

Yet in fact the problem of the old Europe was not only chang-ing, but actually finding a rough-and-ready solution, without their being aware of it. The result of the war was to bring into pre-eminence the two great continental powers, the Soviet Union and the United States, and to place these two super-powers in a position of proximity which they might otherwise never have known. Between them lay Germany, and by that fact alone – far more than by its defeat – Germany acquired a totally different aspect. Germany became in fact like Poland of the eighteenth century, and its partition was equally inevitable. Germany united on either side of the new balance of power would destroy the balance; while an independent middle power would be a constant threat to its neighbours on each side. The mores of the twen-tieth century, the commitment at least of Britain and America to principles of order and good conduct in international affairs, pre-vented their agreeing to a partition of Germany in a cold-blooded manner, and the special arrangement thought necessary for Berlin deprived the partition of the advantages of tidiness; but the partition itself was inevitable none the less.

Such a view of the development of international politics is tempting in its simplicity and its sense of inexorable momentum. As an explanation of events it is unverifiable, and the importance attached to it will vary from one individual to another. In any case the propounding of such a theory is no substitute for a closer examination of the events themselves, and of the decisions which were taken.

There is necessarily a marked imbalance in an examination of the way in which decisions were taken in the West and the East, because of the inaccessibility of sources on the Soviet side. But as far as America and Britain are concerned, one can say with certainty that it was the intention of statesmen and the expectation of the public that Germany would remain a united country, and would, after a suitable period of disarmament, democratisation and re-education re-enter the community of nations. The essence of this view is of course that Germany was a special case, but that, as the wartime suggestion that Germany should be dismembered had gone by default, it should be treated as a whole. Its former leaders would be brought to trial; the United Nations would be devised in such a way as to be effective against Germany, Italy and Japan alone amongst the great powers, and Germany would receive special treatment as the main instigator of war in the past and the principal threat to security in the future.

Stalin's views of the German problem are more difficult to determine. He shared his allies' fears of Germany, and probably set the potential threat even higher than they did. But his immediate aim was to secure the maximum recompense from Germany, for the cost and sacrifice which the war had meant for Russia, by removing capital equipment from Germany under the guise of reparations – a policy the dangers of which the Western powers had learned at the conclusion of the First World War. Between Russia on the one hand, and Britain and America on the other, France shared her Eastern ally's extreme caution about the future of Germany, and sympathised with its demands for reparations – a view which put France, uncommitted as she was to the Potsdam decisions, in the advantageous position of being able for a limited time to seek the support of both sides in the emerging conflict between her allies.

However, the governments of Britain and America soon found

47

it impracticable either to treat Germany as a whole, or to regard Germany entirely as a special case. To some extent the principle of the unity of Germany under allied occupation was sacrificed at Potsdam, in an attempt to meet Russian demands on reparations; and this was followed by the French veto on the setting up of all-German administrative agencies. But a more decisive event implying the abandonment of the economic unity of Germany was General Clay's announcement on 3 May 1946 that no further transfer of reparations would be made from the American to the Russian zone.

Clay's decision was prompted by the fact that while the zonal boundary was open for the export of equipment and goods from the West on reparations account, it was closed to interzonal trade, and particularly for the import of agricultural produce by the West to maintain a reasonable standard of living in the Western zones. It was the more striking since it came only five weeks after the four powers had, after months of bargaining, at last agreed on a fixed level of German industry, which would permit both dismantling of armaments industries and a long-term reparations settlement. But the level of industry agreement placed as limits what might well have been goals for a German industry struggling to reconstruct itself. It was eroded by the acceptance of the division of Germany into distinct units. And six months later it was to be further undermined by the agreement of Britain and America to merge their two zones.

At least as significant as the proposed merger itself were the terms in which it was viewed, as they were expressed by Secretary Byrnes in his speech of 6 September. He then said:

> Germany must be given a chance to export goods in order to import enough to make her economy self-sustaining. Germany is part of Europe and recovery in Europe, and particularly in the states adjoining Germany, will be slow indeed if Germany with her great resources of iron and coal is turned into a poorhouse.

With this speech the special treatment of Germany began to end and the idea of a West German contribution to the recovery of Western Europe as a whole began to replace the supposition that Germany must make some payment for the cost of the war, and must be hamstrung economically so as to lessen its threat to the security of Europe.

To accept the division of Germany was even harder for the Western powers than to see the rest of the world falling into two. The war had been fought against Germany; Germany was thought to be at the root of Europe's security problem, the threat of Germany had been the most solid link between Russia and its western allies. More than that, the division of Germany between East and West was thought to be a most potent source of danger in the future, and an element of instability which must provoke violence. The control of Germany, and its unity under allied administration, were therefore principles which the Western powers would surrender with great reluctance. Dismantling of German industry in the Western zones continued until 1949; and when the Western powers adopted currency reform in their own zones in June 1948, they still sought agreement with the Russians on the introduction of the new currency into Berlin – this being the immediate background to the Berlin blockade.

Across the zonal boundaries a similar development, *mutatis mutandis*, was taking place – even though Molotov still pressed the Foreign Ministers to agree to the setting up of a central German government. Whatever else Stalin had foreseen for Germany, his immediate aim in occupying the Eastern zone was to remove its industrial potential for the benefit of the Soviet Union. By the summer of 1946 this special treatment of Germany was coming to an end from the Russian side too. This did not mean of course that Stalin looked for the co-operation of Eastern Germany in the reconstruction of Eastern Europe. Co-operation had never been Stalin's strong point. But the striking inefficiency, muddle and wastage of the removals from the Soviet zone quickly revealed themselves, and the alternative policy of leaving capital equipment in

Eastern Germany to produce for export, especially to the Soviet Union, was self-imposing. At the same time the political development of Eastern Germany followed a pattern exactly similar to that in the other Russian occupied countries of Eastern Europe. The political control of Eastern Germany was established through the Socialist Unity Party, the police and the Russian occupation forces, just as it was in Bulgaria and Rumania, Poland and Hungary. In this respect too Eastern Germany, for Stalin, rapidly came to be less of a special case.

The most significant and far-reaching of all the changes of policy towards Germany was that carried through by France. Resisting in the first instance co-operation with Britain and America and the fusion of its zone of occupation with theirs, France was won round to close co-operation by the necessity of taking sides in the cold war, and by the fact that for a short time the British and American Governments were prepared to support French claims on the Saar. None the less, the overtaking of French policy towards Germany – including its dismemberment and the 'international nationalisation' of the Ruhr industries – by Anglo-American development of the bizone provided the French Government with a challenge to which it responded in May 1950 with the Schuman Plan. The proposal for a European Coal and Steel Community was set in the context of the development towards European unity, and would have been impossible without it. But its supranational aspects, on which the French insisted so strongly, derived directly from the desire to subordinate the coal and steel industry of the Ruhr, no longer to the four power control which the French had originally pursued with the support of the Russians, but to a supranational body in which Western Germany would itself participate.

The claim of the German problem to early consideration in an account of the transition from war to cold war derives from the immediate confrontation of the four powers in Germany, and from the fact that the acceptance of the division of Germany was an indication of the extent of despair on the Western side at the possibility of agreement with the Soviet Union. But it does not by itself explain the development of the cold war. This is attributable in the first place to the obvious and incontrovertible fact of Russian control over Eastern Europe, and in the second place to a series of moves which with equal certainty indicated an attempt on the part of the Soviet Union to extend its influence marginally in Germany and elsewhere, and which were interpreted by the Western powers as implying a general aggressiveness on the part of the Soviet Union, which must be contained.

The explanation for Soviet policy in the two years after the war remains to be given in the unforeseeable future, when the materials are available. On the one hand Stalin seems to have pursued the traditional objectives of Tsarist foreign policy. The Baltic states were absorbed into the Soviet Union, the frontier of Poland pushed westwards and Bessarabia reclaimed from Rumania. The settlement in the Far East belonged in all its aspects more naturally to two old-fashioned diplomatists, rather than to a Communist dictator and an American President. The Soviet Union pressed on Persia and Manchuria, the Straits and the frontier provinces of Turkey. Stalin even evoked memories of Alexander I's offers to suppress the Barbary pirates by indicating his readiness to take on the trusteeship of Libya. None of these traditional pressures was pushed very hard when it encountered resistance. Even so, the pressure against Greece and Turkey, coinciding as it did with the first of the British financial crises, was sufficient in March 1947 to bring the most startling departure from traditional American foreign policy in the Truman doctrine, when the United States in one move abandoned its isolationism, and asserted its influence at the very point which history showed to be the one of maximum sensitivity for Russia.

It is striking that in these respects Stalin's policy should so closely resemble that of his Tsarist predecessors. In Eastern Europe

51

he went far beyond anything they had achieved. The opportunity to do so derived initially from the Russian liberation of the countries of Eastern Europe from German occupation. This was not followed by the immediate subordination of all the occupied countries to monolithic Communist rule. Thus while effective Communist rule was established from the start in Poland and Rumania, and only formally modified in response to Western pressure, relatively free elections were held in Hungary in November 1945, and a genuine coalition goverment, albeit subject to pressure by the Communists and the Russians, was established as a result.

Only in 1947-48 was the establishment of Communist control taken through its final stage. This has given rise to the suggestion that Stalin interpreted his wartime discussions with the Western allies as implying that he would have a predominant influence in Eastern Europe in exchange for American and British influence in Western Europe. The fact that the Communist parties of France and Italy did not seriously attempt to take power at the end of the war, in spite of their unprecedented strength, is adduced as evidence of such a view. And it follows from this argument that the intensification of Communist control over Eastern Europe was the consequence rather than the cause of the breakdowns of relations with the West.

There may be some truth in this view, to the extent that Russian action was accelerated in response to British and American moves in Germany, to the Truman doctrine and the Marshall Plan. But beyond this the most plausible explanation for the establishment of Russian Communist rule in Eastern Europe appears to be the simplest: that Stalin found himself effectively in control of Eastern Europe, and established there the only form of government acceptable to him. The whole of his career testifies to his successful aspiration to ever-increasing personal power, and this could only be achieved in Eastern Europe through the dominance of the Russian Army and security services, supporting local Communist

leaders amenable to Stalin's wishes. Once this was done there was
no reason or incentive for Stalin to surrender any part of his
personal power in this area, any more than any other.

Whether or not this explanation is correct, the evidence of Communist rule in Eastern Europe profoundly affected the attitude of
Western governments towards Russian actions in Germany, as
well as to the probing which went on in the rest of the world,
which might have been taken more lightly were it not for events
in Eastern Europe. Both the American and the British Governments thought that their countries had fought a war in support of
free and independent governments. The British had joined the
war with the immediate aim of defending the independence of
Poland, and Roosevelt, instinctive politician though he was,
had not needed the pressure of immigrant voters to make him
increasingly disillusioned in the last months of his life with Stalin's
actions in Eastern Europe.

Even so, public opinion in the two countries was understandably loath to accept that the world was dividing into two,
and that negotiation with the Russians was difficult if not impossible. On 5 March 1946 Winston Churchill said at Fulton
Missouri:

> From Stettin, in the Baltic, to Trieste, in the Adriatic, an iron
> curtain has descended across the continent. . . . All these famous
> cities and the populations in them lie in the Soviet sphere, and all are
> subject, in one form or another, not only to Soviet influence, but to
> a very high and increasing measure of control from Moscow.

But commenting on the speech *The Times* said:

> Mr Churchill was perhaps less happy in the passages in his speech in
> which he appeared to contrast 'western democracy' and 'Com-
> munism'. . . . While western democracy and Communism are in
> many respects opposed they have much to learn from each other,
> Communism in the working of political insitutions and in the

establishment of individual rights, western democracy in the development of economic and social planning.

Only in 1947 did the current of opinion begin to change rapidly. The Marshall offer, its rejection by the Soviet Union, and even more its rejection by Czechoslovakia on the instructions of the Soviet Union, seemed to be the turning-point in the division of the world into two. But these events were also followed by a rapid acceleration in the pace of the cold war. The *coup d'état* establishing Communist government in Czechoslovakia in February 1948, the expulsion of Yugoslavia from the Cominform, the Berlin blockade from June 1948 to May 1949, and finally the attack on South Korea in June 1950 were interpreted by Western governments and by a majority of their people as a series of deliberate acts designed to increase Russian power, and as a prelude to more extensive aggression. In response, they devised the Brussels Pact – an alliance between Britain, France and the Benelux countries which still named Germany as the possible aggressor, but in all else was obviously directed against the Soviet Union; to be followed a year later in April 1949 by the North Atlantic Treaty; and in 1950 by the dramatic proposal and lengthy negotiations for the rearmament of Western Germany.

In retrospect the historian is bound to ask how correct the assumptions which stimulated Western reaction were. He will be unable to give any verifiable answers. But he will ask the questions none the less. Did Western governments make the mistake of exaggerating the extent to which these events were directed from Moscow, and therefore attributable to the aggressive designs of Stalin? Obviously their alarm did not derive solely from their interpretation of Stalinist policy. They felt themselves confronted with a more amorphous force, the 'spread of communism'. They recognised that this was to some extent attributable to the just demands of the under-privileged, and met this danger by promoting economic recovery and political stability. None the less, it was assumed that the centre of the international Communist movement was in the Kremlin. How justified was this assumption? The Berlin blockade and the expulsion of Yugoslavia from the Cominform are presumably directly attributable to Stalin. But are the Czech *coup d'état* and the Korean War? It can be argued that the Czech *coup* arose out of purely local circumstances, and that the lack of cohesion amongst the non-Communist parties, together with Benes' indecisiveness, played into the hands of the Czech Communists, so that they needed neither help nor direction from the Soviet Union. It can certainly be argued that the North Korean Government and Army were responsible for the attack on South Korea, and that, had Stalin planned or directed such an attack, he would not have made possible the one successful action by the United Nations in accordance with its original concept by boycotting its meetings at this time. And it is argued on general terms that one too easily falls into the error of exaggerating the competence of a single man, simply because he is a dictator surrounded by secrecy.

For all that, it seems more plausible to assume Russian, and therefore Stalinist, responsibility for these events. Stalin had throughout shown a strong interest in the future of Czechoslovakia, from the time when he had insisted that the Russian zone of occupation in Austria should extend the whole length of the frontier with Czechoslovakia (and Hungary) to his direction that Czechoslovakia should not accept the Marshall offer. As the temperature of the cold war rose, Czechoslovakia was a great salient into Communist Eastern Europe. And Zorin was present in Prague during the *coup d'état* itself. While it is true that a Stalinist directed attack in Korea is difficult to reconcile with Russian absence from the Security Council, it is more plausible that the latter should result from oversight than that the former should be the result of inadequate control. And while it is true that Stalin's record shows a general avoidance of military aggression this is as much an argument for his not having allowed such action to occur without his sanction, as it is for saying that he would under no circumstances have directed military attack, even by a satellite.

But if it was the case that Stalin directed the Czech *coup d'état* and the Korean War as much as the Berlin blockade and pressure on Tito, it none the less seems likely in retrospect that Western governments exaggerated the immediate danger of continuing expansion on the part of the Soviet Union. Even as the Western powers girded their loins and strengthened their military defences they were aware that it was easiest to prepare against straight-forward military expansion, but that this was at best only one of the dangers which they had to face. In fact it may have been the least. Impressed as they were by Russian divisions in Eastern Europe, they were probably not more impressed than was Stalin by the atomic bomb. Sensitive as they were to the weakness of Western Europe they were probably not more alarmed by a war-torn economy than was Stalin: the strength of Communist parties in Western Europe was matched by the weakness of newly established political control in the Russian satellites. Stalin was a cautious man who had never taken risks in international diplomacy; who had avoided war with Germany as long as possible and with Japan almost entirely.

Yet the most cautious man can be transformed by unexpected success, and the world would surely have been different had the expansion of Communist rule met with as little resistance as had Nazi aggression. As events turned out it was only in Czechoslovakia that Communist or Stalinist moves achieved success. Stalin's arrogance led him to underestimate Tito's strength in Yugoslavia. Perhaps he also overlooked the significance for his opponents of the practices which he had established – whatever risks Tito may have faced in opposing Stalin, there was no reason for him to expect political or any other sort of longevity if he submitted.

By blockading Berlin, Stalin provided the world with a type case of the cold war – semi-military pressure for limited ends, met by limited measures of self-defence aimed at nothing more than restoring the *status quo*. At the beginning of the blockade the odds must surely have seemed to be in his favour; either the Western powers would halt the development of Western Germany or they would abandon Berlin; and with good fortune they might do both. And if the enterprise became too risky the clamps on Berlin could be loosened, without prejudice to the future. What Stalin failed to foresee was that he would evoke the technical means of supplying Berlin by air – and this is not surprising since the Western powers themselves did not think this could be done until four-engined aircraft, and their own experience, showed it could. The status of Berlin did indeed change after the blockade, as East Berlin was separated from West. But as later events showed, a blockade was not necessary to achieve this, and it was a poor substitute for driving out the West altogether.

In Korea the miscalculation, whoever was responsible for it, was less than sometimes appears to be the case. Without the presence of American forces in Japan and without the decisiveness of President Truman, North Korean troops would have overrun the whole peninsula. And the political and military difficulties of making landings on enemy territory to reverse a *fait accompli* would have been disproportionately greater than those involved in going to the defence of the existing order.

The failure of three out of the four most important forward moves for which Stalin may be thought responsible must surely have been in part the cause of the change of policy foreseen in the Nineteenth Party Congress in 1952. On the other side, the effects of Communist policy could scarcely have been greater in stimulating the support for a policy of strength to contain the Soviet Union. Before Czechoslovakia, it was possible to argue that the conflict with communism had been exaggerated, and that the example of co-operation with Communists demonstrated internally in Czechoslovakia could be extended to the international sphere. Before Tito's expulsion from the Cominform, it was possible to argue that the conflict with Russia derived from the conservative and reactionary policies of the Western powers and could be obviated by the establishment of true social democracy. Those who argued that the policy of strength made it more difficult to talk with the Russians appeared refuted by the readiness of Stalin to negotiate after the failure of the Berlin blockade. The outbreak of war in Korea invalidated the arguments of those who wanted a concentration of resources on economic and social development at the cost of military preparedness.

As a result the cold war had taken definite shape within five years of the ending of the war in Europe. The world was divided in two, and a line drawn in Europe the crossing of which was recognised as a *casus belli*. The line was drawn through Germany, a fact which was recognised as the failure of a wartime alliance, and thought in the West to contain a most potent threat to security: for all that had been said about dismembering Germany as a solution to the German problem, this unforeseen barrier to German aspirations to unity was thought to invite as violent a reaction as a vacuum in nature. The initiative in the cold war remained on the Communist side, in the sense that it could make forward moves in a way in which others could not (while still claiming to be as pacific as Picasso's dove).

The reaction to this initiative on the Western side was the wholesale abandonment of traditional foreign policies. The United States and Britain joined the European powers in forming the North Atlantic Treaty Organization, which, as a peacetime alliance between democratic states, would have been unprecedented even had it not established entirely new institutional and procedural arrangements, and the movement towards unity in Western Europe was given greater urgency by pressure from the East. An 'arms race' of an unprecedented scale – and nature, since it was concerned with qualitative rather than quantitative improvement – was embarked upon. And yet for all this, the initiative, the reaction and the counteraction remained limited in means and in ends. The Americans did not send tanks along the autobahn to break the Berlin blockade; the Russians did not shoot down the aircraft which turned the flank of the blockade; neither side regarded the total defeat of the other as an attainable objective in the immediate future. In the Far East the Communist world was strengthened to an extent difficult to calculate by the success of the Chinese Communists, and although the division between the Communist and non-Communist world was for most of its length a broad band with blurred edges rather than a sharp line, it existed none the less.

The question will always recur about any period of history as to whether it could have been different; more so with a period so swift in movement and decisive in outcome as this. We have already suggested that there does appear to be a certain inexorability about the division of Germany. It is true that an example of another possibility clearly exists in the case of Austria. The occupation of Austria, its division into zones and the further division of the capital, lying within the Russian zone, exactly paralleled the occupation of Germany. But there the similarity ceased. An Austrian government under a non-Communist Chancellor was established by the Russians as they liberated Vienna. Free elections were held in November 1945, which strengthened the democratic government while permitting the inclusion of a Communist minister on the basis of a mere 5 per cent. popular vote. The statute under which Austrian government was established was so devised that the veto power vested in each of the four occupying powers was a veto on interference with what the government wished to do, not a veto on their action. The actual occupation of the country lasted, and a peace treaty could not be signed, until 1955; but long before that date Austria had moved far towards the neutral status which it finally secured.

The pattern for a neutral state in the centre of Europe was thus established. But could the pattern drawn for a small country, which was not regarded as an aggressor, be enlarged to fit its large, powerful, traditionally expansive neighbour? Could this have been done even if 'unconditional surrender' had never been mentioned? It was an idea which was widely canvassed at the time of the disengagement debate in 1957-58. But the combination of two emerging power blocs, with the fact that they faced each other on the territory of precisely that power which both sides regarded as having in the past been most unscrupulous in the pursuit of its own aggrandisement, makes the possibility seem remote indeed.

Was there an alternative to Russian domination of Eastern Europe? Again the pattern exists in the case of Finland. It is surely the case that the Western powers would have tolerated Russian influence over the countries of Eastern Europe comparable to that exercised over Finland, and regarded it as the legitimate outcome of Russia's anxieties for her own security. The motives behind Stalin's tolerant attitude towards Finland are as much in need of explanation as those which permitted the relative independence of Austria (unless we assume that his fascination by his Tsarist predecessors extended to copying the autonomy of Finland). Whatever the explanation may be, the Finnish case belies the contention that there was no meeting-point between the Western powers' view of the 'independence' of Eastern Europe and the Russian demands for the safeguarding of their own security. For all that, it is improbable that such a solution, resting as it does on a high degree of sophistication amongst the Finns, and of tolerance on the part of Stalin, could be extended along the whole frontier of the Soviet Union, particularly in its relations with countries nurturing a long-standing sense of rivalry with and antipathy towards Russia.

To this extent the territorial arrangements in Europe, and the new state of international relations which came to be known as the cold war, have a self-sustaining force. If one starts from the nature of Communist rule in Russia and certain assumptions about

Stalin's passion for personal power; from the old anxieties about the threat of Germany, and the disposition and confrontation of forces, which resulted from the last war, fought against that threat, then the basic elements of the cold war seem a necessary sequel. Beyond that, in the sequence of events which form the fabric of these five years, almost everything might have been different. From the technical achievement which made the Berlin airlift possible to the personal decisiveness of Truman or the old age of Benes, from the historical accident of Britain's financial weakness in March 1947 to the collective decision of the electorates of Western Germany or Italy – all these are variables characteristic of human affairs. They make it possible for the historian to establish landmarks at which the course of events might have been significantly different.

2 THE RISE OF COMMUNIST POWER IN THE FAR EAST

Geoffrey Hudson

Before the Second World War there was outside the Soviet Union and its protectorate of Outer Mongolia only one country of the world in which a Communist party controlled a tract of territory with an army and civil administration of its own. This was China, where ever since 1927 the Communists had maintained their local government and military forces in defiance of the weak and distracted central government. For the decade from 1927 to 1937 they had been in open insurrection; driven from their original stronghold in South China, they had established themselves in the north-west after the famous 'Long March' of 1934. Then, during the eight years of the war against Japan, they had formed part of a national united front against the invading foreign enemy under the nominal supreme command of Chiang Kai-shek, but had in practice retained their independence as partners rather than subordinates of the internationally recognised National Government, which moved up the Yangtse from Nanking to Chungking under the impact of the Japanese invasion.

Although the Kuomintang party, which controlled the National Government, and the Communists had combined to oppose a Japanese conquest of China, their operations against the common enemy could not be harmonious, because each side foresaw that the post-war relations of power in Chinese domestic politics would be determined by the strategic positions held by their respective forces at the end of the war. The Japanese occupation of a large part of North China, from which the regular troops under the authority of the National Government had been driven out, had provided the Communists, as specialists in guerrilla warfare, with opportunities for infiltrating behind the Japanese lines and organising centres of resistance under their own political control; thus in the event of a Japanese collapse the area of Communist ascendancy would be several times as extensive as it had been at the beginning of 1937, before the outbreak of the war. Alarmed at this development, the Kuomintang tried to limit the growth of Communist power by preventing supplies of arms from reaching the Communist areas. Such measures, however, did not meet with the approval of the Americans, who were a factor in Chinese politics from the end of 1941 onwards. The war between the United States and Japan had made the former the military ally of China, and China became an American 'strategic sphere' for assistance to the Chinese Army in training, supplies and overall operational advice. Wishing to maximise the Chinese war effort against Japan, the American Government and its representatives in China were unsympathetic to the Kuomintang's purpose of containing communism and diverting man-power and resources to this end. It became American diplomatic policy to try to bring about a reconciliation between the National Government and the Communists, while General 'Vinegar Joe' Stilwell, as American military adviser to Chiang Kai-shek, urged the sending of supplies of American arms to the Communists to enable them to attack Japanese bases in North China. This advocacy caused Chiang to demand his recall, and although President Roosevelt acceded to the request and replaced Stilwell with another and less provocative American general, the episode had far-reaching consequences, for Stilwell, embittered by the rebuff, carried on a campaign of vilification of the Kuomintang régime after his return to the United States. In particular he had the ear of General Marshall, who was to play so large a part in the formation of American policy towards China during the three years after the end of the war.

The war ended with unexpected abruptness, for the atomic

bomb had been a secret withheld even from high-level American commanders, and it had been generally assumed that Japan would hold out until actually invaded. But just before Japan's surrender the Chinese Government had reached agreements with both the United States and the Soviet Union, which, if they had been properly carried out, would have given Chiang Kai-shek a probably decisive advantage over the Communists. The Americans agreed that when Japan surrendered he should have the right to take the surrender of all the Japanese forces in China, except in the Russian zone of operations, and that American sea and air transport should be made available to move Chinese Government troops to the principal Chinese cities under Japanese occupation. The Russians agreed, in the treaty by which China confirmed the concessions in Manchuria granted to Russia at Yalta as the price of Russia's entry into the war against Japan, to evacuate Manchuria within three months of the end of the war, to transfer administrative control to agents of the Chinese National Government, and to confine material assistance under the treaty to that Government. On paper these two agreements left the Chinese Communists with no internationally recognised right to take the surrender of Japanese troops, or acquire their equipment: they also appeared to ensure that the Chinese Government would regain control of all important places under Japanese occupation with either American or Russian co-operation in the area concerned.

The agreements were reflected in the so-called Order Number One issued to Japanese Imperial Headquarters by General Mac-Arthur as Supreme Commander for the Allied Powers after Japan's surrender; Japanese troops in Japan and South Korea were ordered to surrender to the Americans, those in Manchuria and North Korea to the Russians, and those in China outside Manchuria to commanders designated by Chiang Kai-shek. The Communists in North China refused to recognise the Order; Chu Teh as their Commander-in-Chief commanded them to take the offensive and force the surrender of Japanese units wherever they could. He also ordered part of the Communist forces to move into Manchuria, where the Russians were in process of taking the Japanese surrender. The effect of these operations in North China was very slight; the Japanese were far better armed than the Communists and stood their ground, waiting for Chinese Government troops to come and take over, so that only a few outlying Japanese garrisons were captured with their arms by the Communists. In Manchuria, on the other hand, where the Communists did not have to do any fighting because the Japanese Army had already surrendered to the Russians, they obtained a rich haul of Japanese equipment. The Russians, contrary to the treaty which Stalin had just concluded with the Chinese Government, admitted them into Manchuria, allowed them to share in the occupation of the towns, and permitted them to help themselves from the arms. and munition dumps captured from the Japanese.

While the Communists were thus in effect taking over Manchuria with Russian connivance, American ships and transport aircraft were moving Chinese Government troops to Nanking, Shanghai, Tsingtao, Tientsin and Peking. Similar transport was provided for the Government troops who were in accordance with the treaty with the Soviet Union to take over Manchuria. But when the American transports arrived off Dairen, the principal Manchurian port, the Russians refused to allow a landing, referring to their special rights in the port under the recently concluded treaty, although these did not provide any legal grounds for preventing the transit of Chinese regular troops. The American admiral in charge of the transports therefore went on to two other Manchurian ports, Hulutao and Yingkow, but found that the harbour areas in both places had been turned over by the Soviet military authorities to Chinese Communists. His orders prohibited him from forcing a landing at any place occupied by 'dissident Chinese forces', so he had to go south and land the Chinese Government troops at Chingwangtao, south of the Great

Wall and outside Manchuria. From here it was possible for the Government troops to march into Manchuria overland, but they had to go through the Shanhaikwan Pass between the mountains and the sea – a very strong defensive position which the Russians had also turned over to the Communists. They attacked, forced the pass and captured Chinchow in southern Manchuria on 26 November, five weeks after they had been turned away from Dairen. The Russians then changed their policy and allowed Chinese Government troops to take over Mukden without opposition. The attempt to keep them out of Manchuria had failed, but the Communists retained the Japanese arms they had acquired and not only used them to equip their units in Manchuria but distributed them to their forces in North China. These supplies were of very great importance to the Communists because they had hitherto been poorly armed; their great skill in guerrilla warfare had enabled them to survive and extend their control in rural areas, but for weapons they had depended on village workshops or captures from Kuomintang or Japanese units. Now, thanks to the Russians, they had an abundance of arms, including artillery and tanks, which they had never previously possessed. Their haul of Japanese arms was not greater than that obtained by the Kuomintang forces after Japan's surrender, but it enabled the Communists for the first time to equip the manpower available to them and undertake operations which went beyond guerrilla raids.

It is clear from the facts of the record that the Soviet Union in September and October 1945 did try to use their military occupation of Manchuria to put the Communists in power there, just as they used military occupation for the same purpose in the countries of Eastern Europe. On the other hand, they gave little further assistance to the Chinese Communists after the end of November and virtually none at all after the final withdrawal of Soviet forces from Manchuria in the spring of 1946. Their behaviour must be interpreted in the light of the remarks attributed to Stalin by a Yugoslav biographer of Tito;[1] according to this account Stalin said to Kardelj at a meeting in Moscow in 1948:

> After the war we invited the Chinese comrades to come to Moscow and we discussed the situation in China. We told them bluntly that we considered the development of the uprising in China had no prospect, and that the Chinese comrades should join the Chiang Kai-shek government and dissolve their army. The Chinese comrades agreed here with the views of the Soviet comrades, but went back to China and acted otherwise. They mustered their forces, and now (1948), as we see, they are beating the Chiang Kai-shek army.

This often quoted passage does not specify the date of the consultation, which is given simply as 'after the war'.

In view of the Soviet actions in Manchuria during the three months immediately after Japan's surrender Stalin could hardly then have been convinced that the Communist uprising 'had no prospect', at any rate as far as Manchuria was concerned. Hulutao, Yingkow and Shanhaikwan were handed over to Chinese Communist forces, evidently in the expectation that possession of these places would enable them to keep the Kuomintang Army out of Manchuria without direct Russian military intervention against the internationally recognised Government of China. But the Communist defeat at Shanhaikwan must have been proof for Stalin that the Chinese comrades were not equal to their task. Stalin was never sentimental about foreign Communists; he judged them strictly on their actual performance. Since the Chinese Communists were incapable of holding an almost impregnable position, which the Russians had given them, he naturally came to the conclusion that they were not worth supporting, and since he was unwilling to risk a major conflict with America by the use of Russian troops to oppose Chiang, it was logical for him to advise the Chinese comrades to accept defeat and make the best terms they could with the National Government. There can be little doubt that Stalin gave such advice, but not until after the Shanhaikwan disaster.

It was not only at Shanhaikwan that the Chinese Communists were meeting with reverses in the autumn of 1945. In North China they were being driven from the railways by bestriding which they could block all overland communications between the Yangtse Valley and the Peking-Tientsin area. It was vital for the National Government to clear the main north-south lines if the cities it had taken over from the Japanese in North China were not to be isolated from the core of Kuomintang-governed territory in Central and South China. By December, Kuomintang troops had cleared the east-west Lunghai railway and were making progress on the Peking-Hankow and Tienstin-Pukow lines. The Communists had not yet had time to consolidate their recent territorial gains and were in danger of being pushed back into the remote area from which the Japanese invasion had enabled them to emerge. Help reached them, however, from an unexpected quarter: the American Government had made up its mind that the civil war in China must be stopped, and at the beginning of December, President Truman announced that he was sending General Marshall to China as his personal representative on a mission of mediation. It had already been decided that American aid to China would be suspended if it was going to be 'diverted for use in fratricidal warfare'. Truman publicly told Marshall that his task was first to arrange a cessation of hostilities between the Chinese Government and Communist armies and then to convoke a 'conference of representatives of major political elements . . . to develop an early solution to the present internal strife'. Privately, the President instructed his envoy:

> In your conversations with Chiang Kai-shek and other Chinese leaders you are authorised to speak with the utmost frankness. Particularly you may state . . . that a China disunited and torn by civil strife could not be considered realistically as a proper place for American assistance along the lines enumerated.

Chiang Kai-shek had not asked for American mediation nor did he desire an unconditional armistice in the civil war at a moment when his troops were winning, but he could not disregard the advice from Washington, backed as it was by the threat to cut off all American economic and military aid if he would not desist from 'fratricidal warfare'. He had to agree to a truce which was to be supervised by American officers. Marshall treated the internationally recognised Government of China as on exactly the same footing as the Communist insurgents, and leant over backwards in his endeavours to show his complete impartiality between them. What, however, had escaped the notice of Truman and Marshall was that, in trying to bring about a unification of China without civil war, America had no means of pressure to exert on the Chinese Communists similar to those which it could use to coerce the Chinese Government. The Government was dependent on American aid, particularly after its recovery of the cities from Japanese occupation; the Communists, with their dispersed, self-sufficient economy, were not. The Americans, therefore, were able to stop the civil war when the Kuomintang was winning; later, when the Communists were winning, they had no way of stopping it.

Marshall arrived in China on 20 December 1945; he left in January 1947 to become Secretary of State, having totally failed to bring about any agreement between the National Government and the Communists. Later he was reported to have said about China: 'I wash my hands of a problem which has passed altogether beyond my comprehension and my power to make judgements.' The year of fruitless mediation was put to good use by the Chinese Communists in consolidating their strategic position in North China, and when the civil war was renewed at the beginning of 1947 it was soon evident that time had been on their side. On the morrow of Japan's surrender Chiang Kai-shek had enjoyed high prestige as China's national leader through eight years of war against a foreign invader, which had been brought to a victorious conclusion, but this was a wasting asset and by 1947 it no longer counted for much. The Kuomintang

Army in the autumn of 1945 had shown considerable fighting spirit, stimulated by taking the surrender of a million Japanese soldiers; a year of passive inaction completely demoralised it. The administrative defects of the Kuomintang system of government had become only too apparent in a year and a half of endeavour to restore the Chinese national economy with a top-heavy military budget and essential communications interrupted by rebel forces. Unchecked currency inflation disorganised productive enterprise, promoted speculative hoarding and aggravated official corruption; disappointment following in the wake of victory over Japan destroyed the popularity of the régime among the middle classes, who had originally provided its main political support. Last but not least as a factor in its decline, the Kuomintang itself, frustrated in its hopes of reunifying China under its leadership, depending on American aid and yet bitterly resentful of American interference in Chinese politics, became a prey to factional dissensions in ominous contrast to the cohesion and discipline of the party organisation of the Communists.

During the first half of 1947 the Kuomintang still gained successes in the civil war, but the impetus of 1945 had gone, and in the second half of the year the tide definitely turned in favour of the Communists. The year 1948 was one of disasters culminating in the loss of all Manchuria and nearly all North China to the Communists. South China still held out for a while, but fell to the Communists in the course of 1949, except for the island of Formosa, whither Chiang Kai-shek had removed the residue of the Kuomintang military forces and an apparatus of central government which was superimposed on the local provincial administration. Separated from the mainland by 100 miles of sea, he was safe for the moment from the march of communism, which had overwhelmed the rest of China, but it seemed to be only a matter of time before the Communists would organise a military and naval strength sufficient to pursue the defeated party into its last stronghold.

The Communists did not proclaim their own central government of China and seek international diplomatic recognition for it until they had completed their conquest of the Chinese mainland. The Central People's Government of China was set up in Peking, not Nanking, which had been the Kuomintang capital, in October 1949, nominally as a coalition of Chinese left-wing parties under Communist leadership, but actually under the absolute control of the Communist party. It was at once recognised by the Soviet Union and the Communist-governed states of Eastern Europe. Soon afterwards Britain accorded recognition; this was not at the time regarded in London as a move contrary to the policy of the United States, because the British Foreign Office had been given to understand that the American Government would do the same after the mid-term Congressional elections of November 1950, it being thought dangerous for the electoral prospects of the Democratic party to do it before. But by the time the elections were held, America was already involved in the war in Korea, and as a result of commitments which the American Government then undertook the recognition of Communist China was postponed indefinitely.

By 1950 indeed policy towards China had become an acute issue in American domestic politics. In 1945 hardly a voice had been raised in protest at Marshall's commission to mediate in China; in the American political climate of that time nothing seemed more natural than to suppose that a civil war in another country could be exorcised by the wisdom of 'the greatest living American' and a formula of coalition government. But after the failure of the Marshall mediation a section of the Republican party began to voice increasingly severe criticism of the China policy of the Truman Administration. Marshall, after his return from China and his appointment as Secretary of State, was in favour of complete American disengagement from China. He personally disliked Chiang Kai-shek and he did not see the situation in China as a danger to American interests; moreover, he held that American

71

economic and military resources were not sufficient for large-scale involvement in both Europe and Asia and that Europe should have the prior claim on them. But when the Communists began to win victories in China, American public opinion became apprehensive at the prospect of Communist rule over a nation which had been regarded as a special friend and ally of America, and after the proclamation of the Truman doctrine in support of Greece and Turkey it was difficult for the Administration to explain why communism must be contained by American economic and military aid on the shores of the Mediterranean but not in Eastern Asia. Marshall had to compromise; in order to obtain sufficient support in a Republican-dominated Congress for the Truman doctrine and Marshall Aid to Europe, he had to make concessions to those who urged more American aid for Chiang Kai-shek. But a China policy based on a compromise between the advocates and opponents of intervention could hardly be a success. Congress passed a China Aid Act in April of 1948, but the assistance given to the Chinese Government was too little and too late to alter the outcome of a civil war in which the decisive battles had already been fought. The only effect of the belated China Aid Act was to intensify Chinese Communist hostility to the United States, already developed on theoretical Marxist-Leninist grounds which classified America as the foremost imperialist power after the elimination of Nazi Germany and Japan.

The debate on China continued in America after the final victory of the Communists in the civil war, and became increasingly embittered, although it now took the form of a *post mortem* rather than of an argument about what was to be done. The hopes of those who had regarded the Chinese Communists as 'agrarian reformers' rather than 'real' Communists, or expected them to follow the path marked out by Tito, were disappointed when Mao Tse-tung went to Moscow and concluded a treaty of military alliance with the Soviet Union. It was the news of this treaty which more than anything else brought home to the American public the hard fact of what had happened in China. A nation which had been regarded as a reliable friend and had long been a special sphere for American missionary, philanthropic and educational activities had been taken over into the camp of America's great adversary in world affairs. The policy towards China pursued by Byrnes, Marshall and Acheson as successive Secretaries of State under Truman now appeared in retrospect to have been incredibly stupid. Moreover, just at this time Alger Hiss – who had been a personal friend of Dean Acheson – was convicted in a court of law nominally on a charge of perjury, but actually for having acted as a Soviet agent in the State Department; to charges of mismanagement of foreign policy were henceforward added suspicions that it had been influenced by persons who were dedicated, not to the national interests of the United States, but to the cause of international communism. With Congressional elections only a few months away the domestic political situation became very serious for the Truman Administration during the early part of 1950. Accused of having 'lost' China, it could not afford to tolerate any further Communist conquests in the Far East, and it was in this position when the army of Communist North Korea crossed the frontier of South Korea on 25 June 1950.

Korea, unlike China, had not been an ally of the United States during the war, nor had it had an internationally recognised Government. It had been a territory under full Japanese sovereignty since 1910, and although Korean nationalists had maintained a shadowy 'Provisional Government' in exile in China since 1919, this had not received diplomatic recognition by any state. At the Cairo Conference in 1943 it had been agreed between America, Britain and China that after the Pacific war Korea should 'in due course' become free and independent; later plans were drawn up for a four-power trusteeship of America, Britain, China and Russia to administer Korea until the Koreans should

73

have learnt the arts of democratic self-government, and properly elected rulers of their own. But meanwhile, when Japan's surrender became imminent, arrangements had to be made for a military occupation of Korea and the disarming of the Japanese troops there, so it was agreed that American forces should take over to the south of the 38th parallel of latitude and Russian to the north of that line. This demarcation was not regarded on the American side as in any sense a political division; it was assumed that for political reconstruction Korea would be treated as a unit, and in this, as in so many other cases at that time, high hopes were entertained of Russian co-operation. But the course of events followed the pattern of occupied Germany; a Communist-controlled administration emerged in the Soviet zone, while in the American zone attempts were made to lay the foundations for a liberal democracy. It soon became clear that no fusion between the North and South Korean authorities would be countenanced by Russia, except on terms which made the Korean Communist party predominant in the South as well as in the North.

After two years of fruitless negotiation the American Government referred the problem of Korean unification to the United Nations. An international commission was sent to Korea; it was refused admittance to the North, but in the South it supervised elections, and the Korean Government which emerged from them was recognised as the lawful authority in Korea by the United Nations and by most non-Communist states, while the Communist government in North Korea received *de jure* recognition from the Soviet Union and other countries of the Communist bloc. Both Russian and American troops were then withdrawn from Korea and two mutually hostile Korean governments were left confronting each other across a line of military demarcation which had become in effect a frontier between two states. It was only to be expected that they would fight. But this, although a war between Koreans, would not be merely a civil war like the struggle between Chiang Kai-shek and the Communists in China; the two Korean régimes had been brought into being under Russian and American administrations, and South Korea had become a ward of the United Nations. It was less likely than in China that a war could be fought out in Korea without intervention from outside.

Initially, however, after the departure of the Russian and American troops the fighting would have to be between Koreans, and it was therefore in the first place a question of military power as between North and South Korea. As South Korea had a larger population than North, it had an advantage in potential military manpower, and America was at least as well able as Russia to provide equipment. But whereas the Russians provided the North Korean Army with heavy artillery and tanks, the Americans denied all heavy weapons to the South Korean forces. It was subsequently explained that American policy had been inspired by fear lest, if the South Koreans possessed powerful armaments, they would attack the North and thus bring on a war with Russia. American officials who thought along these lines, however, apparently failed to realise that an army which is too weak to take the offensive will be too weak to defend itself either. But in any case, the American Government at the beginning of 1950 was as anxious to disengage from Korea as from China. On 12 January 1950, Acheson as Secretary of State, made a speech in which he declared a line from the Aleutian Islands to Japan and Okinawa to be America's 'defence perimeter' in the Pacific; Formosa and South Korea were left outside this line. It was an assurance to the Chinese and Korean Communists that they need not fear American intervention if they were to overrun either.

But when in the last week of June the North Korean Army crossed the 38th parallel and drove ahead with 150 Russian-built tanks against the tankless forces of the South, the United States at once intervened to rescue the South, and the Security Council of the United Nations, freed from the Soviet veto through a temporary boycott of its proceedings by a Soviet delegate, authorised military assistance to South Korea as a victim of aggression. Fifteen other nations joined the United States in the first war waged by a world security organisation to beat back an armed attack. At first it seemed that the intervention would fail because the momentum of the North Korean invasion nearly overwhelmed the whole peninsula before enough United Nations troops could be landed. But the Pusan area was held against North Korean attacks, and General MacArthur, appointed to command the United Nations as well as American forces in Korea, repeated the amphibious strategy he had used so effectively in the war against Japan. He took the North Koreans in the rear by a landing at Inchon on the west coast and decisively defeated them. The question of policy was now whether to confine the objective of the war to the liberation of the South Korean territory from the invaders or whether to go on across the 38th parallel and take advantage of the North Korean military collapse to re-unify the whole country. A decision in favour of unification was taken in Washington with the concurrence of Britain and other Western powers and endorsed by a vote of the United Nations Assembly. MacArthur's army swept on northward towards the river Yalu, the frontier between Korea and Manchuria.

But if in the end the United States had refused to tolerate a forcible Communist seizure of South Korea, would the Soviet Union tolerate a forcible anti-Communist seizure of North Korea? With American and allied European troops on their way to the Yalu a Soviet military intervention could only have meant direct hostilities between the two power blocs and a world war in which both sides would now be in possession of nuclear weapons. But there was an alternative to Soviet intervention and this was Chinese Communist intervention under Soviet protection. Chinese forces could be used to drive back the United Nations Army in Korea, while the threat of Soviet intervention would deter America and her allies from retaliation by bombing against

Chinese territory, particularly the area of Manchuria, where the greater part of China's heavy industry was located. This at any rate is what happened, and it is only reasonable to suppose that it was intended, for intervention without an assurance of Russian support in the event of all-out war by the Americans would have been too great a risk even for Mao Tse-tung to take. As it was, the risk was very serious, and the decision a hard one; it is said to have cost him three sleepless nights. Fortunately for him, the military operation was facilitated by the certainty on the American side that there was no risk of Chinese intervention. MacArthur incredulous of reports of Chinese preparations to intervene and unaware until it was too late that more than a quarter of a million Chinese soldiers were enveloping his right flank pushed his army up to the Yalu. The result was a heavy defeat for the United Nations forces and their hurried retreat back again into South Korea.

The Korean War began as one between North and South Korea; it then became in effect one between North Korea and America; by the end of 1950 it had become one between American and Communist China. Fear of a fourth stage in which it might become one between America and Russia caused the American Government to confine the struggle against China to the Korean peninsula, so that China was able to wage war against three Great Powers outside her borders with complete immunity for her own territory against their counteraction. This was not in accordance with the wishes of General MacArthur, who was in favour of using American air-power against Manchuria in spite of the risk of Russian intervention. His attempts to appeal to the American public over the head of the American Government produced an impossible situation for President Truman, who finally dismissed him from his command in April of 1951. Meanwhile, the Chinese, encouraged by their initial victory, had become hopeful of driving the United Nations forces out of Korea altogether, and ten days after MacArthur's dismissal launched a great offensive against positions which the UNC (United Nations Command) had taken up close to the 38th parallel. The offensive failed, with very heavy casualties for the Chinese, and the UNC began counter-attacking. The Soviet Union now put out peace feelers on China's behalf, and on 8 July negotiations for an armistice were begun in Korea between representatives of the opposing armies.

The American Government expected the truce talks to go on for about three weeks; in fact, they lasted for over two years. It was assumed in Washington that, if the Communists wanted to end the war, details of a cease-fire agreement could be worked out in a short time; there was a failure to recognise the capacity of Communists, and especially to Chinese Communists, for using endless talk as an instrument of policy. In order to reduce casualties with a truce already in view, the UNC desisted from further offensive operations against the Chinese, and gave the latter time to recover from their defeat and dig themselves in. Thereafter, the Communist delegates to the armistice negotiations felt no need for haste. Most of the armistice terms were at last agreed, but no way of compromise could be found on the Communist demand that all prisoners of war, including those who had manifested anti-Communist sentiments in captivity, should be forcibly repatriated to their homelands. The war dragged on without any more great battles – for both sides now held strongly fortified lines across the peninsula – but with much bloody local fighting for tactically important positions.

In America the Truman Administration incurred fresh unpopularity on account of the prolongation of the war, which it was unable to terminate either by victory or cease-fire. General Eisenhower as Republican candidate for the Presidency in 1952 made a pledge to bring the war to a speedy end a principal part of his campaign. After his election he set about redeeming his promise. As a simple soldier he believed that more than verbal argument at the conference table was needed to persuade the Communists to conclude an armistice on acceptable terms. A major offensive with ground troops would be too costly in casualties, even if successful, but there were possible uses of American airpower which had not yet been tried. In May 1953, a warning was conveyed to Communist China through Indian channels that, if the truce talks finally broke down, the UNC would strike at targets within China and would not refrain from the employment of nuclear weapons. This was a return to the strategy which had been advocated by MacArthur, but rejected by Truman, two years earlier. It was now less risky than it had been then because of the death of Stalin and the domestic political disarray in Moscow which had made the Soviet attitude to the conflict slightly less truculent. At any rate the threat had its effect. The Chinese gave way on the issue of prisoner repatriation and an armistice was signed on 27 July 1953, three years and one month after the day when the North Korean Army had first crossed the 38th parallel.

An armistice, however, was not yet peace, and an international conference was projected for ending the Korean War with a formal peace treaty. It was intended that this conference – which met in Geneva in 1954 – should also settle two other Far Eastern issues involving the Western and Communist power blocs. One of these was Formosa and the other Indo-China. The question of Formosa had arisen as a subject of conflict between Communist China and America as a consequence of the outbreak of the war in Korea. As already mentioned, Acheson, early in 1950, had put both South Korea and Formosa outside the American 'defence perimeter' and indicated that the United States would not take any action to save either from Communist conquest. But when policy was reversed on South Korea, it was natural that it should be reversed on Formosa also; it did not seem to make sense to fight the Communists in Korea but allow them to take Formosa and capture half a million anti-Communist troops there. President Truman therefore ordered the American

79

Navy to 'neutralise' Formosa, preventing any invasion of the island from the mainland, but also restraining the Kuomintang forces in the island from attacking the mainland. This policy, however, did not, like the intervention in Korea, have any endorsement from the United Nations, and it was opposed by the British Government, which sought to limit the war to Korea and avoid hostilities with China. Even after the Chinese had intervened in Korea, Britain continued to disapprove of any irrevocable commitment with Chiang Kai-shek which would make it harder to obtain a settlement with Peking after the war. The United States, on the other hand, became more and more deeply involved in the defence of Formosa and finally concluded a treaty of military alliance with the surviving Kuomintang Government in Taipeh, which it continued to recognise as the *de jure* Government of China.

The question of Indo-China had been brought within the sphere of Communist-Western world conflict because the Vietnamese nationalist movement for independence from French colonial rule had fallen under Communist leadership and had since the end of 1949 been given material assistance across the border from Communist China. What had been, therefore, essentially a colonial war, in which no country but France had an interest in preserving French control there, came to be regarded in Washington as a sector of the world-wide front for the containment of communism. American arms were made available to France for carrying on the war against the Vietminh, the Communist-led guerrilla organisation which employed political and military techniques learned from China. When a large part of the French army was surrounded in Dien Bien Phu early in 1954 and could not be supplied from the air because the relieving planes were shot down by Chinese anti-aircraft guns, direct American intervention was considered in Washington, but the idea was abandoned, because intervention with ground forces would be too unpopular with the American people after the experience of the war in

Korea, and 'massive retaliation' with nuclear weapons, as theoretically advocated for American strategy by Secretary Dulles, could find no suitable targets in the Vietnam jungles. Dien Bien Phu surrendered on 6 May 1954, ten days after the opening of an international conference in Geneva intended to bring about peace settlements in both Korea and Indo-China. America and Britain, Russia and China were there, as well as France and representatives of both the Vietminh and the French-sponsored Government of Vietnam, together with all the states which had taken part in the Korean War. The Korean phase of the conference ended in complete deadlock and no peace treaty was signed; the war was not renewed, but it remained suspended merely by the armistice agreement, with two halves of Korea still separated and the armies which had fought each other for three years still confronting each other from fortified lines across a deserted demilitarised zone which, since nobody lives there, has become a sanctuary for all kinds of birds. The bulk of the American and other non-Korean components of the UNC were withdrawn, but two American divisions remained – which have been ever since the only American troops in the world technically on active service. The Chinese 'People's Volunteers' were withdrawn across the Yalu, but strong Chinese forces were held in Manchuria ready to re-enter Korea at any time.

With regard to Formosa, there was likewise a failure to reach any treaty settlement, but a *de facto* truce was established in the Formosa Straits, with the Chinese Communists deterred from any attempt to invade the island by the presence of the American Seventh Fleet. Twice – in 1955 and again in 1958 – probing operations against the Kuomintang forward positions on the small islands of Quemoy and Matsu off the South China coast were undertaken, presumably in the hope that the American Government would advise Chiang Kai-shek to abandon them, but the attacks were discontinued when it became clear that the Seventh Fleet would intervene. On the diplomatic plane, Washington and

Peking carried on prolonged negotiations through their ambassadors in Warsaw and elsewhere, but found no basis for agreement, because the Chinese Communists steadily refused to give any undertaking not to try to take Formosa by force, claiming that it was their inalienable right as the central government of China to bring all Chinese provinces under their authority. The United States continued to recognise the Kuomintang Government in Taipeh as the Government of China and mustered sufficient votes in the United Nations to keep China's seat there for its delegate.

For Indo-China a treaty did indeed emerge from the Geneva conference, although the United States was not a signatory of it. Vietnam was divided territorially between a Vietminh régime in the North and an anti-Communist one in the South; since there was not, as there was in Korea, a definite front line between the contending forces, it was necessary to carry out parallel withdrawals and regrouping in order to achieve the partition. The partition was not represented in the treaty as more than temporary for it was laid down that elections should be held throughout Vietnam after two years. As there was a larger population in the North than in the South and as it was under the totalitarian control of the Vietminh it was a foregone conclusion that such elections would establish Communist rule over the whole country. This appears to have been accepted as inevitable by the French, who, having suffered military defeat, were disposed to cut their losses and make the best of the existing situation. The Americans, however, declined to regard South Vietnam as lost, and in opposition to the French, they supported the political faction of Ngo Dinh Dien, who refused to take part in nation-wide elections on the ground that they could not be free in the North, and built up an army with American aid to resist a Vietminh take-over in Saigon.

As a result of events in Eastern Asia from 1945 to 1955, there were at the end of the decade four Communist states in existence there apart from the Asian territory of the Soviet Union. These were Mongolia, the Chinese People's Republic, North Korea and North Vietnam. Mongolia had already been Communist before the Second World War and remained a Soviet satellite, but the other three régimes – among which Communist China was, of course, immeasurably more important than the other two – owed their being to the circumstances of the collapse of Japan's imperial power. But North Korea and North Vietnam, however, owed their survival to some degree of Chinese intervention, for North Korea would certainly have been completely overrun by the UNC in 1950 but for the Chinese rescue operation, and the Vietminh would probably have been overwhelmed by the Navarre offensive in 1954 but for the Chinese help which gave them victory at Dien Bien Phu. The Chinese Communist revolution had thus – even though thwarted in Formosa – extended its action successfully beyond the frontiers of China, and a new Communist order had come into being, which, unlike the new group of Communist states in Eastern Europe, was not subordinate to Moscow, but a system of power in its own right.

3 GERMANY

Donald Watt

If the 'cold war' is to be considered as a description of the
relationship between the Soviet Union and the Western powers
in the years since 1945, it might be held that it took its origins
in the break with the Polish Government in 1943, spread in 1944-
45 to the Balkans and Greece, but then came to centre for the
next decade on the control of Germany. The struggle for Germany as such is of course of longer duration. It has been claimed
that it was taking place throughout the inter-war period.[2] But
there is a significant difference between the struggle for Germany's
allegiance in the days when she was a united power, and that
which took place in the power vacuum of the post-war years with
Germany divided and defeated.

The struggle for Germany, which constitutes the German
phase of the cold war, began in 1945 with Germany's surrender
and occupation and ended at the Geneva Summit Conference a
decade later with the Soviet withdrawal into the fortress of the
'Two Germanies' policy, and the diversion of the main Soviet
diplomatic offensive to the Middle East. It was not to be revived
until November 1958 – in so different a form that its discussion
belongs to a separate chapter of this book. Its course can be
divided into five main phases: the period of nominal collaboration
from 1945-46 which ended with the cessation of reparations
deliveries from the Western zones to the Soviet Union in April
1946; the period of the main crisis which lasted from 1946 to the
end of the first Berlin crisis; the period of Western consolidation

and integration from the end of the Berlin crisis to the signature of the Paris agreements and the treaty of the European Defence Community; the period of the Soviet defensive action from 1952 to the admission of Western Germany to NATO; and finally the phase of Soviet withdrawal, the Soviet recognition of Western Germany and the Geneva Summit Conference.

The history of the German phase in the cold war is complicated not only by the conflict between the four occupying powers – the Soviet Union, the United States, Great Britain and France – but also by conflicts within each grouping, and between the various German political parties of whom five main groups are significant; the three mass parties and their allies, the Christian Democrat (CDU), the Social Democrat (SPD) and the Socialist Unity (SED) parties; and the two lesser groupings of the non-party neutralists and the nationalist right, both of democratic and of neo-Nazi colouring. The interaction between those groups and one another, and their effects on the relationships between the occupying powers, make the course of events often extremely complicated to follow.

To take the policies of the occupying powers first: Soviet policy has suffered a gradual diminution of its aims from the hope of a unified, Communist-controlled Germany held in the 1945-49 period, through successive phases of aiming first at a disarmed, neutralised and united Germany, then at an armed, unified, but neutral Germany, to the final retreat into the policy of the Two Germanies. Throughout, they have been imprisoned in the consequences of their initial occupation policy, their deal with Poland in 1945 over the Oder-Neisse line and the establishment of the German Democratic Republic. By contrast, Britain and the United States began with no overall German policy other than a punitive one, and changed at different speeds and times to a policy of maintaining the balance of power in Central Europe. With both the reparations issue was crucial, and this, taken with minor military considerations, led inevitably to the acceptance of a division of Germany, already recognised in fact in the American compromise proposals on the reparations issue made at Potsdam. Once Germany's division was apparent the pressures of the cold war led them to a position where ultimately they were bound to prefer the integration of Western Germany into Western Europe to any serious move towards German unification. Inevitably, the result was to make of the demarcation line between the Western and Soviet zones of occupation in Germany a frontier between East and West. The 'truce lines established in 1945', as Dean Rusk has called them,[3] hardened into barriers, not only to the passage of Germans but to the exercise of power by the great powers themselves. The 'reach' of the two blocs terminates at the truce-line, as the failure of the Western powers to take any action in 1953 at the time of the East German rising amply and tragically demonstrated.

The only dissentient note in the West has been struck by France, the main complicating factor in Western policy. French policy from the beginning was concerned with French security against Germany and France's status as a great power. Fears for Europe under the Soviet threat were to put her government in the forefront of the integration movement, but these fears had always to be balanced against France's own internal weakness and the traditional dislike of Germany. Not until 1955-56 did France commit herself to the idea of a Franco-German condominium, which now so dominates French policy on German issues.

It is necessary, first, to consider the wartime origins of the struggle for Germany.

Of all the allies in the grand coalition against Nazi Germany, only the Soviet Union seemed in 1945 to have developed a policy designed not so much to prevent the repetition of the events which had led up to the outbreak of the Second World War as to influence decisively the post-war balance of power. During the war it was possible to argue that the Soviets were pursuing two contradictory policies: that of the dismemberment of Germany as advanced in the various inter-allied conferences from Moscow in 1941 to Yalta in 1945, and that of a German-Soviet *rapprochement*. The Soviets were unique among the allies in conducting separate armistice negotiations with Nazi Germany during the war[4] and unique in their overt support for a Free German movement. They seem at one time to have hoped to influence a sizeable part of the German Army into a repetition of Tauroggen, but the failures of the Russian-controlled National Committee for Free Germany and the much-publicised 'Appeal of the Fifty Generals' in December 1944 to affect German morale on the Eastern Front apparently led them to abandon this. At the same time they were building up Communist cadres for a return to Germany. The common denominator to all these policies was clearly a wish to create a weak Germany ripe for the extension of Soviet influence, whether divided or not. A dismembered Germany would make an excellent field for a new Soviet-led movement for German reunification.

The new line adopted in early 1945 was to prepare Germany for a thorough 'bourgeois-democratic' transformation. Germany in this view still suffered from a kind of industrial as well as agrarian feudalism, and had not completed the bourgeois revolution essential as a preliminary to the introduction of socialism. The group of German Moscow-trained Communists under Ulbricht who were to accompany the Soviet troops into Germany were instructed not to set up a separate Communist party but to work for a broad-based anti-Fascist movement, a 'bloc for militant democracy'. This was in fact the policy followed in the first few months of occupation, though in practice great care was taken to see that there was a trusted Moscow-trained German Communist in each position of importance. Attempts to revive the native German Communist party and attempts by members of the Communist underground in Germany to challenge the leadership of the Moscow reimmigrants were severely dealt with.

In June 1945 the line changed again, as a result of a visit by Wilhelm Pieck to Moscow. A separate Communist party, the KPD was established and the Socialists were allowed to form a party of their own, though in much of the Soviet zone it was heavily infiltrated by fellow-travellers. The experiment was very nearly disastrous, despite the political facilities made available to the KPD and denied to their opponents by the Soviet occupying authority, since it was impossible for the KPD either to cause the abandonment of or to dissociate themselves from the wholesale Soviet plundering of their Zone's economic resources for reparation payments, let alone to undo the effect of the behaviour of the Soviet Army's rank-and-file in the aftermath of victory. In November 1945, therefore, the line changed again with the formation of the Socialist Unity Party, the SED, and the *Gleichschaltung* of the Socialist Party in the Soviet Zone. The SED were built up steadily for the holding of all-German elections, elections which both they and their Soviet sponsors were sure in their mind of winning. Not until their defeat in October 1946, especially in the election of the City Government of Berlin, were they to be disillusioned.

Of the Western allies, Britain was perhaps the most concerned with the post-war balance of power and anxious as to the possible courses of action the Soviet Union would follow. The most perceptive (and prophetic) contributions to the back-stage debate on the future of Germany came from the Chiefs of Staff and the Treasury. In September 1944, the Chiefs of Staff advised that the dismemberment of Germany would on balance be to Britain's advantage, both as a sure means of preventing German rearmament and a renewal of aggression and as a means of guarding against a hostile Soviet Union. A unified but disarmed Germany would possibly fall into Soviet hands and would never be permitted to rearm. A divided Germany would offer much more prospect of the Western and Southern share coming within the orbit of a West European grouping. The actual issue of dismemberment seemed to have been settled in a positive sense at Yalta by the decision to refer the means of implementing such action to the European Advisory Commission. The British Government at this stage were still divided, Churchill and Eden still generally supporting the idea, although the former was greatly perturbed and restrained by his anxieties over Russian behaviour. It was at this stage that the Treasury intervened with an impressive survey of economic arguments against dismemberment. The British zone of occupation, they pointed out, was largely industrial in character and was not self-sufficient in food supplies, which it drew in part from Eastern Germany, in part from overseas. It could probably be expected to contain a large number of refugees in addition. Experience with the occupation of Italy had already shown that to maintain a minimum standard of living under such conditions could be enormously costly to the occupying power. It was essential that Germany should be permitted to import at a given level and that German deliveries of goods should be sufficient to pay for these imports. These relief imports must be the first charge on German deliveries, otherwise Britain would find herself paying for them. If th: first claim on these deliveries was to be to meet reparations payments, Britain would in fact find herself paying Germany's reparation bill. Germany was an economic whole and must be treated as such.

Their analysis of the reparations issue was prophetic. They warned against 'once and for all' deliveries from particular zones of occupation, unless the Allied Control Commission, in agreement with the occupying power, had decided that these could take place without risk of creating conditions contrary to the administrative interests of the occupying power. They warned against any commitment to secure reparations deliveries beyond the limit judged to be within the capacity of the British zone of occupation. If the zone was stripped of its capital resources, someone – presumably the occupying power – would have to provide the large sums needed to restore its working capital. If the Soviet Union claimed that any deficiency in deliveries from the Soviet Zone could be made up by deliveries from other zones, then Britain's liabilities would be infinite. The cost of the Soviet proposals would be social disturbance in Germany and the endangering of Western political institutions.

If the plans for dismembering Germany included not only the transfer of part of Eastern Germany to Poland but also the establishment of three or four self-supporting states, with a prohibition on currency and customs unions and the break-up of the existing transport and communications services, then Britain would face a financial and economic liability only dischargeable by making her pay for the revival of Germany. American aid for the whole area was essential to help towards the solution of Germany's economic problems as a whole. In a final and even more prophetic passage, they warned that, if the Soviet Zone was likely to develop into a system amenable to Soviet policy, then Britain would have to consider the development of a unified Western Germany to be fitted into the economy of Western Europe. This memorandum the Cabinet accepted, concluding that the result of current Soviet policy if left unopposed, would be to leave Great Britain occupying an area for which imports would be required, which neither Germany nor Britain would be able to afford. It did not, however, finally convince the advocates of dismemberment, who were to find themselves shortly faced with a *fait accompli*.[5]

Those memoranda were predicated on an outright break between East and West of a kind which Britain was still determined to prevent if this were possible. No one in Britain relished the idea of a confrontation between East and West, especially as evidence was mounting of a return to isolationism and a reluctance to accept long-term involvement in Europe on the part of the Roosevelt administration. For the moment the moral drawn in Britain was that German dismemberment was to be resisted at all costs, and that it was preferable only to a total abandonment of Germany to the Soviet orbit. By March 1945, the American

administration had been largely won round to this British way of
thinking, one which the State Department, and the few long-
sighted realists within the Administration anxious about Soviet
ambitions, like Stimson, Harriman or Forrestal, already shared.
The dominating considerations in American policy, however,
were two in number: that there should be no American commitment to a lengthy occupation, and that the American Government
should under no circumstances undertake to underwrite the bill
for German reparations and for the recovery of Europe. In
President Roosevelt's mind and in the attitudes of his principal
advisers can be found the conviction that the end of the war would
find Europe in a state of turmoil and near civil war; that it was one
of the main aims of Britain to involve the United States in the
reconstruction of Europe; and that the end of the war could be
expected to lead to a major resurge of isolationism in the United
States which it would be folly to oppose. The United States could
not agree to commit either troops or money to the post-war
reconstruction of Europe on any but the shortest of terms – two
years was the period Roosevelt named to Churchill and Stalin at
Yalta. Where Germany herself was concerned Roosevelt was
greatly influenced by the populist Germanophobe circle around
him, headed by Hans Morgenthau, the Secretary of the Treasury.
The idea of allowing Germany any but the most marginal of
industrial recoveries or of protecting German industrial plant
against the Soviet demands for reparations was thus entirely
contrary to the dominant school of thought in the United States.

There were clearly inconsistencies in the American as well as in
the Soviet position, just as in their punitive approach to German
reparations, the two seem to have had more in common with each
other than either with Britain. Indeed there is a good deal to be
said for the view that, had the two realised their full identity of
views, the idea of dismembering Germany would not have been
as casually dropped as it was in March 1945.[6] Only their determination to avoid footing the bill for German reparations united

the British and American Governments and was to unite them the following year. In the meantime, the prospect of American withdrawal spurred the British Government to urge and to win acceptance of French participation in the occupation of Germany and admitted to the negotiations over Germany a new and disturbing factor.

French policy on Germany at this time was governed by two factors also: de Gaulle's determination to accept nothing which put a barrier in the way of France's behaving like a great power, and a general French conviction that only a permanent detachment of the Rhineland and the Saar, as well as the Ruhr basin from Germany could grant France permanent security. The French programme in fact outdid even Foch's demands at Versailles in 1919. French military policy in the last days of Germany's defeat was largely influenced by the determination to seize as much of German territory as possible as a gage to be used in subsequent negotiations.[7] General de Gaulle refused to accept for France any agreements in the reaching of which France had not participated, a refusal which was largely to invalidate those reached between the other three occupying powers at Yalta and Potsdam. Only the agreements reached at the European Advisory Commission, in which French representatives did participate, remained valid for France.

The French Government objected particularly strongly to all those clauses of the political and economic 'Principles' agreed on at Potsdam which looked towards the treatment of Germany as a unity. Even more than the Soviets they were to disagree to anything likely to prevent them treating their zone's economic resources as a source on which France's economic deficiencies and the effects of war's devastations in France should be a first charge. Even more than Poland they were determined to secure the detachment of the Rhineland, the Saar and the Ruhr from Germany, and to resist all Allied policy measures on Germany until this was granted for them. Unlike Poland, however, they were playing as a would-be great power, not a satellite. For that they often lacked the power to withstand the pressure of their Allies, on whom they were often dependent for more than was safe for the maintenance of an independent position.

The three Allies thus approached the Potsdam Conference with very different outlooks and policies, making further trouble for themselves by their refusal to admit French participation. The outstanding issues to be settled were those of Germany's eastern frontiers, and the payment of German reparations to the Soviet Union. The British Government had already concluded in advance, and the United States administration came very quickly to realise, that the issue of the German-Polish frontier was of great importance in the issue of reparations. The Potsdam settlement of these issues by default was in fact to deprive each side of any real freedom of manoeuvre, and therefore to set the whole pattern for the clash over Germany which was to follow.

The Soviet Union approached Potsdam as the prisoner of its Polish policy. By its reassertion of the annexations originally agreed on with Hitler in August and September 1939, its break with the London Polish Government and its reluctant acceptance of Mikolajczyk, it found itself saddled with an unwilling and potentially hostile satellite, in which its own nominees, at the head, were saddled with responsibility for a fifth partition of Poland. Its remedy was to move Poland's western frontier bodily as far west as its pre-1939 eastern frontier had been moved and so to seek in East and West Prussia, Silesia, Stettin and all the land east of the Oder and Neisse rivers compensation for Poland's losses in the East. The action made Poland their certain ally as long as the settlement lasted. At the same time it made it impossible for the Soviet Union to tolerate any government other than one friendly to them in Poland – as it was subsequently to bind them equally to their nominees in the German Democratic Republic. Any step back could not be anything but a loss and a sacrifice.

The British Government found in the Soviet action confirmation of their gloomier fears. Before arrival at Potsdam they had concluded that there was little means available to them to influence the Soviet Union into changing its policy on Poland's western frontier. In practice this meant, however, that the whole basis on which Germany's capacity to pay was calculated had been destroyed. The move of the Polish frontier meant in practice a withdrawal from the German economy of one of its main sources of grain and coal, a great increase in the number of refugees to the West, and a great increase in the cost of supporting the Western zones. The British delegation in fact came to Potsdam determined to use the threat to withhold or release reparations deliveries to secure their own requirements of food deliveries from the East to their zone.

The stage was thus set for a head-on collision. The Soviet Union proved adamant on the Oder-Neisse line, on its refusal to negotiate a trade treaty or to agree that Germany's needs to pay for her imports should have priority over reparations deliveries from current production or stocks. Instead, it demanded $2,000–$3,000 million in deliveries of machinery from the Ruhr in reparations.

It will be clear that the different attitude of the Soviet and the British Governments to their zones already meant in practice separate treatment of the two parts of Germany, in fact their physical separation, and that despite their hope that Germany would be treated as an economic whole, the British Government, faced with a conflict between an agreed overall inter-allied policy on Germany and a separate individual treatment of their zone from the other zones, was forced by sheer economic necessity to plump for the second. Their choice was made more unavoidable by the fact that control over reparations deliveries to the Soviets from the British Zone was the only diplomatic weapon to hand with which still to strive for a single Germany organised economically in conformity with British views of what was most in Europe's and in her own interest. Separation was at Potsdam still a weapon to be used within a framework of unity, the framework set by the agreement reached between the three Powers to establish centralised German administrative departments run by German administrators in the fields of finance, transport, communications, foreign trade and industry. The Soviet desire to see Germany geared to one thing only – unlimited reparations payments for the reconstruction of western Russia – which ruled out any deliveries of food or raw materials from their own zone to the West, took place within a similar framework.

The compromise agreed on the reparations issue, nevertheless recognized the economic division of Germany *de facto*. American initiative secured agreement that the bulk of Soviet and Polish reparations claims should be met from the Soviet Zone. In addition the Soviet Union was to be entitled to 15 per cent. of all industrial capital removed from the Ruhr as unnecessary to its peace economy in return for Soviet deliveries of food, coal, fertilisers, zinc, timber and clay products of equivalent value from their zone, plus a further 10 per cent. without any such exchange. The idea of each zone drawing its food supplies from the area of Germany from which they had come before 1939 was dropped. Britain and the United States were left to supply the remaining needs of their zones unless German production there were allowed to rise to a figure adequate to cover these needs. The compromise amounted virtually to a barter treaty between the Soviet Zone and the West.

Economic separation was, however, to take place within an agreed framework set by the Control Commission and by all-German administrative bodies. But the failure to bring the French in at Potsdam enabled the French to refuse to accept any of the Conference's agreements if they chose not to, and the outright desire to dismember Germany, which continued to dominate France's policy in Germany for another eighteen months, destroyed any possibility of these all-German agencies being set up. The division of Germany was brought one stage further.

The actual physical act which precipitated the break, the firing on Fort Sumter, as it were, did not come, however, until April 1946. It came because the Soviet authorities preferred a free hand in their zone, or rather to refuse accountability for the policy of dismantlement there, to the chance of economic control of all Germany. They consistently refused to give any account of the raw materials and finished produce, the capital goods and equipment dismantled and removed from their zone, thus rendering it useless as an earner of foreign exchange. The level of German industry to which the industries of the Ruhr were to be reduced was based on a balanced import and export plan to cover all Germany, which the Soviet action made meaningless. The British and Americans found themselves willy-nilly pouring money into their zones, which were forced both to supply Soviet reparations in dismantled equipment, and with what was left, to earn the foreign exchange necessary for foreign imports. Bevin for Britain proposed an international consortium to manage the Ruhr, but neither the US nor the Soviet Union would play. The British were in fact having to find £80 m. a year in dollars mainly to feed their zone, 'paying reparations to Germany' in the disgruntled words of the Germanophobe Chancellor of the Exchequer, Hugh Dalton,[8] and American expenses were running equally high. In April, therefore, General Clay, the US High Commissioner, executed the threat envisaged by the British at Potsdam the previous summer and broke off all reparations payments to the Soviet Union. The severance was now complete.

This first period had already established what was to be the overriding pattern of the struggle for Germany. Both sides were bidding for complete control, to be found in an agreed German policy which would most accord with their long-term aims. Both were equally matched – masters in their own zones, powerless outside them. When faced with the choice, both sides, driven by overriding economic reasons arising from their post-war economic weakness, preferred to integrate their own zones into their section of the world economy rather than to avoid means likely to prejudice their chance of winning control of all Germany at the opening of the next stage in the struggle.

The next phase was characterised by a position of unification in theory and separation in practice.

The break over the reparations issue ushered in the first and most serious stage in the German phase of the 'cold war', that which included the Berlin crisis of 1948. This period was marked in the larger sweep of the cold war by the decline of Britain's economic position to one where a withdrawal from the European continent appeared seriously on the cards, by the United States' grasp of the initiative in the emergence of the Truman doctrine and the European Recovery Programme, and by the final abandonment by France of her attempt to pursue a separate foreign policy. These larger movements in the alignments and policies of the powers could not but have their repercussion in Germany, where they led inevitably to the formation on both sides of the demarcation line in Germany of opposed German régimes which, while they hardly deserved the title of puppets ascribed them in the press of the powers sponsoring their opponents, represented the extension into Germany of the ideological aspects of the cold war. In each case the creation of these régimes was intended to provide a base by which the political support of all Germany might be attracted to one side or the other. But their creation had three consequences for the future development of Germany.

Firstly, it heralded the end of the period when Germany was merely a passive object of international politics. Secondly, it inevitably reinforced and made more permanent the arbitrary division of Germany along the demarcation line. And thirdly, since, after all, only two years had elapsed since the defeat of Germany's bid for world dominion, it led inevitably to proposals for the tighter integration of the future Germany into the existing political organisation of her victors, as the only way in which the revival of German economic power could be so organised as to avoid a recurrence of the economic and political nationalism which the victors believed to have underlain the German support for Nazism.

This period of the cold war over Germany took the form of a kind of 'constitutional struggle', centring less around the actual unification of Germany, to which ideal all participants in the struggle still genuinely subscribed, than around the kinds of rules which were to govern the process of unification. Both sides appeared to believe that if the rules could only be set up aright, their nominees in German politics were bound to win. This 'constitutional debate' still tends to impose its form on any negotiations on or discussion of German unification to this day. What most alarmed the West in this period was the abandonment of this struggle for most of 1948 by the Soviet Union in favour of a direct blockade of Berlin and the forces of the Western allies occupying Berlin. The blockade represented in fact the Stalin régime's preference for the use of force where geographical circumstances seemed to favour it, just as its defeat tended to argue a failure to understand the overwhelming technological advantages enjoyed by the United States and the manner in which these could then be employed in any direct confrontation of power.

In this confrontation of power between the United States and the Soviet Union the position of the two other Western powers was an uneasy one. British policy since 1945 had concentrated on building up a network of alliances in Western Europe which was to constitute for some time Britain's major contribution to the movement towards European unity. The essential basis of this was the closest Anglo-French co-operation, and the fear of a German revival. The need to redevelop German strength was therefore unpopular at all levels of British politics.[9] Against this had to be set the undoubted fact that it was principally the expense of occupying and supporting the British Zone in Germany which had, as the Treasury had prophesied in January 1945, defeated all Britain's efforts to achieve a speedy post-war recovery, and had exhausted the American loan of 1945 without ending Britain's economic weakness. With America's return to the European scene, Britain moved willy-nilly away from her alignment with France towards one with the United States, opening the way for that loss of contact with France which was to prove disastrous a decade or more later. On their side, successive French Governments saw themselves confronted with a revival of German strength with British and American support on a scale which rendered the neo-Fochism of the de Gaulle governments simply irrelevant. They turned, therefore, almost in desperation, to the idea of integration, the idea of integrating German physical and industrial resources so firmly into Western Europe that any chance of their future use *against* Western Europe could be eliminated. So that just as French resistance to the idea of all-German administrative agencies had thwarted German unification prior to May 1946, so the French policy of integration was to perpetuate Germany's disunity in the future.

The 'constitutional struggle' was fought out mainly at the Foreign Ministers' conferences at Paris in July 1946, at London and Moscow in January and April 1947, and at London in November-December 1947. It was accompanied *pari passu* by the encouragement of political parties in Germany and the development of rival German institutions in preparation for the political struggle which would come once the two Germanies were reunited. Here again the Soviet Union, which, so long as it remained confident of victory in Germany, showed little sign of the suspicions of a revival of German power which hampered the Western powers, made the running – only to suffer a major setback in October 1946, in the municipal elections in Berlin. Throughout 1946, the SED had been built up with Soviet aid, while its rivals had been harassed by the Soviet occupying authorities; and both the Soviet policy-makers and the SED leadership seem to have expected an overwhelming victory,[10] analogous to those scored with the aid of similar methods in Eastern Europe. The result was an overwhelming defeat, the SED scoring only 19·8 per cent. of the total vote. Thereafter, to expect the Soviet Union to place any reliance on free elections was to expect the Soviet Union to admit defeat.

The Soviet defeat was the more upsetting in view of the sacrifices Molotov had made at Paris in July 1946. There France had proposed the internationalisation of the most important enterprises in the Ruhr, its political separation from Germany, the detachment of the Rhineland, the dismemberment in fact of Germany, a programme which offered the Soviets a permanent foothold in West Germany, and lasting control of its economic growth. Confident of electoral victory, however, Molotov had spurned the French, and made himself the advocate of German unity and an end of the occupation. In a bid for German support, he had demanded an all-German government, a plebiscite, a peace-treaty, an increase in the permitted level of industrial output, all measures which the French regarded with horror. All this now proved of no avail. Instead, the Russians were faced with a public setback, above all in Berlin where a Social Democrat anti-SED City Council was established which was to defy all the Soviets' subsequent attempts to destroy the will and morale of Berlin.

In the meantime, the Anglo-American powers were going ahead with their own plans for a German bridgehead. At Paris in July, James Byrnes, the US Secretary of State, had proposed the economic fusion of the Western zones, a proposal which the British had accepted. At Stuttgart in September, he had foreshadowed the association of German figures with the government of the Bizone. This was translated into practice in May 1947 with the establishment of the Economic Council for the Bizone, an organ which had the functions of a government, though its appearance was avoided. Bizonia, and the development of a German political system within it, were no more intended to lead to the separation of Germany than was the Soviet development of the SED and, a more sinister development, the People's Police. The intention was to build a bridgehead, or rather the first pier of a bridge by which Germany could be reunited. But the bridge was never to be completed.

Confirmation of this can be found in the continuing pre-occupation with the reparations question and the course of the Moscow Conference of April 1947. It was here that the French made their last serious bid for German dismemberment, relying on Soviet goodwill for their resistance to the proposal to merge their zone with Bizonia, their proposal to associate the Soviet Union with control of the Ruhr and their support of the Soviet position on reparations. The French proposals were, moreover, supported by the French Communist party which did not leave the Government until 4 May 1947. The Russian Government were still, however, bidding for a strong centralised Germany, the government of which would be easier for them to bring under their control through control of its key positions. The West were by contrast agreed on the need for a federal structure in Germany capable of withstanding the centripetal forces which Bismarck and Hitler had used to make Germany so dangerous to her neighbours. Britain and the United States in addition were most anxious to achieve the economic unification of Germany, so as to end the drain on their own financial resources necessary to keep their zones from starving. The Soviet demand for continued reparations from current production and their refusal to account for what they had already taken from their own zone, or to allow a resumption of the pre-1940 pattern of food distribution, made them totally unwilling to accept any Soviet proposals for German political unity. They therefore moved steadily on with the fusion of their zones, and were joined, a new development, in the summer of 1947 by the French. 'France is no longer a mediator' declared M. Bidault, the French Foreign Minister, on 20 June 1947.

A major factor in the British and French support for the unification of the Western zones was the conviction that the Soviet Union had determined to see Western Europe in economic and financial ruin. Secretary of State Marshall's speech in June 1947 at the Harvard graduation ceremonies provided them with a guarantee against this, provided that Western Europe could work as one. Moreover, it removed one of the major motivating forces in the French opposition to the development of Western Germany by no longer making exploitation of German resources the only way in which France could rebuild her own economic strength. In the move towards fusion of the three zones, however, it was the British and American Governments which forced the pace. The Frankfurt Charter of January 1948, promulgated on 9 February, faced the French Government with the immediate actuality of a German government. In London, at the end of February 1948, France, later to be joined by the Benelux countries, embarked on the road to fusion of the French Zone with Bizonia and the creation of a West German federal republic. But before this could be reached, the most serious Soviet challenge of the cold war in Europe had to be faced and overcome, in the blockade of Berlin.

By March 1948 the fundamental contradiction in the Western position over Germany had in fact forced the Soviets into a direct trial of strength. The Western powers, especially Britain and the United States, were committed fundamentally to the idea of a unified German state. As shown earlier, the British Government had resisted the arguments of those within their own ranks who had argued for dismemberment in the latter half of 1944, and had succeeded in overcoming both American and Soviet preference for dismemberment in the negotiations in the European Advisory Commission even before the Malta Conference. French resistance had prevented the political implementation of the Yalta and Potsdam decisions. And Soviet selfishness had forced Britain and the United States to decide against its economic implementation so long as the question of reparations and German export levels remained unsettled. From that time total unification could be achieved only if Soviet policy was fundamentally altered, and the Soviets persuaded or forced to leave Eastern Germany. The power to force them to leave, the British and American Governments did not possess. The means to persuade them were also lacking, at least in the judgement of London and Washington. The logical consequence could only be a return to partition,[11] a return which would be enhanced by the development of a West German state. The fact that the Soviets left it to the Western powers to make the running towards partition, preferring still to build up the SED and to encourage the right-wing and nationalist elements in Germany into a neutralist position, was indication enough of this.

The overriding factor in dictating British and American policy was still the impossibility of ending their own economic weakness, of preventing a total breakdown in the economic system of Western Europe, without an end of the drain in their resources caused by German economic weakness. The Economic Councils of Bizonia themselves were not strong enough to carry out the task of German reconstruction, and there was above all the need to remove from the German financial system the immense surplus of currency which pressed so heavily on its existing resources. The Marshall Plan and the Six-Power Western conference at London in February 1948 made it clear that the West had decided to consolidate the economic partition of Germany forced on them in 1946. The urgency of a currency reform, and the need to retain control of the new currency in the West, led directly to the Berlin blockade. Marshal Sokolovsky had already left the Allied Control Council in March 1948 on the grounds that the agreed quadrupartite basis for governing Germany had been destroyed. His answer to the currency reform, the proclamation that inter-zone commerce would thereafter be conducted as commerce between separate states, was therefore only logical. The Russian attempt to force the West out of Berlin by blockade followed at once.

The case of the Berlin crisis and its special importance for the cold war are discussed elsewhere. Its significance for the development of the cold war in Germany was threefold. Firstly, it marked a change from deadlock on the pseudo-constitutional issues of German unification to the use of the threat of violence. Secondly, the threat focused the attention of the West on its military weakness, which, coupled with European fears of a revival of German militarism, was to lead through the Brussels Treaty of West European Union to the formation of NATO. Thirdly, the Soviet failure to hold up the formation of the West German federal republic either by the demonstration of Western weakness, which Soviet victory over Berlin would have provided, or by bargaining over access to Berlin in the talks by which the Berlin crisis was resolved, threw the main weight of conducting the cold war in Germany on to the German political parties and groupings themselves.

One can distinguish at this time no less than five significant political groupings in Germany. Firstly, there were the Christian Democrats and their allies, who were to take Western Germany into NATO in preference to making for German unification. Secondly, there were the Social Democrats, who preferred to press for a reunification they had no really significant way of effecting. Thirdly, there were the SED, part Communist, part fellow-traveller, committed to a Germany in alliance with the Soviet Union. Fourthly came a curious grouping of old-style nationalists attracted by analogies with the *Ostpolitik* of the 1920s, favouring essentially a policy of German withdrawal from the cold war by agreement with the Soviet Union. Herr Nadolny, the former German Ambassador to Moscow and one of the four senior German diplomats in the Nazi era to resign on a straight policy issue, with Herr Nuschke and Professor Noack, led this group, whose strength lay in the respect on which its leaders could count, rather than on its electoral organisation or popular support. Lastly came a group of right-wing nationalists, more concerned to seize power in Western Germany and free it from its position of subordination to the West, no doubt as a prelude also to a revival of the policy of balance between West and East, characteristic of the Weimar Republic.

Of these five groups, the only ones to be in an effective position to carry out their own policies were the SED and the Christian Democrat coalition led by Dr Adenauer. The Social Democrats have not yet succeeded in achieving an electoral majority in Germany to enable them to execute their own policy, and in time their search for a means of unifying Germany by taking her out of the cold war has been modified into its present position of staunchly supporting NATO and Western Germany's part in the movement for European unity. The neo-nationalists were so close to Nazism as to invite police action to suppress them, action in which pressure from the British High Commissioner was necessary to overcome the reluctance of the West German authorities to admit the presence of enemies to their right as well as to their left.

That left the group of would-be neutralists as embodying the only alternative policy to that of the two groupings to achieve power. Their rise and fall illustrates the continuing operation within the German body politic of the same factors which governed the policies of the great powers. The outcome of the first Berlin crisis had shown that neither of the two blocs was prepared to use force to achieve their aims in Germany (in using the geopolitical position provided them by Berlin's position inside the Soviet Zone to blockade the Allies the Soviets were conforming to rather than breaking that rule). War was for both blocs tacitly ruled out. To manoeuvre one's opponents into a position where they are faced with the possibility of having to use force, is a dangerous tactic, which on two occasions, 1948 and 1961, has also proved unprofitable. Failing that, the situation could not but stabilise into a division of Germany.

In March 1948, the Soviet authorities took a step which when copied by the West was to make a policy of disengagement as a means to German unification unrealistic for the political leaders in either of the two Germanies. They instituted the establishment of an East German élite army with the establishment of 'police' units, the *Bereitschaften*, which were in fact armed, equipped and organised on army lines. Their establishment meant that a unified Germany would face civil war unless they were disbanded prior to unification; that Germany in fact could only be unified by a Soviet abandonment of their own creation. There was nothing that a unified Germany could offer the Soviet Union comparable with the problems which such an abandonment would raise. The Soviet Union had equipped the SED leadership with the means of waging civil war in Germany. The West German political parties and the neutralists were faced with a situation where German unification meant either the abolition of the SED and the People's Police or their own defeat and disappearance. Compromise became impossible. Willy-nilly the West German parties were forced towards the West and NATO. Only the Western powers could protect them against the threat to their existence. Only through the acquiescence of the West could they achieve the full exercise of German sovereignty. Moreover, where the Soviets could freely arm and establish the East German leadership, conscious of the political control they could exercise through the party and the political police, the Western leadership had their own fears of German strength, and memories of the uses to which German strength had been put in the past to overcome, let alone the similar emotions rooted within the breasts of their electorates. The closest unity and co-operation with the West became for the West Germans the only realistic policy. The alternative policies eventually perished of their own impracticability.

Leaving the Western powers to make the running in the constitutional establishment of two Germanies, the Soviets were in fact still concentrating on ways and means of taking over a unified Germany. But the skill of Dr Adenauer in winning a gradual revival of Germany's sovereign rights for the régime he headed made it impossible for them to deny the SED leadership similar concessions. During 1948 they were still able to pose as champions of German unity. Nadolny, Nuschke and Noack took part in the Volkscongress movement and its call for a plebiscite throughout Germany on unity and joint peace. But the Volkscongress in fact easily developed into a constitutional assembly for East Germany, evolving a draft constitution which was approved in March 1949 for the establishment of the German Democratic Republic (DDR) the following October.

The talks arising out of the Berlin blockade in fact established the *status quo* in Germany. The Soviets were unable to obtain recognition for their claim that Berlin was part of the Soviet Zone. Even on the establishment of a single bank of issue and export-import agency for Berlin and the Eastern Zone the four powers proved unable to reach agreement. The establishment of the two German states followed automatically, leaving only the status of Berlin unsettled by the Western allies' refusal to risk a new crisis with the Soviet Union by accepting the West German claim that Berlin be recognised as part of West Germany.

The next phase saw the gradual envelopment of the two Germanies into the blocs of East and West. The end of the Berlin crisis marked a return to the pseudo-constitutional cold-war methods employed by the two blocs in Germany before March 1948. But the establishment of the two German governments involved two new parties in the game, and further limited the freedom of action of the policy-makers in East and West. By the Petersberg agreements of November 1949, the Western powers came formally to recognise the claims of the new government in Bonn to be the only legitimate government in Germany, and ruled out any recognition of its alternative in Potsdam, which came to be regarded as an illegitimate extension of the Soviet occupying authority.

But the Berlin crisis had effects beyond purely German ones. Seen in retrospect, the events of the year 1948 mark the final establishment of the 1945 truce lines between East and West. The Soviet coup in Czechoslovakia, the defeat of the pro-Soviet elements in the Italian elections in 1948 and in the strike movement in France, the enactment of the Marshall plan and the Yugoslav defection from the Cominform combined to make a change in the *status quo* impossible without general war.

But the revelations of Western military weakness on the ground in Europe had in fact given the Western governments a bad shock and opened the way to their success in locking the United States for two decades into the balance of power in Europe through the North Atlantic Treaty Organisation, the military counterpart of OEEC and ERP. West Germany necessarily became part of the second at once and was soon to become part of the first. Britain and the United States came to be dominated by the need to maintain the unity of the West, and unwilling to risk anything which might impair its cohesion. The possible loss of the West German glacis came to be regarded as a military disaster of the first magnitude.

In this first period the Soviets still played on the theme of allied unity in the hope of reversing the trend of 1948. Too late in the day they began to preach the values of the Potsdam agreements, their failure to observe the reparations clauses of which had been the occasion of the initial break in 1946. The Potsdam system they praised, however, had never existed. And their attempts to obtain entry to the international Ruhr authority and to revive the Berlin Kommandatura were blocked by the unwillingness of the West to admit a Soviet footing across the demarcation lines without a *quid pro quo* that was never offered them.

Central to the Soviet attempt to return to the Potsdam ideal were their proposals to create a German State Council as a prelude to the establishment of an all-German government. But the form their proposals took showed how the establishment of the two

German authorities by the separate systems used by West and East to establish legitimacy and sovereignty, free elections and controlled plebiscites, had altered the situation. The German State Council, so ran the Soviet proposals, was to be established by nomination from the existing political bodies, i.e. from Bonn and the government of the DDR. The West, still committed to the idea that their policy of setting up a West German government was a prelude, not an alternative, to German unification, insisted on free elections throughout Germany, something which the development of the *Bereitschaften* and the *Volkspolizei* in the Soviet Zone made inconceivable.

This division between West and East was reflected at the party level in Germany. Despite their disagreements on priorities, Adenauer preferring that alignment with the West should precede unification, Schumacher and the Social Democrats insisting on the priority of unification as the greatest deterrent to Soviet aggression, neither party would accept that the SED represented anything with which they would hold conversations. They were thus driven to insist on free elections in East Germany, with all that that implied in the dismemberment of the SED's apparatus of political persuasion, as the precondition for German unification. Thus Grotewohl's overtures, as for example in his letter of November 1950 to Dr Adenauer, were left unanswered. Moreover, the West came to insist on the continuation of the occupation, as a guarantee against civil war, until the 'free' elections had been held and an all-German government established. The Western powers and the Bundestag launched the first Western counter-offensive in the autumn of 1951 with an appeal to the United Nations to establish a neutral supervisory committee to supervise the all-German elections. The Committee, consisting of representatives from Iceland, the Netherlands, Pakistan, Brazil and Poland,[12] was in fact set up. But the DDR government refused to recognise the UN decision, Poland withdrew and the Commission was denied entry into East Germany the following year.

The opening of the Korean War in June 1950 introduced a new stage in the development of the German phase of the cold war. By intensifying the fears of Western military planners of a similar Soviet use of conventional war in Europe, it led in a matter of three months only to the United States demanding the revival of German military power within NATO, and threatening withdrawal from integrated European commands if NATO flinched from this issue. The proposal faced both her European allies and the Adenauer government with an agonising situation, which could only be resolved by actions likely still further to prevent any unification of Germany. The West German Government had in fact made the strictest of declarations against the establishment of a German Army at the time of the signature of the Petersberg agreements, although Dr Adenauer had declared (4 December 1949) that if necessary German units could be raised for service in a European army. If given a choice he would probably, as he told General Robertson in June 1950, have preferred a militarised police on the model of the DDR's *Volkspolizei*. But although Dr Adenauer's drive for German *Gleichberechtigung* would have been certain to include the re-establishment of German military authority sooner or later, the making of the proposal only a year after the solemn declarations made at Petersberg cannot but have been unwelcome to him.

The proposal was a good deal more unwelcome in France, already restive under the pressures the cold war was establishing. The ensuing debate on neutralism had led already to the emergence of a new school of thought, whose main aim was the securing for the European side of NATO and the economic partnership set up by OEEC of control over the vagaries of American policy and the instabilities of the American economy. This had led in April 1950 to Georges Bidault's proposal of an Atlantic Supreme Council; and with this an obvious corollary was the need for a common European viewpoint, the first step towards which was a Franco-German entente. Robert Schuman developed the idea of newer and bolder safeguards against the emergence of a traditional German menace in the idea of an economic partnership with Germany through European union, the principal French and German war-making resources, coal and steel, being abstracted from national control. The Schuman Plan, out of which was to emerge the European Coal and Steel Authority, had been launched in May 1950.

M. Pleven's proposals for a European army, the European Defence Community, launched in October 1950, thus represented the culmination of a development which much antedated the American move of the previous month. The idea of 'economic internationalisation' of the Ruhr had in fact first been elaborated by the French Socialist leader Felix Gouin[13] during his premiership of January-June 1946. At that time no corresponding internationalisation of the French equivalents to the Ruhr came into question; Germany was still the object rather than the subject of international politics. The new proposals, however, were a logical development given the fact of West German sovereignty. Unhappily, here as elsewhere, the French Government, like its British counterpart, was dangerously, almost fatally, ahead of its own public opinion.

The French plan took eighteen months to implement, eighteen months during which it proved impossible to secure British membership, even despite the change from Labour to Conservative leadership in Britain in October 1951. The EDC agreements of May 1952 nevertheless marked a further stage towards rendering permanent Germany's divisions. It was a step made unavoidable by the continuing pressures of the cold war, and it developed logically and inevitably, both from the failure of the Allies to treat Germany as a whole in 1945-46 (a failure for which France carried a major responsibility), and from the pressing need felt by the North Atlantic powers to end the drain put upon their economies by the isolation and sterilisation of Western Germany. The Soviet encouragement of North Korean use of force in June

1950 faced the NATO powers with a similar need to alleviate the drain on their military position caused by the demilitarisation of Western Germany. Just as their economies had borne the strain of Western Germany's economy in 1946-48, so now their defences laboured under the strain of West Germany's defence. The revival of West Germany's capacity to defend herself was a logical counterpart to the revival of her capacity to produce, to trade and to finance that trade. And just as Marshall's ERP had led to West German economic revival within a framework of European co-operation, so the proposal to revive West Germany's military forces seemed logically to necessitate this taking place within as tight a framework of integration with the West as could be achieved. Despite Soviet propaganda to the contrary, no one on the West wished to solve the Soviet problem by reviving that which Germany before 1945 had constituted.

The effect was nevertheless inevitably to render the truce-lines and postures of 1945 still more difficult to unscramble. The inexorable logic of the situation continued to operate. Neither bloc could afford to seem to be against the unification of Germany. Neither bloc could face a revival of the policy of holding the balance followed by Germany between 1918-41 which the constitution of a genuinely independent unified Germany could involve. Each bloc was forced therefore to seem to play for a gain of all Germany, while in practice employing measures designed to secure the allegiance of the half they occupied, even at the cost of making a gain of the whole impossible.

From this point the Soviet Union began to be on the defensive in Germany. The imminence of the signature of the EDC treaty led the Soviet Government to revive the policy they had abandoned in 1948-49, of making themselves the champions of German unity. In 1949 they had attempted to forestall the creation of a West German state by an appeal to the allies in the West to return to the spirit of the Potsdam Agreements of 1945. The new offensive launched in March 1952 took a two-fold form. In Britain and France the utmost was done to encourage the Germanophobia of the common people and the attempts to exploit it by those out of office on the left in each country. Within Germany the offer of a genuine unification with almost total *Wehrhoheit* was made, a national state with its own land, sea and air forces, far more sovereign in the military sphere than it would be within the framework of a European army of units integrated down to battalion or company level envisaged by the EDC treaties. The Soviet Note of 10 March 1952 made further concessions to German nationalism by its plea for the full rehabilitation of former Nazis. And a second Note of 24 April emphasised its point with the direct warning that the signature of the treaties with the West would create 'new difficulties in the path of unification with the eastern part of Germany'. The moral was underlined by the sealing off of the inter-zonal demarcation line with wire and minefields, and the establishment of a 500 metre forbidden zone and a three-mile security zone on the East German side of the new border.

The Soviet initiative caught both the Western occupying powers and the Bonn government on the hop. The Western powers were determined not to allow the Soviet initiative to delay progress on EDC and postpone the integration of West European troops. In order, however, to seem to support the idea of German unity, they were forced to counter with the one card the Soviets could not overtrump, that of free elections to create an all-German government and the ascertaining by a UN Commission that adequate safeguards for the political liberty of the individual existed in the Soviet Zone.

The effects of the Soviet initiative in Germany were more far-reaching. A new neutralist grouping, *die Notgemeinschaft für den Frieden Europas*, came into existence, which attracted for a time the actual support of a political party in West Germany, the *Bayerische Partei*, as well as that of the German hero, Pastor Niemoller. Much more serious, however, was the fillip given to the revival of extreme nationalism by the lure of sovereignty and freedom. The main instrument of pressure on the Adenauer government was the right-wing Free Democrat Party, an essential part of his coalition. One of their areas of complaint inevitably was the hostage given to France for her past acquiescence in Germany's revival, the Saar. Nor could Adenauer count on the support of public opinion to the left of his coalition. The Social Democrats regarded EDC as one-sided and discriminatory against Germany, as long as Britain and the Scandinavian countries were not members. Direct Soviet pressure Adenauer could resist by refusing to accept neutralisation and the Oder-Neisse line and insisting on free elections under international supervision. But the concessions made to the Free German Party, coupled with a temporary revival of extreme German nationalism, reacted on French opinion to make immediate ratification of the EDC treaties by the National Assembly impossible.

The second stage in the Soviet defensive action against ratification of the EDC treaties opened with the death of Stalin and the East German rising of June 1953. This last revealed the complete unreality of the Soviet position in Germany, a position which rested solely on the military strength of the Soviet occupying forces, and the unwillingness of the West to challenge them. The government of the DDR were revealed as complete Soviet puppets maintained in power only by Soviet tanks. The focus of the Soviet defensive had, however, shifted away from Germany to the field of intra-NATO relationships. Here it was proving much more successful, so much so as to lead Western Foreign Ministers into deciding to probe Soviet intentions on Germany and a European settlement anew. The post-Stalin government was able to make encouraging noises in answer to such tendencies, and to have these win a good deal of acceptance by all but the new Republican régime in the USA. In October 1953, the three Western Foreign Ministers met in London and proposed a four power conference on Germany. In December at the NATO

Council discussions occurred between the new British Foreign Secretary, Anthony Eden, and Dr Adenauer on some form of security declaration to allay Soviet fears of a resurgent Germany.

The degree of Western anxiety can be seen in the threats issued by Secretary Dulles of an 'agonising reappraisal' of America's foreign policy, leading to a withdrawal from Europe into Fortress America and action in the Far East, if the French Assembly failed to ratify the EDC agreements. We know from Lord Avon's memoirs,[14] that British policy was dominated by the twin fears of losing Germany to the Soviet Union, or to a position where she could play East against West, and of divisions on Germany destroying the unity of NATO. This dilemma led Eden to evolve the policy pursued over the next eighteen months, months in which the bankruptcy of American policy and the crisis in France placed the initiative in formulating policy in the West firmly in Britain's hands. Eden assumed Soviet policy to be to obtain an American withdrawal from Europe and to prevent the emergence of a strong united Germany integrated with the West. To achieve the latter he regarded as the main aim of Western policy. If he realised that Soviet policy was aimed to operate both on French and German public opinion, this does not emerge from his memoirs; these show his tactics to be aimed principally at alleviating Soviet fears of Western power and German fears that integration with the West would preclude the attainment of unity. Western tactics, he wrote, must be 'to avoid creating the impression that we (and more particularly the Americans) are in such a hurry to get on with EDC that we are not aiming at serious negotiations on Germany and Austria. We must therefore establish the position that we, unlike the Russians, have a practical plan for German reunification which will produce a representative all-German government with which alone a peace treaty can be negotiated. This must be based on free all-German elections as the first step.'[15]

The course of the Berlin conference in January 1954, however, showed that there was no real way of removing the direct conflict between the Soviet aim of achieving all its objectives at one stroke, a neutralised Germany and a Europe from which America could be excluded, with the determination of the NATO powers to retain the existing balance of power. Moreover, all present knew that, given her head, a reunited Germany would join up with NATO either via EDC or directly, so that neutralisation was out of the question except to provide a plateau on which the cold war could be continued. As Eden said, 'If Germany is to be neutral and disarmed, who will keep her disarmed? If Germany is to be neutral and armed, who will keep her neutral?'

The summer of 1954 saw both the victory and final defeat of Soviet policy. In August 1954, the French National Assembly rejected the EDC treaties. This was followed by Eden's brilliant stroke in reviving the Brussels Treaties of 1948, in bringing Germany and Italy into a revived West European Union and in securing through this the entry of West Germany into NATO as a full partner, precisely what the Pleven plan and the EDC agreements had been designed to prevent. Soviet policy had overreached itself, since French action was at this time no longer decisive in NATO. Dr Adenauer had in fact outlasted his nationalist critics on the German Right and the new gains for German sovereignty more than matched those offered by the Soviet Union. Only atomic weapons remained beyond Germany's grasp.

The ratification of the Paris agreements by which Western Germany joined the North Atlantic Alliance gave rise in Britain to the hope that a genuine German peace treaty would now be possible. Soviet policy was in ruins, defeated. Surely now was the time, while showing lenience and magnanimity to the defeated, to ensure a perpetuation of the victory in a treaty of peace. Such at least were the sentiments of Sir Anthony Eden. Added to them was the conviction that Western supremacy in nuclear weapons was now at its height and likely to decline. If one was to 'negotiate from strength' now was the time to do it. To secure such a peace, Eden was now even prepared to cast Germany loose from NATO as the price of her unification, secure in the confidence that she would return to the Western fold, provided only the peace treaty left her free to do so. He recognised that there were 'legitimate' Soviet fears. These he was magnanimously disposed to meet by the offer of a demilitarised zone in Central Europe, an agreement to limit armaments in specified areas, and the conclusion of a European Security pact, a new Locarno in fact.

These proposals, however magnanimous they might sound, were those of victor to vanquished, especially the proposal that the Soviets might gratefully accept from the West the security they could not achieve on their own. But the diagnosis that underlay the proposals was fundamentally false. Soviet policy had been defeated, but not the Soviet Union. The West were in the position of besieged soldiers who, having caused their enemy to raise the siege, expect him to sue for peace. In this latter-day Peninsular Cold War in Europe, Massena's troops had just recoiled from Torres Vedras. But many victories had to be won before they were to withdraw across the Pyrenees.

The Soviet Union had in fact failed in achieving the aims of her forward policy. Despite all her efforts Western Germany had entered NATO. But Soviet hold on East Germany had increased considerably since the rising of 1953, and the West had not even begun to think of means of prising it out of their hands, since the assumption was that they would vacate the fortress voluntarily if sufficient guarantees were given them.

The failure of this assumption to accord with the facts was the real reason why the Geneva Summit Conference of July 1955, envisaged by the West as the Versailles of the cold war, proved a complete failure. While it is possibly true that a genuine fear of Germany underlay the Soviet Union's policy on Germany,[16] Western guarantees of her security were hardly likely to satisfy a nation whose historians preached that the West had for six years done its best to turn Hitler's Germany against her. Nor was the moment when the struggle for the succession was at its height in Russia a good time to press for concessions. Lastly, the Soviet negotiators were immovable in their policy on Germany's eastern frontiers. Could any security pact allay their own fears as annexors of Königsberg, still less those of their Czech and Polish satellites? The Soviet leaders could be forgiven if they held privately to something like the ninepin theory put forward by US analysts in relation to South-East Asia.

Whatever the reasoning underlying Soviet policy, they had in fact destroyed the basis of Western policy the month before the summit with their recognition of the West German Government and their invitation to Dr Adenauer to visit Moscow. By this they had initiated their new policy, that of the 'Two Germanies', now reinforced with the Berlin Wall from which it has until this day proved impossible for the West to shake them.

The Summit Conference of 1955 in fact proved not to be the treaty of peace the West had hoped for. Rather it marked an armistice. The truth is that it was to prove impossible to define a state of security which should be attractive to both sides. A state of security which is stable in the Western sense is no security at all for the Soviet Union, since to them it threatens permanent instability – and vice versa. The point of the balance is so narrow as continually to try nerves on both sides whenever the smallest oscillation takes place. Both West and East preferred a balance based on the division of Germany to any risk of losing control of their own half. Forward tactics for each always embodied a set of proposals for a unified Germany, designed to secure its inclination towards, if not its adhesion to, their own side. But behind these always lay their real position, a policy of the two Germanies. German unification, by comparison, was desirable but unattainable.

The Geneva Summit Conference of 1955 in fact marked the end of the cold war in Germany. It was followed by three years in which the question of East-West relations in Germany hardly stirred. In November 1958, after the defeat of the Soviet policy of penetration in the Middle East, Khrushchev returned to the Berlin issue, mainly so far as one can judge, to force the abandonment of Berlin and the recognition of the East German régime. His own position in East Germany is an unstable one as the Wall itself, and the refugee flood it dammed, shows. But the course of the Berlin crisis of 1958-61 is another story, which must be considered separately.

4 BERLIN

Philip Windsor

To distinguish between the question of Germany and the problem of Berlin in the evolution of the cold war is a difficult task. But it is a necessary one if the special position of Berlin in that conflict is to be understood.

Germany has always been the heart and central subject of the cold war if the cold war is to be appreciated as a definable struggle, separate, for example, from colonial independence movements, or revolution in the 'third world'. In a sense, indeed, the cold war began in 1939, when the prospect of a war involving Germany and all the major European powers determined the Nazi-Soviet Pact. Since then, the Soviet Union and the Western powers have been united only against Germany. They have never found it possible to agree on a common policy towards Germany. Germany's potentialities as a great power accentuated the division between the two sides: both required her as an ally against the other. But the division of Germany has made that impossible. And both parties have come to accept this, because they recognise that it enables them at least to stay apart, and draws a clear frontier between their spheres. The cold war has been a perpetual conflict between these two positions. On the one hand, it was a competition for the alliance of a reunified Germany; on the other, it was, far from a pursuit of conflict by diplomatic means, an agreement not to go to war but to maintain the *status quo*, based on a divided Germany.

In fact, though not in name, the cold war has evolved in the second of these directions. But at the beginning of the post-war period, on the surface at least, this was not the case. The Soviet Union, it seemed, was still pursuing a fundamental objective of Russian foreign policy since the days of Lenin: an alliance with Germany, if possible a Communist Germany. It does not appear that the Western powers distinguished this very clearly from Stalin's extension of Soviet rule over the Eastern European countries: and indeed it was difficult to distinguish these two at the time. But there does seem to have been a difference. The second can be regarded as a primarily defensive measure, undertaken against a possible recrudescence of German military power, or against a German alliance with the West. The first would have meant a political and diplomatic offensive, and would almost certainly have ensured Soviet domination over the whole of Europe.

In general, after the first few years, the Soviet Union appears to have abandoned any immediate design of bringing the whole of Germany into the Communist camp. It has, at least since 1955, appeared reconciled to the division of Germany, and to a stabilisation of the cold war along these lines. The Western powers, on the other hand, though their whole post-war policy has been based on the division of Germany, do not accept that division. And although, in real terms, this has been the pattern of the cold war throughout the 1950s, the ostensible objective of the cold war from the Western side remains the reunification of Germany.

Throughout these developments, Berlin has been both the symbol and the instrument of the policies of each side. It was in the first place the existence of Berlin as a four-power enclave in the Soviet Zone which prevented the division of Germany from becoming the basis of a European settlement. It was the seat of an all-German government set up by the Allied powers, and it seems clear that at the beginning both sides hoped to use this government as a lever for the creation of a reunified and disarmed Germany. In the Western view, this would presumably have been a neutral country at first, perhaps the special protégé of the United Nations. In the Soviet view it would sooner or later have become a Communist country, the by no means powerless ally of the Soviet Union, very much as China was presumably expected to be.

In the early years, therefore, Soviet pressure was concentrated on Berlin for several reasons. First, because if the Soviet authorities won the political allegiance of the capital, this would be the greatest step towards securing control of the rest of the country. Secondly, because if they could do this with even the passive collaboration of the Western allies, it would demonstrate that military occupation by the Western powers did not mean protection from political conquest. Thirdly, and when this failed, because if they could drive the Western powers out of Berlin it would demonstrate that in the end neither American nuclear power nor the strategic superiority of the United States Air Force nor the presence in Europe of a skeleton American Army, was enough to withstand the concentrated threat of 175 Soviet divisions.

In all these purposes they came within an ace of success, and this was because the Western powers regarded Berlin simply as a separate problem, an inconvenient legacy of wartime arrangements, which had no relevance to the future of Germany or of Europe, and in which even as late as 1949, they still seemed to regard it as their primary task to pave the way for co-operation with Russia in an all-German settlement – even though some of the bitterest battles of the cold war had already been fought.

This then, was the first period in the history of Berlin since 1945. The Soviet Union was still hoping for German reunification, and the East German Communist party was using Berlin, with the active collaboration of the Soviet authorities, as a springboard for a Communist Germany. (It is worth recalling that at the end of the war Roosevelt had declared his intention of limiting the period of occupation in Germany to two years. While this declaration was never enshrined in any statement of policy, Stalin might have had good reason to believe that it was necessary to act quickly so that Germany would fall into his lap when the Americans left. It was of course his very haste and intensity which prolonged the American occupation and created the Atlantic Alliance, but it was not a fantastic hope in 1946 that within a year or two, the whole of Germany, if only its capital were a firm Communist stronghold, could become part of the Socialist camp.) Because the focus of Communist pressure was the city of Berlin the history of the cold war at this time can scarcely be understood without some appreciation of the local history of Berlin: it is hardly an exaggeration to say that at moments events and people in Berlin determined the course of the conflict, and it would be futile to attempt to sketch the history of the 'Berlin problem' in general without regard to local developments.

What then were the methods by which the Russian occupation authorities and the East German Communists attempted to gain control of Berlin, and when did this policy change to a gradual determination to force the Western powers out?

It seems clear that in the first place Soviet tactics were to transfer the effective governing power in Berlin from the Allied council (the 'Inter-Allied Kommandatura') to the organs of representative government in Berlin; and, secondly, to ensure that these were controlled by the Communists. Their allies were the German Communists under the leadership of Ulbricht who had spent the years of Nazi rule in the Soviet Union and returned in the wake of Zhukov's army to organise the Soviet occupation zone, and in particular Berlin, for Communist rule. At first the 'Ulbricht group' intended to take control of the country without forming any open Communist party, or indeed any political parties. All administrative and political measures were to be co-ordinated through an 'anti-Fascist bloc', uniting all who were willing to work with the new authorities, and controlling the economic and political life of the city. Rations were distributed and work was assigned through a system of house, street and block supervisors of the anti-Fascist coalition, appointed by the representatives of the Ulbricht group, and confirmed in office by Russian officers. On this basis, within a very few days of the Russian conquest, and two months before the Western forces arrived to take over their sectors of Berlin, a German city government, the Magistrat, had been formed. The Magistrat was effectively controlled by the Communists, and it supervised the whole administration, police and judiciary of the city.

Shortly after this, however, there was an abrupt change of line that is still difficult to understand. In June 1945, Zhukov ordered the formation of free political parties and trade unions throughout the whole of the Soviet Zone. The Communists now emerged into the open alongside the Liberals, the Social Democrats and the Christian Democrats. In fact all these parties became, willy-nilly, members of the anti-Fascist coalition, and it is worth recalling that this was the time that Stalin was preparing to go to Potsdam. The Russians might well have hoped that, if a centralised political structure was soon to be created – on the basis of the centralised administration which was agreed at Potsdam – the anti-Fascist coalition would be able to take control of the whole country. If it could do so with the open participation of other political parties, the Communist transition to power in Germany would be relatively smooth and quick.

For a time this seemed to be happening in Berlin. The Western representatives, dedicated to the pursuit of Four-Power government, were hardly able to take effective control of their own sectors in the first months let alone obstruct the Soviet authorities or the Magistrat in running the city. The only measures on which the Four Powers seemed able to reach agreement in the Kommandatura were of a negative and limited character, such as denazification and demilitarisation. Beyond this, the Soviet commandant refused co-operation in the name of encouraging the political responsibility of the Magistrat.

In fact, it was not the Western powers who defeated the Russian attempt to gain control of Berlin, but the leaders of the German political parties, whose opposition to the anti-Fascist coalition was daily becoming clearer. Enclosed in a coalition which deprived them of all effective power, forced to append their public agreement to political and economic measures to which for doctrinal or practical reasons they were often strongly opposed, and subject to unremitting Soviet pressure throughout the whole of the occupation zone, they were increasingly determined to assert themselves and win the support of the Western powers.

It was to forestall this that the German Communists launched their next campaign: to merge the Communist party with the Social Democrats. This campaign, which started in earnest at the beginning of 1946, was an acknowledgement of the importance which the political parties were winning – just because the Soviet authorities had opposed German organisations to the Allied government machinery. It was now essential for them to reassert their control over the Social Democrats, by far the most powerful party in Berlin, and the only one which was capable of providing an alternative to Communist government.

In the early months of 1946, the fate of Berlin, and perhaps of Germany, turned on the decision of the Social Democrats. It was they who resisted the merger – with the support of their West German colleagues, but in isolation from the Soviet Zone, where the fusion was rapidly accomplished, and at first with no more than the vaguest moral support from the Western powers. It was only gradually that they won their unofficial backing, and finally their open intervention. The Western authorities at last gave their blessing to the demands of the SPD leader, Franz Neumann, for a referendum, and took measures to protect it from sabotage. The referendum was held in March 1946 (in practice only in the Western sectors) and resulted in the first decisive Western victory in the political battle for Berlin.

The effect was that the covert bid for power on the part of the

German Communists now changed to an open conflict among the allies, which hastened the development of the cold war over the whole of Germany. The dispute in the Kommandatura over the recognition of the SED, the united Socialist party, and the SPD, the independent Socialists, was transferred to the Allied Control Council, where its implications raised the whole question of the government of Germany.

The Russian response in Berlin was to reassert the predominance of the Kommandatura over the Magistrat, and to insist on Allied authority over the German administration. But it was already too late to arrest its development in this fashion: elections had been agreed on, and a constitution drawn up. The elections, which were held in October 1946, marked the turning-point in the struggle. They resulted in an overwhelming victory for the 'Western' parties. An independent government had now emerged in Berlin, and all Russian hopes of gaining political control without a struggle were at an end.

But, at the same time, the city was beginning to split in two. As the Western sectors gained greater political and administrative independence, Soviet control was tightened over East Berlin. Henceforth, the political leaders in the city faced a continuous dilemma: whether to accommodate their Russian and Soviet adversaries from a regard for the population of the Eastern sector, or to split the city finally by resisting them.

In general, they were apt to co-operate on the economic and administrative level, but to resist any infraction of their political independence. This posture grew out of an initial crisis, when the first independent Mayor of Berlin, Otto Ostrowski, lost a vote of confidence on the issue of collaboration with the SED, and was succeeded by an ex-Communist who had just returned from war-time exile in Turkey, Ernst Reuter. The Russian commandant refused to recognise him, and he did not in fact assume office until the city was finally split during the blockade; but from that time on he was the symbol and the leader of Berlin's resistance, and became for a time the voice of all Germany. It was under his direction that the SPD was organised to meet any attempt at a *putsch*, and it was he who for the next five years held the population together.

Meanwhile, two deputy-mayors, Frau Louise Schroeder and Ferdinand Friedensburg, carried on the government of the city. Their task at first was both to maintain the unity of Berlin, and to resist the Russian attempts to exercise political suzerainty: both seemed for a time to be part of the same struggle for independence, but this was only true as long as the Four powers remained on speaking terms. When they came into open conflict, it was impossible to hope that the Berlin government could prevent the division of the city even at the price of compliance with the Soviet authorities in administrative and economic policy.

They continued to try, even after the blockade had been imposed. Most of the House of Representatives was hostile to the extension of the West German currency reform to Berlin, and at first Reuter, and the Senator for Economics, Klingelhöfer, were almost alone in pressing for this move. Even later, Friedensburg and his ministers attempted to maintain a unified administration until a separate government was set up in East Berlin, and the police refused them admission to the City Hall.

The reasons for the blockade and the final division of the city do not seem, however, to lie in developments in Berlin itself, but in the evolution of the cold war throughout Europe, and the relations between Russia and the United States. Here, the turning-point came in 1947. Between January and March, it was plain that the Truman administration was reassessing American foreign policy, and the Truman doctrine which emerged from this discussion was promulgated at the time when the disastrous Foreign Ministers' Conference was convened in Moscow in March. Soviet policy over Germany had hitherto been one of delay while the ground was prepared in Berlin. By the time of the conference it seemed that an open conflict was recognised as inevitable.

The Bizone which the American and British Governments had created in the West seemed to prepare the way for the division of Germany, and this the Soviet Government was clearly determined to prevent. For some months – between March and June 1947 – it seems to have wavered between refusing all discussion of the future of Germany and demanding the creation of a central government, but this hesitation was soon brought to an end – by Marshall Aid. When it was realised that Marshall Aid would also extend to West Germany, delay was no longer possible: the creation in the West of a separate economic entity would precipitate the final division of the country. And as Marshall Aid led to currency reform, the Soviet Government seems to have determined on a showdown, using Berlin as a lever.

By February 1948, Sokolovsky was claiming that Berlin was part of the Soviet Zone, and that the Western powers were endangering their right to stay there by 'abusing their position'. But the Western powers could hardly commit themselves to an open conflict with Russia over Berlin without thereby implicitly making West Berlin a part of West Germany, and so putting an end to all hopes that the Four-Power government of the capital might still constitute a gage for negotiated reunification. They were most reluctant even to appear to accept the division of the country, and for this reason, though both General Clay and the American Ambassador in Moscow, Bedell Smith, had both separately warned Washington in the summer of 1947 that a conflict was bound to come, and that in this case Berlin would probably be blockaded, the extent of the Western commitment to Berlin was never made fully clear until the blockade had actually begun. One suspects that it was not really clear in the minds of the Western leaders either. Certainly, the Soviet authorities must have been encouraged to think that pressure on Berlin might enable them to have their way in Germany, or at least to put off the division of the country. For they do not seem at any stage to have *planned* a full blockade. The blockade of Berlin has become a legend, but it is a mistake to regard it as a single phenomenon with a single purpose. It developed very slowly and it is clear from the behaviour of the SED and the Russians on the spot that though they were hoping to intimidate the Western powers, their original intention was not to force the division of Berlin or of Germany.

Thus, the first steps were taken when the three Western governments finally decided on currency reform. Sokolovsky walked out of the Allied Control Council, and a few days later, in March 1948, the first four trains on their way from West Germany to Berlin were stopped and turned back. But the full blockade was not imposed for months. From April to June, as the siege was progressively tightened, it seemed that its real purpose was to isolate the military governments from the civilian population, and that at the same time the SED was to persuade the Berlin leaders to oppose currency reform and 'maintain the unity of the city'. In this they had some success. The Western powers were divided and had obviously not framed any plans for meeting a full blockade. Most of the Berlin leaders were anxious and uncertain of their power to resist. And although a small military airlift had begun, this was hardly regarded as a means of overcoming the blockade.

The second period was from June to September 1948. The full blockade was now imposed, and the real air-lift improvised. The situation changed completely as it became clear that the Western powers were now prepared to resist Soviet intimidation. For the first time, a full alliance between the Western governments and the Berlin population was created, and in the end currency reform was introduced into Berlin. But at the same time, the three governments regarded the blockade as an instrument to force negotiations. They continued in Moscow throughout this time, and from the Soviet viewpoint came very near success. At the end of August an 'interim agreement' was reached on Berlin. The four military governors were instructed to make arrangements to introduce not the West German currency but the new East mark to Berlin. Negotiations finally broke down only when the Russian demands were pressed further to include practically complete control over the administration of the whole city.

Nevertheless, the governments in Moscow and Berlin both saw that the Western powers, though ready to withstand the most extreme physical pressure, were not yet disposed to maintain the independence of Berlin indefinitely: the final victory might still be Russia's. Hence the target of Soviet intimidation during these months changed from the military authorities to the Berlin government. Throughout the summer the city administration was subjected to a combined campaign, of organised mob pressure on the streets and discreet individual intimidation in the offices of the Magistrat, which was openly designed to force the resignation of the leading Senators and have them replaced by more amenable substitutes. The chief target was naturally Friedensburg, whose deputy, and substitute if his nerves or health had given way, was a member of the SED. There are some signs that the SED was considering a *putsch* towards the end of August: the heroism, in their different spheres, of Reuter who organised the SPD to resist and of Friedensburg who carried on the government in the face of every possible hindrance, was as important in the history of Europe as the organisation of the airlift. Both knew that the negotiations in Moscow were likely to end in a Soviet victory. But between them they preserved the independence of Berlin, and to no small degree forced the hand of their protectors.

The final phase of the blockade lasted from October 1948 to May 1949. After the negotiations had broken down and the Western powers had introduced the D-mark, the blockade and airlift became at last what they are generally thought to have been: a trial of strength between East and West and a decisive battle in the cold war. It was very slowly understood, on both sides, that the airlift could in fact keep Berlin going throughout the winter – that it could be supplied indefinitely from the air.

This unexpected success seems to have caused the final change of plan: the Soviet decision to split the city and consolidate its base in the East before attempting any further advance. Thus a separate East Berlin government was created in November, and the old administration finally migrated to the West. Reuter became the Mayor of West Berlin in a new Assembly. Secret negotiations began in Moscow in February between the United States and the Soviet Union, and continued at the UN. In May the blockade was lifted.

By this time NATO had already been created. On the day that the blockade came to an end the West German constitution was completed. Europe and Germany were divided into two hostile camps, and Berlin was no longer the pivot of the cold war. From now on, an understanding of the history of Berlin and the Berlin crises must be sought in the development of German history, in which the local evolution of Berlin plays a relatively unimportant part. Berlin remained the symbol and was again to become an instrument of the cold war. But the struggle for Berlin was no longer one of its chief objectives.

In the years 1949–52, Stalin's policy towards Germany was thoroughly revised. He now appeared to accept the division of the country, and imposed great exertions on East Germany in the attempt to make it a viable independent state. But this seems to have been conceived as a part of building up a position from which to negotiate afresh for reunification.

This is what he proposed in the Note of 10 March 1952. Some current interpretations of Stalinist foreign policy see in this the beginnings of the change to 'peaceful coexistence'. That would appear a misreading of European history. The reunification of Germany was a prime factor of Stalin's foreign policy, and though he temporarily accepted division after 1949, he was clearly hoping to negotiate to this end. The Note of 1952 indicates a reappraisal of tactics, not a change of objective. Reunification was, and in

Western eyes still is, the fundamental objective of the cold war, and in the search for acceptable terms in 1952, Stalin was pursuing the same policy as that of 1946 and 1948. But Khrushchev's proclamation of peaceful coexistence coincided with his insistence on the division of Germany – and indeed his attempts to force this on the West. This, in Russian eyes, is the only way to liquidate the cold war and to stabilise peaceful coexistence. In other words, the objectives of the two sides switched round in the mid-fifties. That is perhaps why the cold war is still going on.

Throughout this period Berlin was of no great importance in the evolution of the policies of either side. Now that the city was split, and East Berlin had become part of the Soviet realm, it was impossible to make any use of it as a lever for reunification. This was demonstrated to the world after the East German rising of June 1953, when Reuter attempted to use the opportunity to re-open negotiations. But the Western powers showed no disposition to take advantage of the uncertainties in the Kremlin after Stalin's death, or the confusions of the Ulbricht régime after the revolt. They had in fact already excluded any possibility of a German settlement on the basis of neutralisation. The British, German and American Governments all appeared to be equally determined to bring West Germany into the European Defence Community as quickly as possible. Henceforth, German reunification was increasingly identified in the West with the absorption of the whole country into NATO, and, in the years that followed, Dulles, Eden and Adenauer concentrated their diplomatic efforts entirely on the 'German contribution' to Western defence.

Though the Western powers had not abandoned their aim of reunification, they had in fact made it impossible, and though the years between the rising in East Germany and the Hungarian revolt witnessed an almost continuous debate between Russia and the West about the future of Germany, it quickly became apparent that no agreement on reunification could be reached. In fact all hopes of reunification had vanished after the summit conference of Geneva in 1955. The course of Russian diplomacy between May of that year, when West Germany finally became a member of NATO, and July, when the Summit convened at Geneva, is too complex to sketch here, but the Geneva conference made it plain that the Soviet leaders had now finally rejected reunification, and that their efforts would henceforth be bent on securing Western recognition of a divided Germany. If any moment can be called the turning-point of European history since the war, it is July 1955.

After 1955, the basic clash of Soviet and Western policies remained constant. The Soviet Union sought to make the *status quo* into a permanent settlement. It can plausibly be argued that such a definition of spheres of influence was sought by Khrushchev to enable him to withdraw part of his forces from Europe, reduce the risk of war, and concentrate on the 'world revolution'. But whatever the motives behind Soviet policy, Khrushchev was obviously determined on forcing the Western powers to recognise East Germany, and thereby acknowledge the permanent division of the country. Equally, the Western powers were convinced, and still are, that no real settlement could be achieved without reunification. But they had excluded reunification from discussion, and their real position was shrinking to a permanent defence of the *status quo*.

However, it was possible to attack the *status quo* at the point where the West was weakest, and by threatening it there to extort wider concessions. This point was Berlin.

It seems now that the reasons behind the Berlin ultimatum of 1958, and the Berlin crisis of the next three years, lay in a deliberate attempt by Khrushchev to exploit the strength of his local position as part of a long diplomatic campaign which would end in the establishment of diplomatic relations between Pankow and the Western capitals. The moment was well chosen: in 1957, with the launching of the earth's first satellite, and the firing of the first inter-continental ballistic missile, Russia seemed to have established a decisive strategic lead over the United States. At the same time, the local superiority of Russian forces in Europe ensured that whatever it might threaten, the United States was powerless to protect Berlin itself from a *coup de main* at any time the Soviet rulers chose. Equally, the Western presence in Berlin, hitherto proclaimed as a symbol of the eventual liberation of Eastern Europe, seemed to be meaningless after the Hungarian revolt had shown how powerless the Atlantic Alliance had in fact become.

The ultimatum of 27 November 1958 should thus be regarded not as a sudden departure, but as the first step in a campaign which was expected to last for a long period. This is borne out by the nature of the Note itself. It was not a clear demand for the withdrawal of Western troops, it did not insist on the recognition of East Germany within any specified time, and it did not yet threaten the 'separate peace treaty' between the Soviet Union and the German Democratic Republic, which would force the Western powers either to negotiate direct with East Germany or fire the first shot. What it did insist on was an end to the occupation status of West Berlin, an agreement on the eventual creation of a Free City, and the implicit recognition of East Germany as one of the states which guaranteed non-interference in the Free City's 'distinctive way of life'. It was later that the threat of a separate peace treaty emerged as a more direct warning to the West that it would have to negotiate its access rights directly with the East German régime.

The response of the Western powers, then and later, was to refuse any negotiations about Berlin itself, but to attempt a renewed discussion of the whole German problem. This was apparently the object of Macmillan's visit to Moscow in February 1959, where it seems that he tried to approach the German problem through an agreement on reducing forces on both sides of the Iron Curtain in Europe. But this approach was more acceptable to Khrushchev than to Britain's allies, and was dropped before

finally forced the hand of the Western powers, so now the 'Berlin crisis' had generated a local crisis of Berlin which made it impossible to call a halt to international developments. The flood of refugees from East Germany to Berlin was leading to the collapse of the East German state. This flood grew as rumours increased that the way to West Berlin might eventually be barred. The political and economic strains in East Germany forced the government to continue the search for a solution to the Berlin problem, both by creating tension on every possible occasion and through the channels of Eastern bloc diplomacy. And every such attempt stimulated the flood of refugees still further. The Berlin problem grew more intractable throughout 1961, and the contrast between the attempts of both sides to work out a flexible position and the rigidity of the actual situation was borne home in the Vienna meeting between Kennedy and Khrushchev in June. Both were unwilling to contemplate conflict; neither could find a way round the *status quo* with all its latent possibilities of conflict.

A solution was at last found in a meeting of the leaders of the Eastern bloc, in Moscow at the end of July. It appears that it was here that they agreed to seal off West Berlin if all the other security measures of the East German Government failed. And the wall, though it appeared to create still greater tension, was in fact greeted with almost open relief by the Western as well as the Eastern governments. It did nothing to change the fundamental problems, but it averted the immediate danger – at an almost intolerable human cost – of the collapse of East Germany.

Yet the problem had changed in the summer of 1961. It was not the wall that changed it, so much as the weeks of tension that preceded it. Both the United States and the Soviet Union were now apparently convinced that the Berlin crisis had become too dangerous. The risks of bloody incidents along the wall, and the possibilities of a conflict arising out of them, seemed to grow for some months. But after the silent confrontation of Soviet and American tanks at 'Checkpoint Charlie' in October, the tension rapidly subsided. The United States and Britain began to search for a fresh approach to the Berlin problem; the Soviet Union seems to have decided that the best way out of the impasse lay in a *rapprochement* with the Federal Republic. But Adenauer's last government appears to have been equally hostile to both initiatives, recalling its ambassador from Moscow through suspicion that he was lending Khrushchev too sympathetic an ear, and leaking the Anglo-American proposal for an international access authority to Berlin to the press, to ensure that it was killed at birth.

Since the early months of 1962, Berlin has been on ice. The Western powers have not made any fresh approaches for a local solution; the Soviet Union no longer seems concerned to impose a solution of the German problem before discussing other means of reducing tension and the risks of war in Europe. It is clear that no radical measures of disarmament or arms control can be concluded with the Soviet Union without at some stage granting at least a limited recognition to East Germany – Khrushchev's speeches before and after the test-ban treaty bear witness to this continuing preoccupation – but he appears content to let time do his work for him. Berlin is therefore not at present, and is unlikely to become, a significant factor in international relations as it has been in the past. It is not even Khrushchev's local hostage with which to threaten the United States from time to time. There is no close parallel between Berlin and Cuba – because the United States cannot afford to accept local defeat in Berlin as Khrushchev could in Cuba, and this limits Khrushchev's ability to threaten the position.

But it is still extremely valuable to him as a means of demonstrating both within the Communist bloc and the world, the nature and limits of a *détente* with the West. The autobahn incidents of the autumn of 1963 may well have been intended to show Khrushchev's own allies that he was still effectively in control of the situation (the management of this incident, in contrast to those of the preceding years, seems to have been designed to emphasise that it was the Russians and not the East Germans who were responsible for the access routes to Berlin) and at the same time he was not prepared to go too far in his search for a *détente*.

To East Germany, however, Berlin is still a vital problem. It is an active threat to the morale and political resignation of its citizens. The opening of the Wall for a few days over Christmas in 1963 brought hundreds of thousands of people to Berlin from the rest of the country, and even the most fleeting contact with their relations in the West is clearly still of the utmost importance to them. In spite of the general efforts at a more relaxed contact between the two sides in the cold war, the Pankow government was bound to close the Wall again, because even visits from the West implied strain and tension within the régime. Equally they will probably find it impossible to keep the gates permanently shut.

But more important than the practical difficulties which West Berlin presents is the fact that as long as it is occupied by enemy powers, East Germany is transparently an artificial state without a real capital. In terms of intra-German politics and East-West relations, it is impossible both to maintain West Berlin *and* recognise East Germany. Yet there can be no settlement of the German problem, no end to the political and human difficulties of Berlin, until the West does accord some recognition to East Germany.

How can this circle be squared? East Germany, it seems to me, can only be recognised as a public and declaratory step towards German reunification. This would imply a change in the régime, and that at the moment is impossible: as long as the Soviet Union conceives any need for an army in Central Europe, it will need a harsh and reliable régime in East Germany – and equally its position in East Germany enables it to contain the relative liberalism of the other Eastern European countries without difficulty. Ulbricht enables the Soviet Union to encircle Poland, and it is his régime which is the bastion of polycentrism. His warmest supporter is Gomulka.

Any change in the East German régime would probably involve the Communist bloc as a whole in great difficulties, and could not be engineered at the drop of a hint of recognition. But if conditions could be created under which the Soviet Army could be gradually withdrawn from Europe, the possibilities of recognition and eventual reunification would be very much greater.

The best approach to the whole problem seems therefore that of arms control agreements between the two alliances. A detailed policy of linking arms control with recognition, and disarmament with reunification – even many years ahead, but within a specified time – would offer the best hopes of putting an end to the indissoluble problems of Germany and the cold war.

5 THE MIDDLE EAST

Elizabeth Monroe

By comparison with the open combat on other sectors of the East-West frontier, cold war in the Middle East has been waged in velvet gloves. One reason why is plain. When the cold war started, the Middle East was, in contrast to Europe and the Far East, dominated by a single victor, Britain. The British had done the whole of the Middle Eastern fighting, and the Soviet Union, if it wished to challenge their dominance, could do so only by force or subterfuge. Force was out of the question in Russia's enfeebled post-war condition, and, after some feints, all thought of using the Red Army was abandoned. The Soviet Union was therefore obliged to fall back on a mixture of subversion and diplomacy in order to pad its soft underbelly. Yet the threat of Soviet force, as applied to Turkey and Persia at the cold war's outset, was real enough to alarm the Western powers to an extent that made them plan to parry it. For years, elaborate defence schemes shaped their Middle Eastern policy even at times when the threat was more imagined than real.

There was thus, for a decade after the World War, a difference in quality between the cold war as fought in the Middle East and that fought elsewhere. During this decade the two contestants – the Soviet East and the Anglo-American West – were striving for advantage on wholly different planes. The West was working on the material plane of treaties of alliance, bases and military guarantees sweetened with economic aid; the Soviet Union was, by contrast, operating almost entirely in the realm of ideology, in so far as she was operating at all.

In the Middle East, as in Europe, the date at which the cold war began was some months before the end of the war with Germany. In retrospect, it is clear that Stalin expected Churchill and Roosevelt to share his conception of the rights of victors, and to acquiesce in his plans to insulate the Soviet Union in the south as he was insulating it in the west. Both at Teheran and Yalta, he had put out feelers to this end, as well as about Russia's access to the high seas, and he had interpreted the sympathetic answers he then got as encouragement to pursue his aims. By contrast Churchill and Roosevelt, while agreeing that Soviet desires in the south were legitimate, thought that they could be met by 'a favourable régime at the Straits'. This misunderstanding accounts for some moves that the Soviet Union made before the end of the war in both Turkey and Persia.

The Soviet Union had always resented Turkish neutrality, and began to vent its feelings on the Turks in the spring of 1945. In June, three weeks before Potsdam, it invited them to renew a lapsed Russo-Turkish treaty, and in the course of renewal to grant the Soviet Union a base on the Black Sea Straits, and to return to it the two frontier districts of Kars and Ardahan that it had ceded to Turkey in 1921. At about the same time, the Soviet Army of Occupation in Persia (where Allied troops had been stationed since 1942) began actively to sponsor rebellions by the Tudeh party against the government in Teheran. Tudeh means 'Mass', and the masses were Communist, though more out of desire for social change at home than out of love for Russia. In August 1945, Soviet troops actually protected Tudeh insurgents who tried to set up administrative and cultural autonomy in Persia's northern province of Azerbaijan. The same troops later hung on to their positions in northern Persia for some time after the date on which the three major allies had agreed to withdraw from that country.

To Stalin's surprise, these plans and acts shocked his allies. His misreading of their minds became evident at Potsdam, where it was epitomised in an incident that took place on the last night of Churchill's presence as Britain's Prime Minister. Towards the end of a convivial evening, Churchill filled Stalin's glass and his own, and both men drained full beakers of brandy. 'We gazed approvingly at one another.'[17] Immediately, Stalin uttered a thought that must have been uppermost in his mind: 'If you find it impossible to give us a fortified position in the Marmora, could we not have a base at Dedeagatch?' Churchill reports that he fended off this suggestion with some generality about the freedom of the seas. The gulf that separated Soviet from Western thinking was obvious.

Within a matter of weeks, the immense advantage enjoyed by the West over Russia in terms of weapons was made plain by the explosion of the first atomic bomb. In the succeeding months Russia's designs on both Turkey and Persia were thwarted by a combination of Turkish toughness, Persian diplomatic cunning, world pressure applied through the new United Nations Organisation, and growing exasperation on the part of hitherto well-disposed British and American statesmen. Though the world at large was unaware of the East-West tension that was mounting at successive conferences, the men immediately concerned, and notably Truman, Attlee, Bevin, Byrnes and Forrestal, all record their disappointment at Russia's uncompromising attitude over peace plans ranging from reparations to puppet governments.

By 1946, therefore, the Soviet Union was at a double disadvantage on its southern frontier – weak militarily and worsted politically. From a moment late in that year, it gave up the struggle in the south. The Soviets ceased to pester Turkey, left the dissident Azerbaijanis to sink or swim, and dropped a claim that they had laid in September 1946 to a trusteeship over one of the Italian colonies, preferably Tripolitania. In a way that was often characteristic of Russians in Tsarist days, they retired to lick their wounds. They scarcely reappeared in public in the Middle East for a decade; over the Palestine problem, for instance, their only interventions were votes at United Nations meetings un-predictably distributed as between Jew and Arab; in such moves as they made, the one consistent element was intent to do whatever was most likely to damage Anglo-American relations.

In the context of East-West rivalry, the Arab League states and Israel are in a different category from Turkey and Persia. Having no common frontier with the Soviet Union, they can often afford to ignore her. Throughout the years after the World War, they were wholly preoccupied with their own concerns, and notably with the Palestine problem, and scarcely noticed the impact or absence of Soviet policy and pressure. The presence of the West was the incubus of which they were aware – a presence too powerful to resist, other than passively.

In the Arab-Israeli portion of the Middle East, therefore, the cold war falls into three well-marked phases – first, the period of Soviet retirement during which the West had as much of its own way as local public opinion would allow; second, a period from 1955–57 during which the Soviets plumped for championship of the Arabs, and scored great success; third, a period beginning in 1958 and not yet over, in which disillusionment with the Arab world becomes a characteristic not only of Soviet but of United States policy.

A Soviet silence of years about lands seething with social dis-content calls for more explanation than mere pique over two initial setbacks. One reason for it may have been unfamiliarity with the Middle Eastern scene; Soviet literature of the twenties and thirties contains few or no studies of contemporary Middle Eastern affairs. Islam as a topic was frowned on for fear of en-couraging dangerous thoughts in the six Islamic Republics of the Soviet Union. In the early twenties a Kazan Tatar locally known as Sultan Galiev had preached the doctrine that 'national move-ments' in Moslem lands could be 'progressive' and possess 'the character of a true social revolution';[18] for views so awkward, he had been imprisoned, and later executed. Lastly, mistrust of Asian nationalism in general, and notably of nationalist China, was part of Stalin's creed. Almost to the end, he saw Gandhi as a reactionary in the same category as Chiang Kai-shek. Soviet publicists were instructed to describe the Indian Independence Act as a manifestation of 'a national bourgeoisie going over to the camp of imperialism', and the overthrow of King Farouk in 1952 as a 'Fascist coup'. The controlling Middle Eastern bourgeoisie was regarded as unfit to work with; the local Communist parties, which were weak and boasted scarcely any members of note, were sustained on a bare subsistence level with the message that their turn would not come for some time.[19]

In Western minds, this era of blessed quiet induced a sense of complacency. Overworked men were busy at home and in Europe, and had little incentive to devise new diplomatic means of holding their own in the Middle East. British power, though it had diminished significantly on account of Britain's post-war penury, remained outwardly impressive because it was un-opposed. The Labour Government of 1945 was alive to the new thoughts that were coursing through Asia; indeed, in response to them, it offered in May 1946 to evacuate Egypt, subject to certain guarantees. But when its notion of guarantees had been rejected by the Egyptian nationalists, it fell back on old patterns of policy, revealing that even a left-wing Ministry could not abandon Britain's local military privileges. It had more than one reason for its apparent conservatism. By 1947, the Russians were acting so arbitrarily in Eastern Europe that it could not discount the risk of a flash and explosion. Also by 1947, Indian independence, although it had reduced certain British military cares in the Middle East, had created others. For without the central strategic reserve of troops formerly based on India, new means had to be devised for defending new treasure; this was the rapidly rising quantity of Middle Eastern oil on which free Europe depended for re-habilitation under the terms of the Marshall Plan of 1947.[20]

The American assessment of the Soviet danger was if anything more alarmist than the British. As Truman wrote to his Secretary of State, Byrnes, in January 1946: 'Unless Russia is faced with an iron fist and strong language, another war is in the making'.[21] A year later the United States responded, willy-nilly, to an im-poverished Britain's appeal that it take over Western defence responsibilities in Greece and Turkey. This so-called Truman doctrine of 12 March 1947, is a turning-point; it marks the end of all wartime hopes that a trio of satisfied powers might work together, and the end of both British and American illusions that Middle East defence was a matter that could be left to Britain. Yet such was the complacency induced by the local absence of Soviet pressure that the two Western powers for a time felt able to indulge in the luxury of public quarrel about Middle Eastern matters. Their most blatant dispute was over Palestine; they also disagreed, rather less publicly, over British methods of negotiating an up-to-date oil agreement with Persia – the agreement that was to founder at the hands of Dr Mussadiq. Behind doors that were only half-closed, they bickered, too, over British handling of treaty negotiations with the young officers who in 1952 took over the government of Egypt.

Yet the Western partners, though at odds in Middle Eastern eyes, were solidly together on issues elsewhere, and were con-strained by Soviet hostility *outside the Middle East* to co-ordinate their defence planning. Once rid of their Palestine quarrel, they began to plan joint Middle Eastern defence measures that were vital in their own eyes, but that (save in the opinion of a few Arab and Persian elder statesmen of international experience) seemed irrelevant to everyone in the Middle East.

By the end of the forties, the British and Americans had acting separately achieved a defence agreement with Jordan, installed forces in Libya, and retained on short lease a United States air base at Dhahran in Saudi Arabia. But Britain had failed to negotiate new defence treaties with either Egypt or Iraq; though her pre-war treaties with both countries still had some years to run.[22] In 1950, the Korean War gave the Western partners a jolt that quickened their anxieties and impelled them to act together. They tried, but failed, to induce Egypt to agree, with themselves, France and Turkey, to install a 'Middle East Command' on the Suez Canal. They succeeded, jointly with France, in issuing a Western *diktat* designed to prevent fresh outbreaks of fighting in Palestine. This Tripartite Declaration of 1950 was intended to warn the Arab states and Israel not to try altering the armistice lines by force, as well as to preserve a balance in arms supplies to both sides. This scrap of paper served its turn for so long as Western power in the area remained unchallenged.

But all these Western arrangements were out of key with local aspirations. Jews and Arabs wanted more arms; Egypt wanted evacuation of all foreign troops; Asians in general wanted aid 'without strings' and freedom to run their own defences their own way and against their own adversaries. Their attitude is epitomised in a remark made by an Egyptian statesman to Ernest Bevin in the course of the Korean War:

> Your foreign policy is of such wide range that it almost embraces all international problems. But our foreign policy is a very limited one, and can almost be resolved in these two questions under discussion, the question of evacuation, and that of the unity of Egypt and the Sudan under Egyptian crown.[23]

Pursuit of this policy had led Egypt to abstain from condemning the aggressor in Korea: when the Americans criticised this parochial attitude, one Egyptian newspaper retorted that 'Russia and its friends supported the Egyptian case in the Security Council,[24] and they have supported the case of every nation fighting for its independence'.[25]

As this quotation shows, Western irritation with Middle Eastern opinion was a gift to the Soviet Union. The Russians themselves produced a few similar irritants. For instance, in 1951 they addressed threatening notes to Egypt, Syria, Lebanon and Israel warning them against adhering to the West's proposal for a Middle East command, and were locally condemned for attempting to interfere with domestic policy. Yet the volume of Western interference was in Egyptian and Arab eyes so much the greater that the Soviets were presented with an opportunity. They grasped it, though not avidly, because doing so entailed a change in the party line on nationalism, and because the Soviet machine grinds only slowly into gear.

This change in Soviet policy was part of the great change in Soviet theory that took place with Stalin's death in February 1953. But, in retrospect, its coming in the Middle East is discernible for some time before he died. Briefly put, the change took the form of a decision that Asian nationalism, far from giving cause for fear, was so anti-imperialist that it could be turned to account in the cold war. During the Anglo-Persian oil dispute of 1951–52, Soviet propaganda had ceased to flay Dr Mussadiq for condoning American aid, and had converted him into a hero conducting 'the people's struggle against the capitalist-imperialists'. In 1952, the Syrian Communist leader, Khaled Bakdash – who was and is far the ablest Communist in the Arab Middle East – was instructed to proclaim that the Syrian Communists would support a Nationalist Government (*i.e.* would work with the bourgeoisie against a pro-French dictator) without demanding seats therein.[26] As the Cominform journal put the matter in January 1953, Egypt, Persia and Iraq were 'areas of progress in the conflict with imperialism'.

Removal by death of Stalin's monolithic mind, and its replacement by that of the more flexible Malenkov, was probably not the only Soviet reason for coming round to the view that, as an interim measure, Asian nationalists were worth working with even if they were bourgeois and reactionary. Another contribution to the decision was the confidence imparted by achievement of nuclear parity. The explosion of Russia's first hydrogen bomb was announced on 20 August 1953. From 1954 onwards, the tide had turned, and Russia's new interest in Middle Eastern problems became manifest both in Soviet diplomacy and Soviet literature. A decree altered the anti-Islamic propaganda of the twenties and thirties; the Muslim provinces of the Soviet Union were restored to the limelight and presented as a cultural bridge between Russia and Islam; Muslim attachés were appointed to Arab capitals, where they attended the mosque.

In Soviet intellectual circles, orientalism became a respectable pursuit. The orientalist studying for knowledge's sake gave place to the scholar willing to put over the party line. Publications that had been mediocre acquired a new look. A *History of Islamic Studies in the USSR* appeared; the Soviet Academy of Social Sciences gave birth to an offshoot, the Moscow Institute of Middle Eastern Studies, that was to co-ordinate work all over the Soviet Union; new periodicals, notably *Soviet Orientalism*, were put on the market.

These portents of a new policy were little noticed in the West. Both Eden in Britain and Dulles in the United States were deeply preoccupied with the menace of communism, but, at the time, their attention was riveted on South-East Asia. In the Middle East, 1954 was a year of successes for them in the two most important of the shaky countries of the area – Egypt and Persia. The Egyptian revolution of 1952 had placed at the head of affairs soldiers enjoying enough popular support to be able to strike a compromise with Britain over evacuation. The Anglo-Egyptian agreement of 1954 provided for this within a fixed period, but subject to a proviso that the British could 'reactivate' the Suez base in the event of attack on an Arab state or on Turkey. In Persia, the British and Americans, driven into harmony by Dr Mussa-diq's intransigence and the extent to which it played into Communist hands, had helped to promote his collapse and had brought about a settlement of the oil dispute. Eden and Dulles were entitled to pride themselves on patching Western quarrels with rulers whose inclination was to look West rather than East for at least two important kinds of help – educational and economic – as well as for armaments. Their hopes stood high, and even their best observers felt no qualms about the potency of a Soviet appeal to the Middle East on a different plane from their own – an appeal by a power seeking to win a favourable climate of opinion, as opposed to the appeal of Anglo-Saxons, who still wanted a favourable power structure.

Had the West been on the alert in this year of triumphs, it might have seen reason for alarm in the coincidence of the Soviet line with the Arab public mood. It is difficult to single out which of the Soviet and the Arab themes was cause, and which effect; at all events, a cross-fertilisation of anti-Western ideas was taking place. Early in 1954, Nasser summoned his colleagues and ambassadors to a conference at which he proclaimed neutralism as Egypt's creed, and his definition of neutralism[27] was weighted in Russia's favour because it specified freedom from 'imperialist influence', as well as because it seemed to him to tally with the Soviet 'Partisans of Peace' campaign. The Syrian Baathists, led by an older man, Michel Aflaq, who had at the time had wider international experience, did not all swallow the Soviet propaganda line that peaceful coexistence and neutralism were synonymous; they could recall examples, particularly at the time when the French *Front Populaire* of 1936 had endowed the French Communist party with power, of the exploitation of Arabs for Communist ends. But the common man in the Arab world set Soviet doves of peace against Western base-mongering, and Soviet anti-colonialism against dictatorial Western measures such as the Tripartite Declaration on Palestine.

The reversal of Eastern and Western fortunes that took place with the Egyptian-Czech arms deal of September 1955 ended the era of

Western complacency. A new phase of the cold war began. At a stroke, the Soviet Union leapt over the defences that the West had erected along a 'northern tier' – Greece, Turkey, Persia, Pakistan – and had trumped several other Western tricks. Its coup nullified the Western arrangement for an arms balance between the Arabs and Israel; it transformed Western aid from a weapon in Western hands into a bargaining counter for Egyptian or Arab use; and it confirmed all but a few Arabs in the view that Nasser was a new Saladin, giving them dignity and status.

Could the West have forestalled or blunted the blow? The Egyptians had warned the British and American ambassadors that if their governments would not supply arms to Egypt in the quantities that it required, it must turn elsewhere. But they had been paralysed by two handicaps. The first was the permanent incubus of the Palestine problem, that constrained them to keep a balance between Jew and Arab. The second was America's inability to grant arms under the terms of the Mutual Security Act unless Egypt accepted the condition that beneficiaries must accept an American 'military assistance advisory group'. To Nasser, this stipulation spelt a mere change of master, and he rejected it; he would have preferred to buy Western weapons, but had no currency with which to pay for them, so turned to a supplier who would accept payment in Egyptian cotton. Even in retrospect, it is not easy to see how the Western powers could have escaped from their dilemma. They had to decide whether to exchange tried policies, devised partly to suit home politics, for a gesture that might be of transient value. Their conundrum reveals how peculiar had been the monopoly of power that the West had enjoyed in the Middle East since 1921 – the year in which the Bolsheviks had abandoned the pressures exercised by a long line of Tsars.

The early Soviet probes of the Arab world in 1954–55 searched for the countries most worth trying to keep out of the Western orbit. Their spectacular success was with Egypt, but their earliest was with Syria, and illustrates the axiom that Syrian opinion is the best available barometer of the general trend of Arab thought. At the Syrian elections of 1954, the left wing – the Baath and the Communists – had gained ground, though not a majority. The voting showed that the tide of neutralism was running strongly, and towards the end of the year the government somewhat surreptitiously acquired from the East a few second-hand Soviet tanks. In Syria, as later in Egypt, the purchase indicated, not so much a swing towards the Soviet Union, as a move to set the course of Arab neutralism dead on centre.

The Twentieth Congress of the Communist party – the meeting famous for Khrushchev's demolition of the Stalin legend – took place in Moscow in February 1956. From that moment, Soviet policy became assured, and began to radiate confidence. The Congress specified the principles that sounded so attractive to neutralists – peaceful coexistence; cultivation of ties with un-committed countries, which must be free to choose their own 'forms of transition to socialism'; aid to such countries 'irrespective of their political and social structure', and on a commercial basis, without hint of grant or bribe.[28] The new theme was that bourgeois and capitalist democracies, too, were travelling the road to socialism, though Communists were bound to get there first. To the average Arab, listening on his transistor set, the message sounded disinterested, and contrasted favourably with Western proposals hedged about with military conditions, and scarcely distinguishable from British imperialism.

Extraneous events furthered the Soviet cause. In February 1955, a *rapprochement* between Egypt and Syria (an event that worries Israel whenever it occurs) provoked an Israeli show of might, and a military attack on the Egyptians at Gaza that revealed Egypt's military weakness. This experience quickened Egypt's wish to acquire arms, regardless of source. Also early in 1955, Nasser made his first excursion outside the Arab world to attend the Afro-Asian conference of uncommitted peoples at Bandung. Although the notice there served on the great powers by the uncommitted nations was as applicable to East as to West, this fact was blanketed by the Conference's peace slogans. For Nasser, it was unimportant by comparison with the satisfaction of establishing touch with Chou En-lai. Though he realised, as did the Soviet Union, that all sorts of good friends of the West were keeping company with anti-colonials in the Afro-Asian movement, he went home well content with new friendships that were likely to be useful to him.

But perhaps the biggest of all the contributions to the success of Soviet policy between 1955 and 1957 was Western failure to grasp that nothing short of complete Anglo-American harmony would be a match for the new Soviet sense of purpose. By ill luck, the two men in charge of Western policy, Eden and Dulles, did not get on. The subtle diplomat and the righteous lawyer had differed bitterly over Indo-China. Though their countries' interests in the Middle East were now identical, they approached its problems from different standpoints. Eden's was, at bottom, deep resentment at loss of Britain's leadership to, of all nations, Egypt;[29] Dulles's stemmed from antipathy to communism which, in his words, started 'from an atheistic, godless premise' that rendered neutralism 'immoral'.[30]

Dulles was also anti-imperialist, and felt bound to condemn the British whenever he thought that they were becoming too rough with the natives. Had policy been in the hands of men who understood one another, as, for instance, Bevin and Marshall had done, less chances to shine might have been presented to the Soviet Union. As things were, variations, or what seemed to the Arabs to be variations, in British and American policy helped to account for a number of failures. First Britain alone, hoping to retain a power position and to renew an expiring Anglo-Iraqi treaty, induced a single Arab state, Iraq, to snap its fingers at neutralism and join a pro-Western alliance. This was the Baghdad Pact of April 1955, pushed into being by the British and the Turks regardless of one ill-omen – the replacement, in Syria in the previous February, of a pro-Iraqi government by a pro-Egyptian and neutralist one. The Pact, later strengthened by the addition of Persia and Pakistan, was enough of a success to worry the Soviet Union. But the success was hollow because infringement of the popular Arab and Nasserite conceptions of unity and neutrality earned Britain the animosity of the majority of Arabs. Three years later, the Pact's Iraqi adversaries murdered the King, Crown Prince, and Prime Minister who had sponsored it.

As Eden and Dulles grew progressively angrier with Nasser for leading Arabs astray and flirting with the Soviet Union, they perpetrated a notorious series of Western acts out of which the Soviet Union was able to make capital. In July 1956, Dulles abruptly refused loans to finance Nasser's high dam at Aswan, enabling the Soviet Union to offer to do the job. Eden 'would have preferred to play this long,'[31] but he too played short when in November 1956, he fathered the Anglo-French invasion of Egypt in punishment for Nasser's behaviour over the Suez Canal. This act drove the United States and the Soviet Union into voting together at the United Nations, and enabled Bulganin to pose as a saviour of the Arabs by brandishing rockets at London.[32]

Some Arabs accepted this Soviet gesture at its face value; others (of whom Nasser was later to say that he was one)[33] rated it as bluster, uttered for effect. Many attached much greater importance to the American display of loyalty to the United Nations Charter that had caused the United States to denounce an ally, Britain, and a *protégé*, Israel. Egyptians reminded one another of American sponsorship at earlier stages of their revolution,[34] and hoped that the good old days were back, for some of them were growing nervous of their increasing dependence on the Soviet bloc.[35] At the turn of 1956-57, their ideal was an America ready to come to terms with Arab nationalism.

After the world-wide reaction to the Suez crisis had temporarily eliminated the British from the Middle Eastern scene, the United States upheld the Western cause single-handed. But

Egyptian hopes that they would do so in sympathy with neutralism were soon dashed. For the US authorities were concerned about legality, and decided to give Egypt no help pending determination of compensation for Suez Canal shareholders. The form in which this policy was brought home to the Arab world was a United States refusal to go on supplying Egypt with wheat under Public Law 480, and a Congressional order to go slow on the 1966-67 CARE programme for Egypt.[36] There was no doubt about a shift in the direction of Egyptian opinion when, early in 1957, Russian ships sailed into Alexandria carrying the needed wheat and pharmaceuticals; Cairo radio relayed the news to the rest of the Arab world.

The anti-Western trend was enhanced by another well-meant American gesture, the Eisenhower doctrine.[37] Had this doctrine been the impartial gesture for which many Arabs were hoping – that is, the renewal of an earlier American pledge to assist the 'victim of any aggression in the Middle East'[38] – it might have reversed the anti-Western trend. Instead, the doctrine was coloured by American home politics and was an offer to 'co-operate with' nations in the Middle East requesting aid 'against overt armed aggression from any nation controlled by international communism'.

At the American end this offer looked to be value for money; there was no chance of Congressional consent to use of United States forces abroad without the anti-Communist proviso. But at the Arab end the proviso destroyed the whole value of the gesture. For it split the Arab world into two camps – a group that tolerated anti-communism and a group that did not. To most Arabs it bore the marks of a fresh Western move to isolate Nasser and to pit him against Iraq, Saudi Arabia and Jordan; most saw it as a bumbling effort to produce an American version of the Baghdad Pact.

There followed a year of brinkmanship in the course of which the Soviet Union continued to shine. For instance, the Americans drew radio bombardments from Moscow, Cairo and Syria when they moved the Sixth Fleet into the eastern Mediterranean in April 1957 in order to mark their support for King Hussein during a pro-Nasser rising in Jordan. Again in the summer, they dabbled unsuccessfully in a power struggle between Arab rulers for the allegiance of Syria because, mistakenly, they interpreted the Syrian scene solely in terms of the cold war. Syrian advocates of closer ties with Russia were able to point to Western gaucherie.

More than one of these Western schemes stood a chance, at the moment of inception, of turning into a useful stroke of cold war policy. Either the Baghdad Pact or the Eisenhower doctrine might have attracted other states into its orbit; each failed because its sponsor misjudged the strength of neutralism in Asia. The combined effect of a series of Western misjudgements was elimination of British influence from Egypt, and in the end from the whole of the Fertile Crescent (the Arab name for the coast of the Levant and the Euphrates valley), and a branding of the United States as no better than the old-fashioned imperialists. The Sputnik, soaring into orbit in October 1957, seemed to assure the Soviets pride of place in Arab esteem.

But in 1958 the wheel of fortune spun, if not into reverse, at least into neutral. Though the Soviet triumphs had been spectacular because so discomfiting to the West, they had exposed the Soviet Union to risks of a new kind. For the methods used had caused it to quit the safe realm of ideology, and to start competing with the West on a material plane – in a word, to leave the touchline and enter the scrum. Once involved, Russia was to learn the lesson that Britain and America had successively learnt by experience – that no foreigner need expect to be loved in the modern Middle East, and that foreign participants in Arab politics make as many enemies as friends.

Characteristically, Syria set the tone. In 1957, she criticised Soviet hints about great-power management in the Mediterranean area. In 1958, she administered communism a resounding snub.

The Syrian Baath party, reckoning that the pro-Soviet tendencies of some ministers and generals had gone too far, rushed into Egypt's arms and induced Nasser (who had always kept Egyptian communism at bay) to unite Egypt and Syria in the United Arab Republic (UAR).

In the summer of the same year the Iraqi revolution took East and West alike by surprise, and alarmed both. Soviet concern was increased when British and American troops were asked for by Jordan and Lebanon. But as events with some Communist overtones developed in Iraq, Soviet hopes stirred. The pro-British palace clique had been disposed of, and exiles, some of whom had spent years in the Soviet Union, were welcomed home. But the hopes came to nothing. Factional quarrels within Iraq handicapped the would-be ally just as they had handicapped the British in their heyday – more so, because one of them was between rival groups of the Iraqi Communist party.

The Iraqi revolution, far from working out to Soviet advantage, threw a spotlight on to a major flaw in Soviet policy. This flaw was the impossibility of dovetailing open competition with the West for Arab allies with the Communist party line that communism must triumph in the end. Egyptians and Arabs soon saw that 'peaceful coexistence' was a cloak for a policy that was not so disinterested as it had been made out to be. Nasser had always kept communism in check, and by early 1959 slogans such as 'neither with East nor with West' were all over the UAR. The Arabs wanted neither bloc. The Egyptian leaders went on to evolve a 'two stage' theory, according to which Western imperialism had been defeated and now it was communism's turn.

Soviet displeasure with these Arab reflexes was at once proclaimed. In 1958, the Soviet Union began to denounce anti-Communist measures in the UAR, and during 1959 to criticise the Arab interpretation of coexistence, including the 'no bloc' theory. Soviet voices retorted that 'we are not a bloc, but a system' – a phrase that illustrates the difficulty of combining power politics with Communist ideology. Tones grew shriller as more and more Middle Eastern writers joined the fray, and reached a zenith during a tart ideological controversy between Cairo and Moscow in 1961. During its course, *Pravda* (31 May 1961) denounced the UAR as:

> A society in which exploiters rule and people make speeches about democracy, while for their political beliefs progressive people languish in torture chambers.

Examples of Soviet embarrassment occurred from time to time. For instance, in 1963, Outer Mongolia laid before the United Nations Assembly a resolution in favour of the Kurdish uprising which successive Baghdad governments had failed to quell, but had to be told to withdraw the motion, which had got Moscow into bad odour in Baghdad, with consequent crumbs of advantage for the Western powers.

In the third and current phase of the cold war as waged in the Arab states, the governing factor is that the moment of Soviet-Arab common interest is over; it hung on anti-imperialism and the Arabs reckon that except at Aden and in the Persian Gulf they have got rid of the imperialists. Soviet broadcasts of the winter of 1963-64 were full of wistful hankering for the unity of view that prevailed in the good old days of colonialism. The widening gap between their theories and Arab desiderata was especially noticeable in their comment on Arab unity. By their standards, unity was to be deplored if it took on a 'kind of neutralistic slant . . . that ignores the content of the Great October Revolution'. *Pravda* of 14 April 1963, spelt out one theme:

> It all depends in whose hands the banner of unity is carried, and on what basis it will be realised – anti-imperialist democratic and popular or pro-imperialist and anti-democratic?

Another Soviet criticism is that Arab unity is a deviation from the class struggle. As Khrushchev told the Egyptians when he visited them to open the Aswan Dam in May, 1964, the unity theme was acceptable only when it meant:

> Arab workers, Arab peasants, Arab intelligentsia, all working people, unite against the exploiters, including your own Arabs.

Most Arabs rate such remarks as intrusion into their private affairs, and as giving them fresh cause to wish for non-alignment.

Countries that have plumped for East or West afford less scope for cold war competition than do uncommitted Arabs. The facts about Israel, Persia and Turkey are soon told.

Israel is by birth, upbringing and economics a brain child of the West; it is the only country in the Middle East that works institutions of Western pattern – its Parliament, courts and executive. When it was voted into being the Soviet Union toyed with the idea of capturing its imagination and allegiance. Soviet Russia was third in the race to recognise it in 1948. At that time the Israelis too wanted good relations with East as well as West. But bones of contention with the Soviet Union, such as its treatment of Jews, accumulated over the years. They became serious at the time of Stalin's last fling – his onslaught on the Jewish doctors in 1952. So that even before Moscow's decision to arm Egypt, Soviet relations with Israel had become distant. They remain so, and are not improved when Soviet newspapers print complaints from Jews who have tried life in Israel and later returned to Eastern bloc countries because they do not like it.

Turkey and Persia are reckoned by Moscow to be better worth attention than Israel, and Westerners are mistaken to count on either as a permanent bastion.

The Persians thrive on East-West discord. For them, the real black moments in the present century are the rare occasions on which East-West antagonism diminished owing to events in Europe, as it did in 1907, 1914-17 and 1941-45. Their long undefended frontier with the Soviet Union fills them with nagging apprehension, yet their northerly trade connections with Russia are long-standing and natural. They are therefore constrained to rely on feats of balance, and sometimes on guile, to see them through. For generations these skills have served them well. In 1955 the Shah, playing a strong though less than dictatorial role, plumped for the West and joined the Baghdad Pact (now CENTO) and in 1957 he signed a bilateral mutual defence pact with the United States. But many of his Persian critics greatly dislike these firm commitments. They were thus delighted over the announcement of a Russo-Persian agreement in December 1962, and its sequel – Persia's undertaking not to countenance rocket bases on Persian soil. By Persian standards this promise has led to ideal conditions – those in which the Western allies remain handy but in which the Soviet Union cannot do enough to please a neighbour who has given such an undertaking.

The Turks, behaving in their more stolid way, took a tougher line throughout, accepting NATO bases on their soil and the American military and economic aid that has kept them solvent since 1950. But the series of Turkish revolutions and political uncertainties that disturbed national life after 1960 quickened a Soviet hope of 'getting the country out of its political blind alley'. Simultaneously, Turkish qualms about the collapse of authority at home seemed to awaken curiosity about how things were done abroad. More Turks began listening in to Russia. Indeed there have been signs, notably trade signs, of an official desire to improve relations with the USSR. Given peace and political satisfaction over Cyprus, the Turks are solidly with the West. Were shooting to start (and to start elsewhere than in Turkey) they might be as glad as they were in 1939 to save their skins by getting guarantees of neutrality from both sides.

If a balance sheet of Eastern and Western operations in the Middle East is struck, it contains more self-balancing items than is generally supposed. For instance, both East and West have misinterpreted local Arab power struggles – particularly those in Syria – as evidence of their own success or failure in the cold war, whereas these contests are nothing of the sort. Again, both Americans and Soviets have hoped that their championship of anti-colonialism would make them the loved one; instead, both have earned a name for near-colonialism themselves. In the matter of aid, the West should count for most because so much the richer: the United States has given in cash value about twelve times the amount laid out by the Soviet Union in aid to the Middle East, and has made many outright grants, which the Soviet Union has not. Yet volume has meant little or nothing to the recipients. These sums, whatever their size, have won neither side the goodwill they were meant to bring. If anything, the Soviet contribution, though smaller, has been more attractive because it is less hedged about with conditions than are American moneys intended simultaneously to contribute to the security of the Western world. Whatever the reputation earned, each side is committed to continuing with an aid programme that it cannot cancel without handing a gratuitous advantage to its adversary.

The balance sheet also shows, of course, outright credits and debits to both East and West. Of Western credits, undoubtedly the greatest is the superior attraction of Western education, of learning the English language, and of enjoying hail-fellow-well-met conditions in American or British universities that contrast favourably with segregation in Patrice Lumumba College, Moscow. Possibly on account of the failure of Soviet educational efforts in Eastern Europe, the Russians have opened few teaching establishments elsewhere abroad, and are on the defensive about their educational efforts.

A second clear Western asset is immediately apparent in the direction of trade, which flows mainly to and from the West not merely because the Soviet Union, being an oil exporter, has no need of Middle Eastern oil, but because the Middle Eastern merchant has so far been loth to abandon his classic Western suppliers.

Any traveller through the area notices at once how few consumer goods from the East are on show. Middle Eastern trade with the Soviet Union, though rising in both Turkey and Persia, is small except in freak conditions, such as Egypt's sales of cotton to pay for arms in the late fifties, or the occasional disposal of a problem crop such as surplus Cyprus raisins. Until the Soviet Union and Communist China are able to export goods of Western quality, this advantage seems likely to continue.

But against Western assets must be set an immense Western liability in all Arab lands – the responsibility carried by Britain and the United States for founding and maintaining Israel. Again and again this handicap has prevented them from matching or countering Soviet policy in the Arab world.

On Soviet account, far the greatest positive asset is identification with peace and disarmament. All Arabs and many Persians favourably compare Soviet proposals for nuclear-free zones with British and American quests for allies and bases, such as a military foothold at Aden or rocket sites in Turkey. Another advantage to the East – not only to Russia, but to China – is that Nasser's programme of Arab socialism is inching its way towards a totalitarian pattern that is far closer to Eastern than to Western practices. What is more, underdeveloped peoples striving for a better life see far more encouragement in the example of Soviet Russians or Chinese, who are pulling themselves up by their own bootstraps in the present generation, than they see in patented Western models.

Yet the Soviet Union too suffers from offsetting handicaps, and of these the worst, already mentioned, is the impossibility of reconciling Communist party doctrine with Russian power-politics, and the element of duplicity that the latter inject into catchwords such as 'peaceful coexistence'. Seen from this angle, China's pursuit of a 'class struggle' doctrine as monolithic as Stalin's might seem to hold out more attractions than the confused neo-Soviet theme; yet, in the eyes of all Middle Eastern neutralists, China tarnished its reputation when it attacked India. East seems no better than West at pleasing all the Middle Easterners all the time.

Indeed, the anomaly of the cold war as fought there in the middle sixties is that no one can say for sure who is winning, or even gaining ground. The two sides are each of them following costly policies that produce identical local results – the raising of living standards, the spread of education, preparation for 'take-off' – without any assurance that its bounty will work out to its own advantage. On present evidence, the only net gainer by the process is the inhabitant of the Middle East, and the last word must lie with him:

> We treat Russia as a bank. The bank which grants me a loan has no right to interfere in my own affairs.[39]

The words were written of the Soviet Union, but are applied equally to the United States. And the sentiment may be a lasting one. For who can foretell how soon the poorer countries of the Middle East will cease to depend on loans; or how long it will be before two systems as different as those of America and Russia collaborate in order to prevent the Middle Eastern middle-man from turning from one to the other to raise their bids for his favour?

6 SOUTH-EAST ASIA

Brian Crozier

In South-East Asia, the cold war is hot. This apparent paradox is fundamental. In South-East Asia, more than in any other region of the world since the end of the Second World War, Communist parties have sought to further their aims by violence. Periods of violence and non-violence have indeed alternated with such frequency in certain countries that it would be pointless to attempt to disentangle them. Both the 'hot' or shooting phases of the conflict and its phases of relative quiet belong to the cold war, in that both constitute aspects of the fundamental clash of ideologies, still falling short of full-scale military involvement by the major powers (that there has been a degree of involvement on the part of these powers does not affect this argument).

It would be a mistake, on the other hand, to oversimplify situations that are intrinsically complex. In each of the countries of South-East Asia other elements have been at work besides the clash of Communist and Western ideologies. The most important of these are nationalism and the Sino-Soviet dispute. Each has to be given its full weight if a true picture is to emerge.

Between 1945 and 1949, the main outside force at work in South-East Asia was that of the Soviet Union – a compound of Messianism and imperialism; a relatively less important counter-force was that of the retreating Western imperialisms: British, French and Dutch. The most important internal force was nationalism. This in turn took two forms: a generalised anti-Western, anti-colonialist, anti-imperialist current common to all

163

countries in the region except Thailand, which had not been a Western colony; and a specific current peculiar to each country taken individually. The Vietnamese, Burmese and Indonesians, for instance, shared a common opposition to 'Western imperialism'. But their nationalism took wholly different forms.

From 1949, a new and important factor appeared: that of the Chinese People's Republic. The victory of the Chinese Communists over the Kuomintang not only, in effect, restored the imperial unity of China after a century of weakness and confusion. It also brought a major Communist state to the confines of China's traditional vassals in South-East Asia.

From about 1959, another major influence began to affect the cold war, in this as in other parts of the world. This was the Sino-Soviet dispute. By 1962, it had begun to change the character of the cold war in South-East Asia in ways that were not immediately understood, either on the Western or on the Communist side.

Finally, to take the last of the important circumstances that have a bearing on that conflict, the departure of the Western imperial powers created a vacuum that was filled in ways which we shall describe.

It may be convenient to consider in turn each of these influences.

During the immediate post-war years, nationalism was a far more important force than communism in South-East Asia. In all the countries that were breaking away from Western rule, however, the Communists tried to gain control of nationalist movements by identifying themselves with the anti-Western cause. The circumstances appeared to be uniquely favourable from the standpoint of the Communists in that revolutionary situations existed in nearly all the countries that had been under Japanese occupation. Thailand, which had never been colonised by a Western power, is an exception to this and to most other arguments in this chapter. Defeat and humiliation had shattered Western prestige, and local populations were determined to resist any attempt to reimpose imperial authority.

In Burma, the Philippines and Indo-China, the Japanese had set up indigenous régimes which, although their independence was nominal, demonstrated to colonial peoples that they were capable of running their own affairs. In Indonesia, the Japanese set up Indonesian advisory councils which, though they did not amount to a government, were nevertheless an advance on Dutch practice in the direction of autonomy. In Malaya, too, the Japanese had made preparations to launch an 'independent' state.

On the other hand, anti-Japanese resistance movements had been launched in all the countries mentioned, and in each – apart from Indonesia – the Communists played an important part. Moreover, the suddenness of Japan's collapse in August 1945, caused a hiatus between the Japanese surrender and the arrival of allied forces in Malaya, Indo-China and Indonesia – a circumstance that was exploited to the full by local nationalists and Communists. In Burma and the Philippines, circumstances were slightly less favourable to the Communists in that the British and American forces, respectively, had re-established themselves before Japan's final collapse.

It is easier to describe the use made by the Communists of the opportunities offered by this situation than to relate Communist activities to the cold war. It takes two sides to make a war. On the Communist side, the objective was clearly defined and consistently pursued. It was two-fold: to eliminate Western power, in alliance with the nationalists, and to give local revolutions a Communist direction. On the Western side, the outlines were blurred, both by the confusion that arose from the alliance of Communists and nationalists, and by the divergence between the United States on the one hand and the European colonial powers on the other. President Roosevelt had made it clear that the United States would oppose the re-establishment of Western rule over Asian colonies. The British, though willing, at any rate under the

Labour Government that came to power in 1945, to concede independence to Asian dependencies, wanted to do so in conditions of their own choosing, having first re-established their authority. The French, though willing to concede a degree of autonomy within the French Union, were not psychologically prepared to give full independence. The Dutch, broadly speaking, had learnt nothing and forgotten nothing. Allied differences help to account for some curious anomalies, including the now dimly remembered fact that the American Office of Strategic Services (OSS) supplied the Vietminh with arms while it was building up its forces with the aim of resisting the return of French power in Vietnam.

The alliances between nationalists and Communists were marriages of convenience and correspondingly short-lived. In Vietnam, non-Communist nationalists had joined Ho Chi Minh's Communist Party of Indo-China in 1941 to form the League for the Independence of Vietnam, better known as the Vietminh (a contraction of *Viet* Nam Doc Lap Dong *Minh* Hoi). Bao Dai, the former Emperor of Vietnam, himself joined Ho in 1945, becoming 'supreme adviser' to the latter's provisional government. In March 1946, however, Bao Dai, disillusioned with the Communists, went into exile in Hong Kong, and many Vietnamese nationalists followed his example.

In the Philippines, also, the split between nationalists and Communists came early. The Philippine situation was further complicated by early symptoms of the ideological schism between Moscow and Peking.[40] One section of the Filipino Communist Party, headed by Vicente Lava, the party boss during the occupation period, wanted to set up a People's Democratic Government, on lines advocated by Mao Tse-tung. The majority section, headed by Pedro Castro, who succeeded Lava as Secretary-General of the party, followed the then orthodox Moscow line of advocating Communist participation in a coalition government committed to a minimum Marxist programme. This was the

166

situation on the eve of the elections of April 1946, which the returning Americans had decided to hold in fulfilment of their pledge of independence for the Philippines. The Lava group wanted a showdown with the anti-Japanese politicians headed by Sergio Osmena. The Castro group wanted to enter a government headed by Osmena, with the aim of controlling it from within. In the event, however, the elections were won by the collaborationist Liberal party of Manuel Roxas. Since the Moscow-line coalition programme had become impossible, the elections thus had the effect of driving the Communist party towards the violent course which the Lava group's Peking-line tactics would have made inevitable. The instrument of violence was at hand in the theoretically disbanded People's Anti-Japanese Resistance Army, better known as the Hukbalahap, from an abbreviation of its name in Tagalog. The Hukbalahap had been trained under Chinese Communist instructors and, like the Chinese Communist People's Army, thrived on the deep-seated grievances of the Filipino peasants. Some time after the elections, the Hukbalahap's wartime commander, Luis Taruc, set about reorganising this peasant force, with the help of Jesus Lava, a brother of Vicente Lava, who died in 1946. Shortly after, the 'Huks', as they came to be known, were in action again and their numbers and successes grew rapidly in the face of President Roxas's inept attempts at suppression. Roxas, however, died in March 1948, and President Quirino, his former deputy who had succeeded him, granted the Huks an amnesty.

In Burma, the Communist party had split in 1946 into a Trotskyist group headed by Thakin Soe and an orthodox majority under Than Tun. Soe's group called itself the Red Flags and went into armed dissidence. Than Tun's Communists were expelled from the Anti-Fascist People's Freedom League (which later became independent Burma's ruling party) for having fomented labour troubles and conducted anti-Buddhist propaganda. In 1947, however, Than Tun offered to help the government stamp out the Red Flags, apparently as a means of resuming collaboration with the AFPFL on the eve of independence.

In Indonesia, the Communists were relatively weak and in-effectual when the war ended, though one of their future leaders, Sjarifuddin, had taken part in the small anti-Japanese resistance movement. The Indonesian Communist Party (*Partai Komunis Indonesia* or PKI) was formally re-established in May 1946, by returning exiles. One of these, Alimin, had been abroad for twenty years, first in Moscow and more recently in the Yenan caves with the Chinese Communists. By 1948, the PKI had grown considerably, both in numbers and in effectiveness. The Indonesian Communists were, however, working at several levels. Sjarifuddin, concealing his Communist affiliation, had become Prime Minister, working closely with Dr Sutan Sjahrir's PSI (*Partai Sosialis Indonesia*). In February 1948, however, Sjarifuddin broke with the PSI and started organising the FDR (*Front Demokrasi Rakjat*, or People's Democratic Front) which the PKI intended to use to provide the mass support it needed in a forthcoming bid for power.[41]

In Malaya, as in the Philippines, the Communist party had played a leading part in guerrilla activity through the Malayan Peoples' Anti-Japanese Army (MPAJA). The Japanese surren-dered on 15 August 1945, but Admiral Mountbatten's forces did not reach Singapore until 5 September and during the intervening three weeks, the MCP (Malayan Communist Party) guerrillas, emerging from the jungle, started a reign of terror and virtually controlled Malaya. After the British had re-established their authority, however, the MCP devoted its attention to gaining control over the trade unions. Between 1946 and 1948, the Com-munist-controlled Pan-Malayan Federation of Trade Unions successfully launched hundreds of strikes. The MCP, however, was less successful than other South-East Asian Communist parties in identifying itself with the nationalists. There are ethnic as well as political reasons for this. Anti-British Malays, having a political stake in their own country, were nationalists, while anti-British Chinese, most of whom did not identify themselves emotionally with Malaya, tended to be Communists. The MCP, was indeed an overwhelmingly Chinese body, though it did include a small Malay and Indian-Pakistani membership.[42]

We have brought the story to 1948, and this was a fateful year in the history of South-East Asia. At this point, the Soviet Union intervenes more visibly than before. The Asian Communist parties had all been set up by agents of the Comintern, but the dissolution of that body by Stalin in 1943 had led many people to suppose that the Soviet Communists had abandoned their plans for world revolution. In 1947, however, the Cominform, or Communist Information Bureau, was set up, with roughly the same objectives as the Comintern. The launching of the Cominform at a conference in Poland in September of that year really marks the beginning of what has come to be known as the cold war. The main purpose of the new body was to counter the Marshall Plan which, by assisting Western Europe's economic recovery, threatened to frustrate Communist plans.

One of the ways in which the Soviet Communist party proposed to frustrate the Marshall Plan was by fomenting insurrections in Asian colonies or former colonies, thus disrupting local economies and interfering with the flow of raw materials to the West. The Cominform's programme was explained in a momentous inaugural speech by A. Zhdanov who, at that time, stood next to Stalin in the Soviet hierarchy. More precise instructions were conveyed to the South-East Asian parties both by personal emissaries and by delegates to the Calcutta youth conference, held in February 1948. This important event was organised by two of the international front organisations set up by Moscow after the war as 'transmission belts' to convey Communist party directives to the masses while disguising their Communist origin. The two fronts concerned in the Calcutta conference were the World

Federation of Democratic Youth and the International Union of Students. Final plans for the insurrections that broke out almost simultaneously in Malaya, Burma, the Philippines and Indonesia shortly afterwards are known to have been discussed at the Calcutta conference.

The effects of Moscow's new instructions can be clearly seen in each affected country. In Burma the orthodox Communist party had welcomed the Attlee-Nu agreement of October 1947, which foreshadowed independence. On 4 January 1948, however, when independence was proclaimed, the Burmese Communists denounced it; and at the end of March they went into armed dissidence. Thereafter, the newly independent government of Burma was faced with two separate Communist insurrections (as well as a number of separatist ethnic ones): that of the White Flags (orthodox), and of the Red Flags (Trotskyist).

In the Philippines, as we have seen, the Huks had been granted an amnesty. On the Huk side, Luis Taruc himself had negotiated the terms. Almost immediately afterwards, however, Soviet instructions reached Taruc, who thereupon withdrew again to the hills and resumed his interrupted insurrection. It was not until then that he revealed that he was a Communist. In Indonesia, likewise, the crypto-Communist Sjarifuddin, as Prime Minister, had supervised negotiations leading to a truce agreement with the Dutch, but the P K I denounced it shortly afterwards. The agreement, named after the US Navy transport *Renville*, was signed on 7 January 1948. It was unpopular and brought down the Sjarifuddin cabinet who, as we have seen, thereupon organised the People's Democratic Front. The new Front supported the Renville agreement in February, but denounced it in March. By then, the Indonesian delegates to the Calcutta youth conference had returned with their instructions. Sjarifuddin, however, was not the main leader of the insurrection which the P K I duly launched later that year. This was another of Indonesia's Communist exiles, Musso, who had been living in Moscow, and who returned on 12

power. Even today, it lacks the industrial base that would enable it to sustain a protracted modern war. In relative and regional terms, however, the Chinese People's Republic was a great power in 1949. It gave a first demonstration of its determination to re-establish ancient imperial boundaries by invading Tibet in October 1950, and a few weeks later, by intervening on the Communist side in the Korean War, showed, that it was a military power to be reckoned with outside its own frontiers. Thereafter, the presence of Communist China was a factor that could not be ignored by any of the governments on China's periphery.

The consolidation of Mao's military power along the northern border of Vietnam, from November 1949 onward provided the Vietminh Army with a sanctuary and a supply base. The Vietminh's Commander-in-Chief, General Vo Nguyen Giap – a military genius of a high order – used the next year to regroup, retrain and re-equip his forces. Then in October 1950 he launched the offensive that dislodged the French garrisons from the string of forts they held along the China border: Lao Kay, Ha Giang, Cao Bang, Lang Son and Mon Cay.[44] It was a major defeat, in terms of French losses as well as in those of strategic advantage. The dashing General de Lattre, hastily brought over to retrieve the situation, galvanised the defeated French Expeditionary Corps into local success and, while he lasted, the belief in final victory. His illness and death left his less spectacular successors facing the realities of a war 8,000 miles from home against an able enemy with short supply lines. Less than four years later, the ill-starred General Navarre committed the bulk of his (largely non-French) forces to the fortress of Dien Bien Phu, in the hope of luring the Vietminh Army to defeat. Instead, the Vietminh forces, supplied with food by thousands of coolies with bicycles, and unexpectedly equipped with heavy artillery, decisively defeated the French.

China's diplomacy went through several phases.[45] In the first phase, from 1949 to 1954, it was uncompromising and revolutionary. Mao and his subordinates were less interested in establishing good relations with local governments than in encouraging movements that were subverting them. This phase coincided with the period of military involvement in Tibet and Korea and of executions and revolutionary organisation at home. After the Korean armistice (July 1953), however, the Chinese Communist leadership showed signs of wishing to soften China's image in the eyes of the Asian world. The principal manifestations of this softer policy were China's part in the Far Eastern conference at Geneva in 1954, the proclamation of the five principles of peaceful coexistence with India in the same year, and the Afro-Asian conference at Bandung in 1955. In each of these events, the executant of China's policy was Mr Chou En-lai, the most cosmopolitan, the most flexible and the most personable of Mao Tse-tung's senior followers. It was clearly Mr Chou's brief to foster the image of China as a peace-loving and an *Asian* power. Both aspects of the assignment were important and Mr Chou fulfilled them admirably. To be considered peace-loving meant to be accepted as a member of the comity of nations, despite exclusion from the United Nations, which could be represented as the outcome of a vicious American policy. To be in the Afro-Asian movement at the outset (whereas the Soviet Union had been excluded from it) was to acquire a position of advantage among the peoples of the under-developed world who, by definition, ought to be the most susceptible to Chinese influence and teaching.

Studiously unprovocative at Bandung, Mr Chou was, on the whole, unobstructive at Geneva in a situation that offered many opportunities for obstruction. On one occasion, indeed, he rescued the conference from deadlock over the claims of Communist bodies in Cambodia and Laos to be representative, by proposing direct negotiations between the Vietminh and the two governments concerned.[46] After Dien Bien Phu, Mr Chou could doubtless afford to be magnanimous, and it was in a mood of bonhomie that he interrupted his labours at Geneva to fly to

Delhi. There he and Mr Nehru reaffirmed the five principles, which had been drafted in April in an agreement enshrining, in effect, India's recognition of China's Tibetan annexation. The spirit of Sino-Indian brotherhood implicit in the five principles carried over into Bandung conference, in which Mr Chou and Mr Nehru attacked the South-East Asian Treaty Organisation and other American-sponsored alliances, Mr. Nehru supported Peking's claim to Formosa, and Mr Chou endorsed the Indian claim to Goa.

The third phase of Chinese Communist diplomacy, which began about 1957 and was still in progress late in 1963, was marked by a partial return to the hard line of the first revolutionary years. There is no space here to analyse the causes of this regression. But one thing needs to be said: though the honeymoon with India was over, and relations with Moscow were steadily worsening, Peking continued to maintain cordial relations with those South-East Asian nations with which China was in diplomatic contact, and even, in special circumstances, with governments that were thought to be neutrally inclined, such as that of Prince Souvanna Phouma in Laos (1956-58) even though they might continue to recognise the Nationalist régime on Formosa. The most consistent friendship was that of Prince Sihanouk of Cambodia. He and Prince Souvanna Phouma were invited to Peking, as were U Nu of Burma and President Sukarno of Indonesia.

The full force of China's intransigence was felt at the international conference on Laos, which began in May 1961 and did not conclude its labours until July 1962. The conference was in the truest sense a battle in the cold war. As with the 1954 conference, the military position of the 'Western' side in Laos itself deteriorated while the discussions went on, and it was doubtless this factor that persuaded the Chinese delegation to modify its stand on certain details of the proposed settlement which had been delaying agreement. For the first few months of the conference, there is no doubt that the numerous Chinese delegation was making use of it for the conscious purpose of inflicting maximum humiliation on the United States. In the end, however, the agreed settlement was an indirect triumph for Mr Khrushchev, in that it enshrined his 'troika' idea (left-wing and right-wing politicians under a neutral Prime Minister) as a principle of government.[47]

Having considered Soviet and Chinese policies and activity in the area, it is time to consider the intervention there of the United States from 1950 onwards.

The United States, which was at no time interested in maintaining Western imperial positions in Asia, accepted the necessity to help the French fight the Vietnamese Communists from the time Chinese help appeared available to the latter. Accordingly, two American warships were sent to Saigon in March 1950, to demonstrate support for Bao Dai's government, and in May, the American Secretary of State, Mr Dean Acheson, announced that military and economic aid would be granted to Vietnam, Laos and Cambodia to restore security and foster 'genuine nationalism'.[48] The emphasis on 'genuine nationalism' was intentional: the United States wanted to defeat communism, not to restore the French empire. On 27 June, immediately after the Communist invasion of South Korea, President Truman announced that military aid to the forces of France and the three Associated States would be speeded up and an American military mission would be sent to Indo-China 'to provide close working relations with those forces'.[49] The arrival of this mission (Military Assistance Advisory Group or MAAG) in August 1950 was the real beginning of United States involvement in the cold war in Indo-China.

During the first phase, which may be said to have lasted until the signature of the Geneva agreements in 1954, this American involvement was largely monetary. By mid-1952, the Americans were bearing one-third of the cost of operations in Indo-China, and by 1954, this proportion had risen to nearly four-fifths. The conduct of operations, however, remained entirely in French hands, and as we know, these ended in military defeat.

The second phase, which began with Bao Dai's appointment of Ngo Dinh Diem as Prime Minister of Vietnam in June 1954, and lasted until the arrival of the Taylor mission in Saigon in November 1961, was far more active, but still fell short of actual participation in the fighting. President Eisenhower's Administration was unwilling to recognise the Vietminh's military victory in North Vietnam as definitive. In April 1954, Mr Dulles, the Secretary of State, had failed to persuade the British Government to endorse a United States plan for direct intervention by air and naval forces to save the situation at Dien Bien Phu. When the Geneva conference had set the seal on France's defeat, the United States was unwilling to take the responsibility for reopening hostilities. It set about, nevertheless, to consolidate the Diem régime in South Vietnam and deter further Communist aggression in South-East Asia. Thus on the closing day of the Geneva conference, 21 July 1954, Mr Walter Bedell Smith, President Eisenhower's special ambassador, made a unilateral declaration dissociating the United States from the Geneva Agreements, but renouncing 'the threat or the use of force to disturb them'. And at Manila in September, an international conference gathered on Mr Dulles's initiative, approved a South-East Asia Collective Defence Treaty. Under this treaty (later known as SEATO from the organisation set up to implement it), the United States, Britain, France, Australia, New Zealand, together with three Asian nations – Pakistan, Thailand and the Philippines – pledged themselves to collective action to meet Communist aggression in South-East Asia.

In Vietnam, where Mr Diem had inherited a situation bordering on chaos, the Americans took over the training as well as the financing of the South Vietnamese forces from the departing French. Moreover, on the advice of the influential Senator Mike

Mansfield, who had toured the Associated States on behalf of the Senate Committee on Foreign Relations, the Eisenhower Administration made continued aid to Vietnam conditional on the continuance of Mr Diem in office. This proviso, though it helped Mr Diem to weather various challenges to his authority, deprived the United States of much-needed flexibility in the execution of its policy in Vietnam. In Laos, the Americans took over virtually the entire working expenses of the Civil Service and Army, amounting to some $50 million a year.

The results of this policy were disappointing in both countries. In Laos, the Communist-led Pathet Lao forces – a creation of the Vietminh – had emerged from the Indo-China war in control of the north-eastern provinces of Phong Saly and Sam Neua. The country's leading politician, Prince Souvanna Phouma, wanted Laos to be neutral, and tried to secure the integration of the Pathet Lao forces into the Royal Army by negotiations with their leader, Prince Souphannouvong, his half-brother. The Americans tried to frustrate him by setting up an anti-Communist administration which would defeat the Pathet Lao. They managed to get Prince Souvanna sent into virtual exile in 1958 as ambassador to Paris. Their nominees, especially General Phoumi Nosavan, set up a Comité pour la Défense des Intérêts Nationaux (CDIN) and swept into power in scandalously faked elections in April 1960. The success of US policy appeared complete.

The neutralist current was strong, however; and in August, a young Laotian paratroop officer, Captain Kong Lae, set the right-wing ministers to flight with an anti-American *coup d'état*. Prince Souvanna Phouma returned, formed a neutralist government and demonstrated its neutrality by inviting the Soviet Union to set up an embassy in Vientiane. General Phoumi and his friends, on their side, set up headquarters in Savannakhet, in southern Laos, determined to fight their way back to power. At this stage, the American Central Intelligence Agency (CIA) in effect took over the conduct of United States policy in Laos. A few hundred

American 'military advisers', trained in guerrilla tactics and working under the command of the 'faceless' General Hentges in the so-called Programme Evaluations Office, were attached to General Phoumi's forces. In December, General Phoumi, who was getting help from the Thais as well as from the Americans, fought his way back into Vientiane.

Once again, American policy seemed to be succeeding; but once again, success was short-lived. General Phoumi's action had forced Kong Lae into a military alliance with the Pathet Lao. Prince Souvanna Phouma had turned to the Russians for help, and what began as a Soviet food and petrol airlift turned into an arms airlift. And the Vietnamese Communists, who were using Laos as their infiltration route into South Vietnam (the 'Ho Chi Minh trail') came back to advise and lead the Pathet Lao forces. Soon the reinforced Kong Lae-Pathet Lao forces had driven General Phoumi's Army out of two-thirds of Laos.

This was the situation in January 1961, when President Kennedy came to power. The new Administration seemed aware that the Laotian situation was irretrievable. Mr Dean Rusk, the new Secretary of State, tested SEATO's usefulness when that organisation's ministerial council met in Bangkok at the end of March, but found the British and French Foreign Ministers unwilling to recommend collective action on the lines laid down in the Manila Treaty to meet a situation of this kind. This demonstration of SEATO's ineffectualness greatly disheartened the Thai Government, which felt itself the more vulnerable to Communist armed attack. It was against this background that the fourteen-nation conference on Laos opened in Geneva in May, shortly before Mr Kennedy's meeting with Mr Khrushchev in Vienna. While the conference went on, General Phoumi tried to regain lost ground, but a year later, at Nam Tha in northern Laos, on 6 May 1962, his forces were routed. Though the United States, Britain and Australia, thereupon sent forces to Thailand – largely in an effort to reassure the wavering Thais – the collapse of American policy was evident.

In Vietnam also, the turn of events was unfavourable. The Ngo family had established an increasingly unpopular autocracy in which the President's brother, Mr Ngo Dinh Nhu, and Mrs Nhu, acquired growing dominance. Though the French had observed the Geneva Agreements by withdrawing their forces, the unsigned final declaration of the conference, which provided for the re-unification of divided Vietnam by means of country-wide elections, was a dead letter, President Diem having declined elections on the ground that these would not be free in North Vietnam. Now Ho Chi Minh, President of the Democratic Republic of (North) Vietnam, had nursed private and national ambitions as well as strictly Communist ones, ever since, in 1930, he had founded the Communist party of Indo-China – which was to be the instrument for bringing the three countries of what was then French Indo-China under Vietnamese Communist rule. In furtherance of these ambitions, the Vietnamese Communists had set up a Pathet Lao administration in two provinces of Laos by armed invasion in 1953 and 1954. Mr Diem's stubbornness and United States policy, however, were depriving the Vietnamese Communists of the political fruit of their military victory over the French. Hence the Lao Dong party[50] decided once again to resort to armed action. This took the form of an insurrection launched in 1958, with the usual terrorist outrages. In January 1961, on Hanoi's instructions, a 'National Front for the Liberation of South Vietnam' was set up in the south to direct operations and enlist support from non-Communist opponents of the Diem régime.

Less than a year later, the Communist insurrection ushered in the third, and current, phase of American policy. In November 1961, a mission, headed by General Maxwell Taylor, went to Vietnam and recommended greatly increased American military aid to South Vietnam, while calling on President Diem to liberal-ise his régime. During the next few months, the United States military mission was built up from 5,000 men to nearly 14,000 under the command of General Paul Harkins. For the first time, American troops took part in operations and suffered casualties. Despite this increased effort, the Vietcong (Communist) guerrillas increased in numbers and strength and came to control large areas of the countryside. Relations between the increasingly unpopular Diem Government and the United States steadily worsened, and deteriorated dramatically between June and August 1963 when the government, at Mr Nhu's instigation, took various repressive measures against the Buddhist community and political opponents of Mr Diem, who used Buddhist grievances for their own purposes. In September, General Taylor again visited Vietnam, with the powerful Secretary of Defence, Mr McNamara, and on their return to Washington the two men produced a report which, in effect, dissociated the United States Government from the Diem régime, thus reversing the policy in force since 1954. The American military commitment was, however, reaffirmed. On November 1, with evident American approval though not direct participation, the régime was overthrown by a military junta. The war went on.

The ideological rift between Moscow and Peking was bound to embarrass the Communist parties in South-East Asia, as elsewhere. So long as the dispute was confined to doctrinal matters, however, it was possible for them to strike a balance between the rival centres of world communism. But when the dispute began to affect inter-state relations – from 1959 on – it became increasingly difficult for the Asian Communist parties to stay neutral.

All the Communist parties in the area were affected by the dispute, but the most important effects, from the point of view of this study, were felt within the Vietnamese and Indonesian parties. That both parties tried to steer a neutral course is beyond doubt, as a reading of their declarations of policy will show. In the Lao Dong's case, the issue was complicated by Ho Chi Minh's national ambitions, China's proximity and Vietnam's long history of

Chinese domination. As a Vietnamese national leader, Ho could not afford to appear to be a Chinese puppet, and indeed his personal influence was always exerted in favour of dependence on Moscow rather than Peking, whereas the party theorist, Truong Chinh, who had been trained in China, represented the Chinese current within the Lao Dong. The important third congress of the Lao Dong, held in Hanoi in September 1960, produced compromise declarations, but Ho's speech in particular left the distinct impression that the Soviet line was winning. Ho had paid a secret visit to Moscow in August (news of which leaked out in the Hungarian party press) and had later received a letter from Mr Khrushchev, the contents of which were not published. The Lao Dong, however, continued to be subjected to rival blandishment and pressures. Thus Peking sent a military mission to Hanoi in December 1961, and Moscow sent a high-powered party delegation there the following February. Soviet influence began to decline in the latter half of 1962 – after the signature of the Laotian settlement in Geneva, which was against Vietnamese Communist interests. In the spring of 1963, the Russians withdrew their technical advisers from Vientiane and this seemed to confirm the impression that they had lost the power to influence Lao Dong policy in Laos. Finally, the signature of the Moscow nuclear test-ban treaty in July 1963, forced the Lao Dong out of its aspirant neutrality. On 8 and 9 August the party daily *Nhan Dan*, denounced the treaty as a threat to peace; this espousal of Peking's line placed the Lao Dong unequivocally on China's side of the dispute.

In Indonesia, the PKI, like the Lao Dong, tried to steer a neutral course between Moscow and Peking. This took the form of studiously ambiguous statements by the party chairman, Mr D.N. Aidit. While Aidit, however, was careful to praise 'peaceful co-existence' (the Moscow line), his deputy, Lukman, tended to support China's more revolutionary line. It must be assumed that this apparent divergence was concerted between the two men.

The essence of the PKI's dilemma was that, on the one hand, it had adopted constitutional methods after the failure of the Madiun uprising in 1948, while on the other hand, it was aware of opportunities for revolutionary action in neighbouring territories, such as British Borneo. Constitutional methods had been successful in that the party's strength had grown from 7,000 to 8,000 after Madiun to more than $2\frac{1}{2}$ million in 1963. They had proved disappointing, on the other hand, in that, though the PKI was given a place in President Sukarno's 'guided democracy' it had not been given seats in his cabinet. Mr Aidit appeared to fancy his chances as a mediator between Moscow and Peking, and in August and September, headed a PKI mission to both capitals in an unavailing effort to bridge the gap between them. The rival aims of the Soviet and Chinese parties were dramatised in March and April 1963, by the visits paid to Burma and Indonesia first by Marshal Malinovsky, the Soviet Defence Minister, and shortly afterwards by President Liu Shao Ch'i of China.

The Chinese Communists, however, were using methods more subtle than state visits, to undermine Soviet influence in South-East Asia, and indeed throughout the Afro-Asian world. The purport of Peking's efforts became clear in Jakarta in April 1963, when the Chinese delegates to the inaugural conference of a new Afro-Asian Journalists' Association, were successful in having the Soviet delegates excluded from that body. The Chinese had argued that the Soviet delegates, though they came from the Asian republics of the USSR, could not be considered as Asians, Russia having established its rule in parts of Asia by imperialist expansion. The same arguments were used later in the year in attempts to exclude the Soviet Union from further Afro-Asian bodies which the Chinese proposed to set up 'in the spirit of the Bandung'. (The Russians, it will be recalled, had been excluded from the Bandung Conference.)

Something should be said about the end of colonial power and the attempt to continue the attack on the West in the charge against 'neo-colonialism'.

The Communist insurrection had been defeated in Malaya at the price of Britain's withdrawal, though the British for a time retained sovereignty and a powerful naval base in Singapore. In Indo-China, France's withdrawal had been preceded by a military defeat and the United States took up the struggle against the Communists. In Indonesia, Dutch influence was removed by physical expulsion in December 1957. In the Philippines, on the other hand, the United States retained powerful bases and considerable influence, even after independence. The retreat of the Western 'imperialists', which was voluntary in the case of the British and Americans, took the wind out of Communist sails by removing a standing grievance, and threatened to undermine Leninist dogmas.

In tactical terms, this was a dismal prospect for the Communists in that it threatened to isolate them once again. We have seen how most of the countries of South-East Asia emerged from the Second World War with the Communists and Nationalists in alliance. Once independence is won, however, the struggle against the 'imperialists' becomes irrelevant to the Nationalist, however much he may rant against them in public speeches. Hence the coining – by some gifted but anonymous adviser of Mr Khrushchev – of the term 'neo-colonialism'. There is no need to trace the history of this concept here, beyond defining it as the theory that a country is not fully independent so long as it allows 'imperialist' – that is, Western or capitalist – economic enclaves on its territory, and/or is in alliance with the former colonial power or with another 'imperialist' power, for example the United States. The psychological appeal of this theory to the politicians of the new countries, which are often poorer after independence than before, is strong and immediate. Those who accept the 'neo-colonialist' theory admit the need for a *further period of struggle*, designed to get rid of all Western influence.

The most striking instance of the neo-colonialist concept in action in South-East Asia is that of the new Federation of Malaysia. This is not the place to discuss the merits of the Malaysian idea, beyond pointing out that from a British viewpoint it had two powerful political advantages and one strategic one. It enabled Britain to withdraw gracefully from the three Borneo territories, and it provided a future for an autonomous Singapore in an independent Federation; strategically, it enabled Britain to retain the air-naval base at Singapore with the consent of the federated governments. The aspect of Malaysia that interests us here, however, is that though the whole idea, as Lord Home (now Sir Alec Douglas-Home) later put it,[51] was a 'major act of decolonisation', it was immediately denounced by the Communists as a 'neo-colonialist plot'. The anti-Malaysia initiative came from the PKI, whose central committee, at the end of 1961, denounced 'the formation of a new concentration of colonial forces on the very frontiers of our country'. This was a month after the London discussion of November 1961, between Malaya and Britain, which reached agreement on the procedures leading to Malaysia. The 'neo-colonial' argument was taken up *subsequently* by the Soviet and Chinese Communist parties, by the largely Communist Barisan Socialis in Singapore, and in Sarawak by the left-wing of the heavily infiltrated Sarawak United People's Party and the quaintly termed Clandestine Communist Organisation. More interesting still, the Indonesian nationalists, led by President Sukarno, also took over the 'neo-colonialist plot' theory and made it their own. The vindication of Malaysia by a United Nations investigation team in September 1963, and the proclamation of Malaysia on 16 September of that year were defeats, both for the Indonesian nationalists and for the Communists throughout the area.

From the Communist standpoint, however, the term 'neo-colonialism' had paid handsome dividends. Not only had it strengthened the links between the PKI and Indonesia's Nationalists; but it had served to create an improbable alliance between Sarawak's Clandestine Communist Organisation, which is almost 100 per cent. Chinese, and the Indonesian Army.

Some general remarks, of retrospect and prospect, may be attempted.

The Communist insurrections of 1948 were defeated, in the main, because they were irrelevant to the real needs of the countries in which they were launched. They took deeper root in Malaya and the Philippines than in Indonesia or Burma, for special reasons: in Malaya because independence was not in sight in 1948, and in the Philippines because the Communists associated themselves with genuine and deep-seated peasant grievances. It was possible, nevertheless, for the Huk insurrection in the Philippines to be defeated by an enlightened and energetic President – Magsaysay – who made a real effort to attack corruption and deal with landlordism. And in Malaya, an accelerated programme of independence, combined with the regrouping of the population, in the end isolated the Communists, both politically and physically.

In Vietnam, however, the Communists won a major victory, partly because they secured the leadership of a genuine Nationalist movement, and partly because the French Fourth Republic was unwilling to concede the substance of independence. These factors were at least as important as the logistic one of China's proximity, and the ethnic one which enabled the Communists to argue that they were Vietnamese patriots helping to drive out foreign imperialists. Both these factors were denied to the Malayan Communists, who lacked a friendly base near at hand, and who were predominantly Chinese in a Malay country.

In the 1960s, the Americans have been undergoing, to their surprise, the unpleasant experiences the French had had ten years earlier. Despite the superiority of the South Vietnamese forces in numbers and equipment, and the presence of 16,000 United

State troops, the Communists controlled about two thirds of the countryside and were still gaining strength in mid-1964. The fundamental reasons for Vietcong successes were simple: the Diem régime had been repressive and unpopular; and the military régime that succeeded it lacked cohesion. Moreover, the allies of both régimes were foreign and easy to label as 'imperialists', whereas the Vietcong, whatever their politics, were undeniably Vietnamese. In Malaya, the British had been able to offer independence; in South Vietnam, which already had its sovereignty, the Americans had little to offer. The removal of the Ngo family's dictatorship in November 1963, did, however, open up fresh possibilities.

In Burma, General NeWin's second *coup d'état*, in March 1962, was soon followed by a swing to the left. This was almost certainly accelerated later that year by the Chinese invasion of contested territory in the Himalayas, which demonstrated that Burma could not, in the final analysis, rely on Indian protection in the event of Chinese attack. In Indonesia, the Communists thrived within President Sukarno's 'guided democracy'; and were at the same time contained by it. Anti-colonialism and Malaysia gave them opportunities to identify themselves with popular feeling and with the Army, which, in other respects they feared. In Laos, the 'troika' system devised at Geneva in 1962 broke down in effect in the spring of 1963, when Prince Souphannouvong and other Communists left Vientiane. Moreover, the Polish veto on the three-nation Control Commission (Poles and Canadians under Indian chairmanship – another 'troika') for long effectively prevented it from looking too closely at Vietcong incursions into Laotian territory. In Cambodia, the ebullient Chief of State, Prince Sihanouk, clapped his local Communists (Pracheachon) into gaol with gusto, but was on bad terms with his Thai and Vietnamese neighbours, and in international policy, perhaps inevitably, leaned increasingly on China's side from 1962—though General de Gaulle's sympathy with his plan to 'neutralise' continental South-East Asia helped him to preserve Cambodia's theoretical non-alignment.

In June 1961, President Kennedy met Mr Khrushchev for the first time and made Laos a test of Soviet goodwill. The subsequent decline of Soviet influence in Hanoi, however, made this proviso seem irrelevant. It became clearer, indeed, that North Vietnam was pursuing its own policies and that the predominant influence on its execution of them was likely to be Peking – which had at that time no interest in a *modus vivendi* with the United States – and not Moscow.

The situation in South-East Asia in the mid-Sixties was thus one of considerable complexity. Though Soviet influence had declined throughout the area, the Russians had put Indonesia in their debt in 1961 by the sale of at least £130 million worth of arms. American power, with its string of Pacific bases, was heavily involved in Vietnam; and British power, though residual, was committed to the defence of Malaysia. President Sukarno's ambitions and Indonesia's exploding population were important factors.

In the competition in ideas, communism of a kind was gaining ground in Burma and probably in Indonesia; in Singapore, though the Communists were strong, they were being contained by an able Socialist leader, Mr Lee Kuan-yew; in South Vietnam, Communist ideas had gained ground as much by the mistakes of Mr Diem and Mr Nhu as by Communist exertions. Throughout the area, however, the increasing economic and technical influence of Japan provided a powerful rival to Marxist theories of economic development.

In terms of power, the United States, though overwhelmingly strong, still seemed inhibited from deploying its full strength by fear of escalation. Though there might be some grounds for supposing that the Soviet Union was becoming neutral in Indo-China, there was always the danger that a full-scale American military involvement, extending to North Vietnam, might provoke a counter-intervention by Chinese forces, as had happened in Korea in 1950. The overall situation was thus fraught with dangers and one thing only seemed clear: that success was likely to belong to the side that succeeded in identifying itself most closely with the real interests of the peoples of South-East Asia, which were not those of the great powers on either side of the cold war.

Broadly speaking, the peoples of South-East Asia were interested in reasserting their national identities and improving their living standards, usually in that order. The sentimental and cultural links forged in colonial times are stronger than some of them care to admit. They are not particularly interested in emulating the American way of life, and are discouraged by the enormity of the technological gap that separates them from the United States. On the other hand, even those who are most 'left wing', such as the Burmese and Indonesians, are not, in their majority, interested in Marxist forms of 'socialism'; but all are deeply and disturbingly aware of the crushing and permanent presence of China on their northern doorstep. Prince Sihanouk of Cambodia has openly said that he expects his own country, and neighbouring countries, eventually to come under Chinese Communist dominion.

What of the great powers? Some attempt must be made to distinguish between motives of power and those of ideology, and between long-term and short-term objectives. The Chinese Communists have displayed their interest in restoring the furthest frontiers of imperial China, but with the possible exception of Vietnam, this does not necessarily imply a policy of military conquest in South-East Asia. It must be presumed that the Chinese leaders would be content with a string of vassal States to the south. The great barrier to this objective is American power; and a lesser barrier is British power in Malaysia. It is therefore a major policy objective of China to remove American power in east Asia. The violence of insurrection is only one way of doing that: trade, aid and propaganda are others. Maoism is thus an important weapon in the cold war, from China's point of view.

Maoism, however, is in competition not only with Western ideas, but also with Khrushchevism, or 'revisionism'. The ideological division is therefore more blurred than it used to be. As seen from Peking, ideology is an instrument for the achievement of ancient ethnic ambitions, to be asserted in the first instance against the Western powers, but eventually against Soviet influence as well.

South-East Asia is less vitally important to the Soviet Union than to China. Though Moscow must be credited with an enduring interest in the propagation of Soviet Marxism and the leadership of the Communist world, Soviet strategic involvements are more complex than China's. As a nuclear power, the Soviet Union has come to give the highest priority to the avoidance of war with the United States. To the extent that South-East Asia is a possible flash-point, or series of flash-points for a new world war, Soviet diplomacy has an interest in restraining Chinese policies where these seem likely to lead to hostilities between China and the United States. Paradoxically, then, Russia, though interested in the promotion of Communist doctrines in South-East Asia, to the extent that the local Communists might look to Moscow for leadership, is nevertheless in opposition to China in certain strategic and ideological respects.

The Western powers, on their side, are faced with the problem of countering both Chinese and Soviet ideas, while deterring China from major offensive actions and avoiding nuclear war. The formidable military strength of the United States in the Far East, with support from British power in Singapore, seems likely to deter China, and North Vietnam, from overt aggression in the foreseeable future. To counter the appeal of dogma is far less easy. The military support of an unpopular régime, as in South Vietnam, is probably counter-productive – in the ideological sense certainly, and probably in the military sense as well; though if the United States decides to make its presence in South Vietnam permanent, it is hard to see who would dislodge them.

In the long run, healthy nationalism allied to steady economic progress is the best barrier against the spread of doctrines the adoption of which could mean a switch from one side to the other in the cold war. There is still no sign that effective ways of creating such a barrier have been worked out in Washington. Despite the overwhelming military power of the Western allies in South-East Asia, therefore, the long-term outcome of the struggle in that area remains open.

7 AFRICA

Mary Holdsworth

It is tempting, but nevertheless inaccurate, to think of Soviet contacts with African affairs as entirely a post-1949 phenomenon. Some of the early Bolsheviks were knowledgeable about the Maghreb countries in the mid-twenties. A Communist party existed legally in South Africa from 1921 to 1950, and in contacts with it the Comintern were brought up against competing pulls of racial and indigenous loyalties. Three influential leaders of South and West African nationalist opinions, J. T. Gumede, J. A. LaGuma and G. Padmore, visited the Soviet Union between 1927 and 1930, and Mr Padmore even worked there. All three independently of each other turned their backs on Soviet communism. It is interesting to note that until his death in 1959 Mr Padmore was President Nkrumah's adviser on foreign affairs.

But in the early Comintern days the revolution in Asia was a priority. A number of prominent Asian Communists served in the Comintern (as no one from Africa did). Asian Communist parties were founded and became organic parts of the political life of their countries. In the thirties, and in the immediate post-war years, embryonic Communist parties in colonial Africa (the Union of South Africa was also designated 'colonial') became the responsibility of the Communist party of the metropolitan country. The nascent interest in African affairs on the part of the editors of *Novy Vostock* (1919-29) petered out in the intellectual freeze-up of Stalin's purges.

Thus international communism impinged on Africa only

marginally. Even today the dynamism of mid twentieth-century Africa is not primarily a cold-war problem. The emergence of new states is an indigenous political phenomenon of Africa today. But it is not an isolated factor. And it is its inter-connection with the theories and the practices of communism that must be considered here.

The cold war is not central to the preoccupations of most, if not all, of the new African states. Equally, geo-political and historical realities made Africa a fairly marginal, even in a sense an experimental, cold-war frontier from the Soviet point of view. Looking back over the last twelve years, one cannot help seeing, first, that Soviet attitudes to Africa were nevertheless almost wholly governed by cold-war considerations; and secondly, that Soviet leaders launched into this whole adventure from preconceived theoretical premises, rather than from study of empirical situations. Africa, fairly full of surprises for everyone, had some in store for the Soviet leaders and theorists, and may well prove a catalyst for certain relationships and latent stresses within the Soviet bloc itself.

This particular cold-war frontier is one where ideas have to be discussed as fully as political activities, because today's African leaders are themselves concerned with ideas. Moreover, it is in the doctrinal discussions that Sino-Soviet divergences on policy towards developing countries first become apparent. There is indeed as yet little material other than the doctrinal clashes revealed at several Afro-Asian conferences on which to base any study of Sino-Soviet rivalry in the field of applied politics in Africa.

The expansion of facilities for research in African problems in the USSR, and publication in learned journals and at popular level, began just before the death of Stalin, but gained real momentum from 1955. These studies were developed at first in Leningrad and Moscow universities, and at the Academies of Sciences in the two cities. In the former they grew from the

linguistic studies and the studies in material culture in the old-
established schools of Arabic and Asian studies.

Moscow's emphasis on history, geography and social studies
in the reconstituted and very heavily politically tainted Academy
of Sciences meant that 'modern studies' on Africa, which cover
social anthropology, politics and economics, could be easily
developed there. The African Institute of the Academy of Sciences
was established in Moscow in 1959, and now forms a centre for
university teachers and academy research workers whose main
area of interest is the African continent. Africanists from all over
the country (mainly from Moscow, Leningrad and the African
section of the Foreign Ministry and the Institute of World Economics) meet there annually for a study conference, representative of
all the academic disciplines concerned. The Academy journal,
Problemy Vostokovedeniya (Problems of Oriental Studies) began
increasingly to publish articles on Africa: it was renamed *Narody
Azii i Afriki* (Peoples of Asia and Africa) in 1961. Of the semi-
popular journals, *Sovremenny Vostok* (Contemporary East) covers
Africa. It, too, was renamed *Azia i Afrika Segodnya* (Asia and
Africa Today) in 1962. *Pravda* and *Izvestia*, have designated
African correspondents, *Pravda*'s first being appointed in 1958.

The tenor and content of the 'modern studies' on Africa are
important in discussion of the cold war in that continent. Soviet
Africanists see their task as the analysis in Marxist-Leninist terms
of the two interconnected processes of nation-building, and of the
break-up of imperialism. They brought as tools to their task
Marxist dialectic, Marx's historical materialism, Lenin's doctrine
of positive revolution, a good deal of Stalin's insistence on the
hegemony of the working class, and Lenin's concept of imperialism. They brought little empirical research. (Soviet criticism of
current British social anthropology is that it is too empirical and
presents no logical consecutive pattern of human development.)

Soviet views on nation-building (as distinct from those on dis-
imperialism) have in recent years become less monolithic and

have admitted limited possibilities of dialogue. The early comments on African situations in *Narody Afriki*,[52] the first Soviet major works on Africa, kept fairly rigidly to Lenin's assessment of the formative elements of a nation, and bore all the marks of Stalin's uncompromising antagonism to bourgeois nationalism, national deviations or heterodoxy of any kind. Thus in 1954-55, whether discussing the Gold Coast, the Sudan, or the old Afrique Occidentale Française, Dr Potekhin, director of the African Institute, and his colleagues, denied the contribution to nationalist movements of the traditionalist aristocratic leaders, and cast doubts on the reliability of the national bourgeoisie and national intelligentsia as ultimate liberators of their countries from colonialism. They pointed out (with quotations from Lenin) that these two groups could not really be trusted, in that for the sake of their class interests they were always liable to sell out to the imperialists. Dr Potekhin, particularly, in most of his writing was emphatic on the need in Africa, as everywhere else, for a class revolution. He joined issue with Western and African social anthropologists and political theorists, who denied the possibility of analysing African societies in terms of class, and hence of class revolution. He was very critical of the non-violence policies of the African National Congress. He gave a good deal of attention to uncovering an embryonic African proletariat, not only in the Copper Belt, the Congo, the gold and diamond industries of South Africa, and Enugu mines of Nigeria, but in the patterns of migrant labour in West, South and East Africa.

These rigid ideas derived from the Lenin and Stalin classics on the national-colonial question. They were adhered to by Soviet theoreticians, party leaders and journalists in their confrontation with the emergent African states and individual national leaders. When faced with the heterogeneous realities of the African situation, these ideas underwent some modification here and there. In the period of change within the Soviet Union itself, between the end of 1954 and the Twentieth Communist Party Congress of

January-February 1956, rigid attitudes were shaken, and Soviet writing on emergent countries became more relevant to the new world with which it was dealing. The Bandung Conference of independent Asian and African states had taken place in April 1955, and whether Soviet policy advisers had been quick to read the writing on the wall, or whether it was an inspired public relations gesture, the 'Bandung spirit' and the 'five principles of coexistence', filled the Soviet press and henceforward figured in nearly all articles on the emergent countries.

Three doctrinal adjustments were made by Soviet theorists and some of the journalists, and were acted on in selected cases by the Soviet leadership. First, the validity of a 'national' revolution was acknowledged, that is to say of a revolution which is largely the work of a national bourgeoisie and a national educated class. Secondly, it was now generally admitted that the achievement of political independence and status was in itself an all-important milestone in a country's progress on the road to the Socialist revolution, and it came gradually to be suggested that a fairly long pause before the next step might legitimately be made there. Thirdly, it has become legitimate to think that armed conflict might not be essential to a national liberation movement.

In the 1961 Communist party programme an addition to the typology of states was introduced, namely, *national democracies*, designed specifically to meet the needs of emergent countries 'which had chosen non-capitalist lines of development'. This concept was given considerable prominence in Soviet journals and in all discussions concerning Africa, and later Latin America. A description given in *Pravda* in June 1963, in an article called 'Ideology of Neo-colonialism'. reads, 'The Marxist-Leninist parties of the young states of Asia, Africa and Latin America call for the creation of national democracies. The political basis of such states is a bloc of all progressive, patriotic forces struggling for the guarantee of national independence, for broadly based democracy, for the completion of the anti-imperialist and anti-feudal democratic revolution.'

On dis-imperialism, the contemporary Soviet commentators and party leaders have moved very little, if at all, from the basic ideas of Lenin. Today Soviet writers and party spokesmen never entertain the possibility of a negotiated transfer of power, and hold that imperialism is disappearing in the death-throes of capitalism, precipitated by the rivalries of imperial powers, which caused the 1914 war. The October Revolution in Russia of 1917 is presented as the decisive turning-point for Africa and not, for instance, the Canada Act of 1867, or the constitution of independent India of 1946, or the 1946 Brazzaville conference of French African territories, to take more immediately relevant turning-points. In Soviet writing on Africa the growing power of the Warsaw Pact countries is held up as the guarantor for the emergence of free nations from the shadow of imperial exploitation today and not, for example, the existence of the UN. In the manifest changes in the map of the world between 1915 and 1963 the part played by the party of Lenin is given greater prominence than the deliberate evolution of the British Empire into the heterogeneous commonwealth, or of French West Africa and French Equatorial Africa into a series of independent African states *d'expression française*.

In adjusting to the contemporary situation, that is to say to the political independence and international status of the former colonial countries, Soviet theorists have expanded Lenin's ideas into a doctrine of economic colonialism or neo-colonialism, according to which political independence without economic independence is in the long run illusory. They urge that economic independence in erstwhile colonial and weakly developed countries can only be obtained through a strong state sector in the economy, and the swift or gradual elimination of foreign and particularly former metropolitan companies and financial interests. Some of the younger Soviet economists dealing with emergent countries are ready to discuss the advantages and disadvantages of mixed economies, but nearly always Soviet advice to new countries on economic policies is to sever at least financial links with the old metropolitan country, to curtail the activities of foreign-controlled concerns, and to try out new trading patterns. A sustained and vehement critique of the Common Market on these lines, is maintained with very little statistical analysis of actual terms of trade or market potentials.

These kinds of arguments, in their crudest and most intransigent form, permeate most Soviet press writing and comment on Africa. They fill Soviet broadcasts to African countries. These broadcasts started modestly in 1958, with fifteen minutes daily in English and French. By 1963 they had reached a weekly total of 112-115 hours. They then included transmissions in Swahili, Hausa, Somali, Arabic and Italian.

One of the most revealing illustrations of Soviet views on Africa was a pictorial map published in 1960 which, besides showing African economic potential, showed most obtrusively all the military bases on that continent, labelled as 'NATO bases.' It was a vivid, though fleeting, indication of the extent to which Soviet leadership regarded Africa, not primarily as a new political entity in its own right, but as a sphere of influence of the Western alliance. In Soviet theory, such ex-colonial spheres must have a high potential for alienation from Western influence or even for being made actively antagonistic to it. This map showed an organic unity within the continent between Great Britain, France, South Africa, Belgium and Portugal, as NATO members.

The Soviet Union was perhaps quicker than generally realised at understanding, somewhere around 1951, that the next twenty years would be decisive in Africa, and suspected that there would be possibilities of disturbing the hinterland position of the Western powers, largely, but not wholly, by ideological levers. Opportunities for economic action and for direct political action were sought, and taken quickly as and when they arose.

These were intermittent and contingent on other circumstances, but gradually a steady effort to wean away the élites was built up. Did Africa seem a possible break-out from the 'containment' policy of the Baghdad Pact and SEATO? Though this is never stated in so many words, Soviet political and economic writing on Africa is permeated with an obsessive preoccupation with what are labelled 'imperialist' power alliances. These preconceptions are almost as detrimental to any rational assessment of African needs and priorities as the rigid doctrinal positions on the nature of dis-imperialism or of social change.

What success has the Soviet Union had in attempts to pull African countries into a committed position?

Perhaps one could start with Ethiopia, as being the country with the longest independent history in Africa, and with the longest official Soviet contacts. The USSR gave moral and press support to Ethiopia at the time of the Italian Abyssinian campaign in 1935. In 1943 official diplomatic relations were established and have remained without any spectacular ups and downs until today. In 1956 the legations were raised to the rank of embassies. Trade and aid agreements were signed, and reasonable economic objectives seem to be pursued. The Emperor, who usually has a good press, visited the USSR in 1959 and among other things inspected the collections resulting from Russo-Ethiopian contacts in Tsarist days. The Soviet presence in Addis Ababa over this long period has provided a base for the distribution of literature, and for a time at least for the illegal recruitment of students for studies in Moscow. But it seems too, in a peculiar way, to have been a training ground for reasonable behaviour both for Soviet leaders and Soviet staffs. It is the country *par excellence* which is quoted as an example of 'coexistence with states of different social and political system'.

Soviet relations with Ghana formed a pattern which was re-peated with variations in regard to several subsequently established African states. The Gold Coast became formally independent in March 1957, its first government led by Dr Nkrumah. Dr Nkrumah's Convention People's Party in 1955 was described by Dr Potekhin as a screen for British imperialism. This was immediately before the change in the Soviet attitude to nationalist leaders. Dr Potekhin at the end of 1957 pays a handsome tribute in quite another key to Dr Nkrumah in his *Ghana To-day*.

The Soviet Union offered the new state diplomatic recognition and an economic agreement in January 1958; cultural and technical facilities at subsequent periods. A Soviet legation was opened in Accra in 1959, with an initial staff of seventy-five, and a cultural centre two years later. President Nkrumah paid an extensive visit to the USSR in the summer of 1961, when he was received with top honours. He spent a considerable time there studying economic development and social engineering. Ghana is on the itinerary of Soviet touring cruises, and an Accra-Moscow air service via Rabat and Conakry was started in September 1962.

One can now look back over five years of Soviet-Ghanaian contacts and draw up an interim balance. Ghana's trade with the USSR (mainly the export of cocoa) made up 4 per cent. of her foreign trade in 1960, and has somewhat decreased in proportion to her total trade since. She received credits amounting to some $40,000,000, but how much she has actually drawn is not published. Ghana purchased eight Soviet IL aircraft for her air force and for her civil air fleet. The transaction did not prove entirely satisfactory and after a long stalemate, four ILs were returned to the suppliers as redundant in September 1963. Ghana Airways now has four Dakotas, four ILs, two Britannias, and three Viscounts. The Soviet Union is engaged in two or three large-scale projects, and notably on the creation of two state farms, Israel being entrusted with building up a third.

But Ghana has not banned a mixed economy, and relies on trade, aid and technical assistance in training programmes from the UK, USA, and other non-Communist countries, notably

West Germany and Israel. She continues to send sizable groups of young people to the Soviet Union for education and training of all kinds, including some military cadets, but they total hundreds and not thousands. In December 1963, the death of a Ghanaian medical student in Kalinin provoked a mass protest by Ghanaian students in the USSR in Moscow, though the Ghana Government tried to play down the incident. Though Ghana has groups of short-contract Soviet teachers and technicians, she has equally accepted American Peace Corps personnel, and in 1963 asked for more. The Soviet cultural centre in Accra was closed early in 1963. The embassy staff is of a more normal size. Whether the influence on President Nkrumah of his contacts with Mr Khrushchev and with the Soviet way of life generally is deep and permanent, or opportunist and transient, remains to be seen. While in the Soviet Union he went on record as saying that he regarded the CPSU as the best framework for holding a multi-national and multi-racial state together, as well as saying how much he admired a single overall economic plan. He has certainly adopted many features of the totalitarian régime, as he saw it in the USSR, notably that of an official youth organisation closely geared to the purposes of state. But he does not, in spite of the very bad press he has had at times in Britain, seem to have accepted a cold-war alignment. Nor has Ghana been designated a 'national democracy' in the Soviety typology of states – a title which seems to depend on the degree of a state's positive break with Western groupings. President Nkrumah is the leading exponent of a structurally knit United States of Africa, and he probably weighs up his political commitments with that objective well in view.

The Soviet-Guinea story illustrates some special characteristics of the Soviet African encounter. The Soviet Union offered Guinea recognition and credits immediately the results of the 1958 referendum there were announced.[53] She also took up the whole of Guinea's export banana crop when France severed trade links in the first months of total break-off. A renewable bilateral economic agreement was signed as well as a credit agreement in August 1959. Facilities for higher education in the USSR were offered (before the Friendship University was founded), as well as technical aid. President Sekou Touré visited Moscow and Leningrad in December 1959 and September 1960, and was received with immense official acclaim. Guinea used the facilities freely and probably today still has the highest total of technicians and other loan personnel from Eastern Europe and the USSR. Her trade with the Soviet Union stood in 1960 at about 7 per cent. of her total foreign trade, which is the highest percentage of such trade for a country on the African continent other than Egypt.

But inferences that Guinea had either ideologically or economically become committed to the Communist bloc, openly made in the Western press or tacitly assumed by the African specialists in the USSR, were premature. Towards the end of 1961 the Soviet ambassador in Conakry was asked to withdraw on the grounds that the embassy was being used for internal interference. A group of Guinean students were withdrawn from Moscow. And major discussions, entailing a visit from Mr Mikoyan in person, took place before the trade agreement was renewed.

It is difficult to see how it was thought that President Sekou Touré could subscribe to Marxist-Leninist ideology. He has consistently declared that he regards religion as a living force, and that theory exists for the sake of individuals and not the other way about. He has repeated that Guinea must work out her agricultural policy on the basis of peasant land-tenure systems sprung from her own soil. His astringent and discriminating attitude to slogans and high-pressure political salesmanship is illustrated by his remark, 'We must wear our own spectacles', made at the Cotonou Congress of (French) West African Trade Unions in January 1957, before he ever became head of state.

The Guinea banana boats (as well as Ghana cocoa) illustrate an aspect of foreign trade typical of the majority of African states, namely their dependence on the export of primary agricultural products (or a single product). Soviet offers to take payment in kind, or to take up at short notice the bulk of a crop, have offered real economic inducements to countries largely dependent on one or two agricultural cash crops. Eventually, unless the USSR improved her machinery of payment and the availability of suitable goods for purchase, this bulk sale has brought its own disappointments to the selling country (as happened in some Asian countries earlier), but initially it is a tempting arrangement and of real if temporary economic service to the countries concerned. Plans for stabilising world prices for primary products are a high priority in the UN Economic Commission for Africa, as well as being one of the urgent practical problems to which the conferences of African states have addressed themselves. These needs are also being constantly canvassed in the world cocoa and coffee commodity schemes (in the first of which at any rate the USSR participates). Soviet cocoa purchases from Ghana have increased year by year, but have probably now reached a ceiling. Soviet trade with Ethiopia and the Sudan includes hides, and agreements with Tanganyika include coffee. Such purchases are of substantial benefits to the exporting countries concerned, particularly in the early years, until a more varied and flexible economy in the new country is built up. At the same time, the USSR has throughout made bilateral agreements with individual countries, and though talking generally of world markets for primary products has not so far actively co-operated in multilateral agreements. Economic solutions to the problems of the primary producers will strengthen the possibilities of economic choices and lessen the suggestion of political commitment. This will fit in well with today's mood in many of the states concerned.

In the meantime, in considering the overall trade (as distinct from technical aid) performance of the USSR in Africa, it is not surprising that it does not compare favourably with either that of the experienced and highly developed ex-metropolitan countries

which extremist and irresponsible fringes have easy, not to say encouraged, access, may precipitate crises out of all proportion to the actual numbers of their perpetrators. That in fact such disasters have not happened in East Africa (with the exception of the Mau Mau tragedy, which does not come in to this category) has been due to the immense personal prestige of the individual leaders concerned with independence movements, and to the persevering efforts of the UK Government, which is at any rate always seen to be seeking solutions, even if they cannot always be found. The Soviet press and Soviet broadcasts to Africa on East and Central African topics have throughout been violent, irresponsible and ill-informed, particularly during actual constitutional conferences on East Africa or fact-finding commissions on Central Africa. The Kenya coastal strip issue, that of the Somali border, the constitutional issue between KADU and KANU, all these have been grist to the propaganda mill. There has also been evidence of funds and facilities being put at a politician's disposal.

Disturbances early in 1964 in all four East African states, triggered off by a revolution in Zanzibar, demonstrated both the points of instability and the disruptive potential of even unsubtle propaganda. On 11 January 1964, in Zanzibar, the Sultan's government was overthrown by armed insurrection. Power was seized by Mr Abeid Karume (leader of the Afro-Shirazi party), Mr Abdul Rahman Babu (of the Umma, a small Marxist party), and 'Field-Marshal' Okello, a native of Uganda who had trained in the Havana guerrilla school and served as correspondent for the New China News Agency. Mr Okello had under his orders some 700 armed fighters, said to have been trained by him in Kenya. A left-wing member of the Afro-Shirazi party, Mr Adbulla Hanga, acting assistant-president to Mr Karume, has Moscow connections, and his wife, an American Negro research student, worked under Professor Potekhin at the Africa Institute in Moscow. The new government proclaimed the 'People's Republic of Zanzibar' which was quickly recognised by China, Cuba, and the USSR.

Only after some hesitation did Britain, West Germany and other Western countries grant recognition.

On 20 January, two battalions of the Tanganyika Rifles mutinied and evicted their British officers and NCO's. Rioting broke out in Dar-es-Salaam. After two days' silence, President Nyerere asked the UK Government for military help to restore law and order. He disbanded the Tanganyika Army, and at a press conference the following day said that the emergency was at an end. On 23 January, rioting broke out among units of the Uganda Rifles, and at the request of Mr Obote, the Prime Minister, British troops from Kenya disarmed the rioters. The Prime Minister imposed a press censorship. Dissatisfaction spread to African troops in Kenya by 24 January, and here too at the request of Mr Kenyatta, British troops from the British base disarmed the rioters. The proposed visit of President Chou En-lai to Tanganyika was postponed. President Nyerere asked for the situation in East Africa to be discussed urgently at the Organisation of African Unity. A resolution was passed approving the action of the governments concerned in asking for British help.

The Communist front organisation whose activities are the greatest potential danger in many of the new states is probably the World Federation of Free Trade Unions. The WFTU provokes discord at conferences of labour organisations and advocates the use of industrial disputes as a political weapon. Its strength and apparent tasks differ considerably between East and West Africa. In the former, it tried to wean unions away from what one Soviet expert called the 'social reformist traditions of British Trade Unionism' and to detach them from affiliation to the Brussels based Socialist International Confederation of Free Trade Unions (ICFTU), and from a policy, once independence is obtained, of regarding industrial and welfare problems as the union's prime responsibility, rather than the use of strike action for a political purpose. The Kenya Federation of Labour was a powerful force behind Mr Mboya of KANU in pressure for independence. In the Sudan, the unions, developed under the Condominium, were among the most powerful components in the independence movement, and were united in the anti-imperialist front. After the formation of the military government in 1958, the unions continued as one of the centres of opposition. In 1961 General Abboud and the Supreme Council dissolved the Railway Workers' Union. Strikes followed, and today relations between formerly politically strong unions and a guided régime (albeit a national one) is one of the Sudan's major internal problems. In West Africa the struggle for the allegiance of UGTAN (Union Générale des Travailleurs Afrique Noire), the largest intra-African union affiliation, is one of the main objectives of the WFTU. The powerful and politically militant unions of French West African territories (developed in the first place by the CGT and originally WFTU members) have retained their strong political tastes though they have now become the acknowledged unions of the successor states. At the Cotonou congress in 1957 and at a series of subsequent meetings at which UGTAN was founded, opinion was evenly divided within its constituent members as to whether or not to withdraw from all TU affiliations outside Africa, including both WFTU and ICFTU. These issues are by no means settled. Whether or not dual affiliation or only an intra-African loyalty is chosen and enforced, the balance of influence remains precarious and provides an area of activity where deliberate disruption has immense repercussions, not only in direct dislocation, and sometimes violence, which poor societies and precarious régimes can hardly stand, but also in making authoritarian régimes almost a necessity, which brings another whole series of consequences in its train.

Another 'front' organisation, the International Organisation of Journalists, has gathered momentum in its activities in Africa in the last two years and should be mentioned in this context. In 1963, however, it met with two reverses on African territory – in Conakry and Dakar – and the formation that year of the International Federation of Journalists by those who were dissatisfied with the Communist mores of the I O J provides alternative possibilities for courses and conferences for journalists serving African papers. Also, since Africa in the last fifteen years has been hot 'news' and is likely to remain so, contacts with journalists from all over the world are likely to bring their own corrective to influences of the I O J, whether the organisation works actually in African territories or as an agent for training courses for African journalists elsewhere.

In the case of active backing by Communist countries in situations of armed conflict, the overall picture is curiously inconclusive, except for the strong impression that so far African nationalist parties have been reluctant to employ actual military aid from Warsaw Pact countries, whatever they may have accepted or purchased in equipment and weapons. The Soviet Union too, apart from the abortive operation in the Congo, has been reluctant to become openly involved in actual warfare in the three main areas of internal conflict in the last ten years.

In Cameroun, the Soviet Union supported the late Mr Moumié and the UPC (Union Populaire Camerounaise), but did not participate in the protracted guerrilla warfare, and officially recognised President Ahidjo on his establishment as head of state (prior to federation with the British Camerouns in 1962). In Algeria, the USSR gave strident and sustained press support to the FLN, as well as some Red Cross and welfare supplies, but not any trained men or armour. It was suggested at the time in the English press that Mr Khrushchev's precipitate recognition of Mr Ferhat Abbas, practically on the morrow of the Evian agreement, was meant to gloss over his cautious attitude of the six previous years. Today *Pravda* officially states that Soviet arms were supplied to the FLN. An article published on 18 May 1963 for the opening of the Addis conference of African heads of states gave a summary of Soviet action at key moments of African liberation movements, quoting leaders' thanks, and this was one of the items quoted. The embarrassment with independent Algeria is the classic one of relations with a revolutionary national government which, once in power, is suppressing or restricting the official Communist party within its borders. But the main significance of Algeria for the Sino-Soviet rivalries may well be in the differing attitudes and actions of the Soviet Union and China during the war period.

In the Congo, Soviet activity has been and is of the most openly 'cold war' kind. First, the sending of vehicles, aircraft, transport aircraft, provisions and equipment in the summer of 1960 was an act reminiscent of Red Army intervention, on the pretext of a call to aid in countries adjacent to the Soviet Union. The text of Mr Khrushchev's telegram to Mr Kasavubu and Mr Lumumba of 17 July 1960, is instructive:

> It is not difficult to see that those who undertook armed intervention in the Congo and who pushed the Belgians into it want to strike a blow at all the peoples of Africa, and maintain inviolate the medieval slave-owning order on a large part of the African continent. The hand of the aggressor raised against the independence of the Congo is simultaneously raised against Nigeria, Madagascar, Mali, Togo and other African countries which have only just received independence or should receive it in the immediate future. . . . If the hand of the aggressor is raised against the Congo then the Soviet Government declares that the necessity will arise of taking more effective measures. . . .

Though this attempted intervention failed completely, neither the USSR's activities nor potential as a hindrance to a stable solution in the Congo are at an end.

Constant Soviet flaunting of its admiration for Bandung was paralleled by another, almost intuitive, public relations gesture in regard to Africa. This was the renaming of the Friendship University for overseas students in Moscow, the Lumumba University, after the murder of Mr Lumumba in February 1961. This action was in tune with the mood of young nationalists and radicals in many parts of independent Africa, and probably did something to rehabilitate Moscow in their eyes after the ignominy of being evicted from Leopoldville and Mr Khrushchev's miscalculated speech at the Fifteenth Session of the UN Assembly. But besides the naming of the University, the Soviet press keeps constant the image of Mr Gizenga (arrested in February 1962) as Mr Lumumba's spiritual heir and the leader who should be occupying Mr Adoula's seat. The vehemence of Soviet opposition to UN action in the Congo over the last three years, however, and the USSR's steady refusal to pay her share of the UN operation, is not in accord with the majority of African opinion on the UN generally, or with the desire expressed by most independent African states to seek a stable solution in the Congo as an intra-African responsibility. But Soviet linking of the UN armed backing for Mr Adoula with 'the imperialists' – Great Britain, France, Belgium and Portugal – combined with the use of Mr Gizenga as a potential leader or martyr, is an effective way of exacerbating and prolonging a precarious and inflammable situation. Mr V. Maevsky, *Pravda*'s specialist on Africa, in an article on 29 June 1963 called 'Lessons of the Congo', repeats that the Belgian 1960 intervention was planned in advance; that the UN, under Mr Hammarskjoeld, was under the imperialist heel; that UN action was a NATO aggression against the Congo, for the benefit of US monopolies; that the present tentative plans for the restoration of the Congo economy are unequal and binding economic commitments, and that the suggestions for the retraining of the Congo armed forces are merely an attempt to hand the force itself over to NATO.[54]

It is difficult to foresee the definitive Soviet line on the conflict in the three Portuguese territories. The Dakar conference of African foreign ministers in August, 1963, recommended support for Mr Roberto Holden's Angolan party, and on balance came out in favour of Dr Mondlane's freedom party in Mozambique. Of the Angolan freedom fighters, Soviet support seemed on the whole to be for Mr Mario d'Andrade and his MPLA. Soviet reaction to the definitive choice of Roberto was hostile, partly because his group was backed by Mr Adoula. Two Mozambique splinter groups are now established in Uganda and in Cairo respectively, and it remains to be seen where Soviet backing will be active and for what reason, and in what form. The situation may alter radically if the discussions at the UN between Portugal and representative African governments on this issue develop favourably. Whatever decision is made in regard to partisan support, the Soviet press and Soviet broadcasts to Africa take every opportunity to point to the NATO membership of Portugal, and hence to Britain's commitment with the active imperialist on the African continent.

The training and despatch of guerrillas have become important from two aspects. First, because in the last two years a far greater proportion of responsible African opinion has slowly changed over to regarding limited armed conflict as a legitimate and workable means, in the last resort, of hastening independence in those parts of Africa which are still under imperial or white rule. The declared policy at recent African conferences is that when all else has been tried, fighting is a legitimate and proper means to attain the goal of independence. Thus states already independent have a right and a duty to provide facilities and bases for freedom fighters. This is something quite new. The fact that this attitude has been taken by some leaders who in their own rise to power at the head of a nationalist movement did not in fact use violence, is a measure of the pressure of emotion and opinion for an Africa wholly free of white domination. The Soviet and other Communist bloc countries' reputation as training grounds for partisan warfare is well established; this kind of operation forms part of standard military service training, and there is scattered evidence from African students of opportunity in Moscow for this type of thing. UPC Camerouns partisans were variously said to be trained by Czechs and the Chinese, and there are ever-recurrent rumours of partisan training being available either in or through Ghana. But the point is that unless the new intra-African organisations are firm and well organised, it may be difficult to prevent perhaps substantial groups of future 'freedom fighters' from training in Warsaw Pact countries and so becoming liable to back splinter groups whose loyalties for one reason or another lie in the same direction as cold-war objectives. At present it looks as if the African Unity Organisation is taking this danger seriously.

In the last eighteen months several West African countries have had régimes more or less violently overthrown, while others, Nigeria and Ghana, are in the midst of treason trials of high ranking politicians. In fact, each individual case has individual features and individual precipitating reasons. But basic instability, poverty, lack of experience in handling a political opposition, are common to all. A leading article in *West Africa* of 9 November 1963 analyses these situations in terms of power struggles between the 'ins' and 'outs' and of the impatience of a rising generation with cautious political or economic policies of their elders:

> Their criticism is directed against what they consider out-dated foreign policies, and against mortgaging of their country's economy to Western capitalism. Very few of these young men are even Communist fellow-travellers. Many are idealists. They are usually ill organised but when in alliance with the much better organised trade union movements are potentially capable of pricking the insecure government balloon. . . . Foreign intervention has not been proved, although, of course, it cannot be completely discounted. M. Sekou Touré made unsupported accusations in connection with Brazzaville, as did President Houphouet-Boigny recently in connection with the Ivory Coast plot. Chad accused the Sudan of supporting the régime opponents.[55]

Scattered indications of this kind of activity suggest added nuisance in situations which are already unstable, rather than any serious threat to national identity. The new governments are quick to recognise it and deal with it, where there is no fundamental cleavage at the heart of the state itself.

Who are these impatient, young, ill-organised groups? The late Dr Kolarz, in a study of Marxist groups in West Africa concluded that these are *Marxist* (as opposed to Marxist-Leninist) groups, and that African Marxism is still very fluid and spontaneous.[56] Are they trained from Moscow? It is interesting that Dr Potekhin in his criticism of African socialism says that one must wait for the emergence of really well-educated Marxist groups in Africa for the gradual spread of 'scientific socialism'. On the other hand, President Houphouet-Boigny was recently quoted as saying that if you want your son to become an anti-Communist you send him to Moscow; if you want him to become a Marxist you send him to Paris. There is a great deal of truth in this saying, since students, above everyone else, are quick to sense a restrictive situation, and must immediately recognise it in Soviet universities. Nevertheless, Dr Potekhin's words should not be taken lightly, and if he thinks that there are growing cadres of orthodox African Marxists, this is probably true. The nearest to a Communist party in West Africa is the PAI in Senegal, which is a small, frankly Marxist party and follows a 'national democracy' line. Basutoland has an official Communist party. A modestly produced monthly, *African Communist*, deals mostly with Southern Africa, South-West Africa and the Protectorates. It is published by the South African Communist party in London, in best nineteenth-century traditions. In Algeria, Tunisia and Egypt the Communist party is under restraint, while the single party states by definition do not allow one.

We cannot usefully consider here the internal situation in the Union of South Africa. A modern study on the history of the Communist party of South Africa has still to be made. Much activity in opposition to apartheid policies is indictable under the suppression of communism legislation, so it is not easy to tell how far international communism is involved today. It is more relevant to note Soviet attitudes and reactions to the recent efforts for joint policies and actions by African states, at the UN, at the conferences of African heads of states at Addis, and at other conferences. This will be an interesting barometer of Soviet adjustment to the present strong tendency of African states to establish joint initiatives on the affairs of the African continent. Some adverse comment has been expressed by some African papers on the lack of response to economic boycott proposals by both East European countries and China, taking as evidence the Union's foreign trade returns for 1962.

Scattered references have been made in this study to intra-African groupings, and to pan-Africanism, and it has been pointed out that the movement for African unity has gathered momentum, and begun to take organisational shape, in the last two years. An estimate of Soviet success or failure with these groupings contributes to an assessment of Soviet impact on African affairs, and is necessary, too, for a consideration of Sino-Soviet rivalry in the African context.

Broadly speaking, there are four varieties of grouping. First, the pan-African movement, which has a history of congresses beginning with Versailles in 1919, began more as a Negro movement with impetus largely from America and the Caribbean. With the fifth Congress in 1945 in London, at which both Mr Kenyatta and Dr Nkrumah were organisers, pan-Africanism became an effective power in modern Africa, and the conference of heads of states held in May 1963, in Addis Ababa, attended by thirty-two heads of states, can with justification be regarded as the London Congress's ultimate successor. Secondly, an Afro-Asian grouping. This began with the meeting of heads of states, plus observers from as yet dependent countries, in Bandung in 1955. Later came the Afro-Asian Solidarity Conferences with strong Communist influence, first in Cairo, January 1958, in Conakry in 1960 and in 1963 in Moshi. Thirdly there arose conflicting ideas whether the African continent as a whole formed a political, ethnic or cultural entity, i.e. whether Egypt and the Maghreb countries, and perhaps Zanzibar and Madagascar, really formed a unity in any relevant sense with the countries of sub-Saharan or 'Black' Africa. And finally, there has existed since 1959, and exists to some extent today, division between the 'Casablanca' countries – Ghana, Guinea, Morocco, Egypt, some-times Mali – and the 'Monrovia' countries – Nigeria, Ivory Coast, Madagascar, Sierra Leone, Tunisia, and most of the countries of 'expression française', including a more organised inner ring of 'expression française' territories within that group.

From the time of her definitive entry into African affairs, the USSR put her backing into the Afro-Asian grouping, and during the period of close Soviet-Egyptian co-operation, largely through President Nasser's good offices, held executive office in the Afro-Asian organising committee and participated and promoted the various ancillary organisations and conferences, in particular mounting a large and very much publicised Afro-Asian writers' conference in Tashkent in 1958. Care was always taken that the Soviet delegation, whether as members or observers to such conferences, was composed mainly of Soviet Asian nationals and that the leader was an outstanding personality from Central Asia or Transcaucasia. Afro-Asian solidarity organisations were launched throughout the major cities of the Soviet Union, many of the public figures speaking at them being also members of the World Peace Council. Sponsorship of the Friendship University was another function of the USSR societies.

At the Afro-Asian congresses and ancillary group meetings violent anti-Western attitudes and speeches were the rule, more specifically attacks on SEATO, the Baghdad Pact and NATO. These meetings, however, remained largely sounding boards. The clearly growing preoccupation of African states with specifically African groupings, and their increasingly evident potential as political and eventually economic organisations, focused Soviet attention on these groups, and brought both a re-appraisal of pan-Africanism as a philosophy and some degree of backing of intra-African groupings, though of course no longer as a participant. From December 1958 (when the first African heads of states conference took place in Accra) Soviet praise and approval were for the Casablanca group. This was composed of the states which had both broken away most radically from their former metropolitan connections and had adopted more or less guided economies, and had seemingly been most willing to establish connections with Warsaw Pact countries. It looked at one time as if it was for these countries that Soviet theorists and the new Communist party programme had prepared the designation of 'national democracies'.

There is a possibility that when the African Unity Organisation, established at Addis Ababa in May 1963, is effectively set up, and its suggested regional and functional organs working, it may temporarily lean somewhat towards the Communist countries, or at least away from the West. An intense preoccupation with anti-colonialism and anti-apartheid policies promotes at times a homogeneous image of the 'West', made up of nationalist South Africa, Portugal, Belgium, with their allies and supporters in NATO, Great Britain, France and the USA. This is the very picture which Soviet propaganda paints. The Soviet Union, what-ever its imperial activities in Asia (and these are becoming in-creasingly recognised by the African group at UN) is clear of imperial taint in Africa. 'The US and Great Britain, the staunchest friends of our enemies,' said one of the Uganda ministerial dele-gates at Dar es Salaam in June 1963. The *Pravda* article on the Addis conference quoted earlier discussed what should be the conference's aims in terms of African unity, and advocated the liquidation of foreign economic supremacy and foreign bases. Such a programme is attractive in its simplicity and radical quality, when compared with the slow-maturing and sophisticated programmes for economic development and reorganisation which many of the states need. The bitterness with which Soviet commentators denigrate Israeli activity in Africa is due to disappointment that Ghana and Ethiopia, to name just two countries, have found an independent source of economic aid and know-how.

When Mr Oginga Odinga the rather flamboyant left-wing politician of KANU, now Minister of Home Affairs in Kenya and recipient of the World Peace Council medal in 1963, travelled first to Moscow and later to Peking in 1961, he served to focus African attention on the incipient Sino-Soviet divergence. The need felt by Mir Tursun Zade (a poet from Tadjikistan and usually head of the Soviet representatives at the Afro-Asian Solidarity Conferences) to justify the Soviet record in Africa and Asia at the second Afro-Asian writers' conference in Cairo in February 1962, was another such straw in the wind. This was probably the first public occasion in such circles at which the Soviet position was challenged by the Chinese. It proved to be the first of a series of challenges in 'front' organisations mainly concerned with the new states.

A meeting of the International Organisation of Journalists in September 1963 took place on a Mediterranean cruise from which the Chinese were excluded. This was in retaliation for a Djakarta meeting of the Afro-Asian Journalists Organisation in April, which had been prepared the previous year at executive sessions in Peking, and at which the Soviet delegation were given only observer and not membership status, in spite of petitions by twelve delegations (four of them from Africa) for a reversal of this decision. The third full-scale Afro-Asian Solidarity Conference met in Moshi, Tanganyika, in February 1963. In spite of a speech by President Nyerere clearly warning the two protagonists not to treat the conference as a forum for esoteric dispute,[57] the Soviet head of delegation, Mir Tursun Zade, and the Chinese delegates aired their doctrinal differences. It was before this audience that the Chinese delegate (Liu Ning-yi) made the point that Russians were after all 'white' like all the rest of the colonialists, and that China shares the same destiny as other Afro-Asian peoples. There were plans, fostered by the Chinese trade union federation and supported by the Indian Communist party, for a conference of Afro-Asian trade unions to be held at the end of 1963 in Indonesia; the Soviet Union was excluded from the sponsoring powers, which included UAR, Morocco, Ghana and Guinea.

Besides these activities in solidarity and front organisations, China has begun to foster a variety of direct contacts with African states and organisations. Much of this is reminiscent of Soviet activity ten years ago and includes visits by politicians and personalities, cultural missions, the translation of books, exchanges of specialists and broadcasting (in English, French, Swahili, Portuguese, Hausa, Cantonese, a total of some seventy hours a week). Her physical presence in Africa is most marked in the West African states, and in Algeria, where a large trade exhibit was mounted in September 1963. China has a year-old trade and credit agreement with Guinea, and in May 1963 concluded a trade and credit agreement with Somalia. Political discussions continued with Somalia, at the same time as a Somalia military mission was negotiating in the USSR. In October, the Prime Minister of Somalia visited both countries. In November 1963 the USSR and Somalia announced Soviet assistance for a Somali army 20,000 strong, equipped with modern weapons. Mr Chou En-lai visited a number of African states, including Somalia, in the winter of 1963-64.

China bases her claim to support in the Afro-Asian world on her criticism of Mr Khrushchev's policies for pandering to Western governments and for economic and political support of governments which are not clearly committed to eliminating capitalism. She gives her voice much more clearly to Lenin's original doctrine of positive revolution and to the use of arms where the situation demands it. (As recently as May 1963, China openly said that she still backed the Cameroun UPC and Mr

Ahidjo confirmed that UPC guerrillas still receive Chinese training.) China's economic doctrine is more radical than the USSR's: she has no use for mixed economics or for gradual reforms of land tenure systems. Her speakers point out that her pattern of economic and social reform is more relevant to African needs, since Russia had gone some way on the road to industrialisation before the 1917 revolution. In the last two years China has discarded the idea that the Soviet Union is in part an Asian state, and has built up the contention that China is both Asian and a victim of nineteenth-century colonialist attitudes. Russia is placed firmly on the other side of the fence. It was as an Afro-Asian Prime Minister, though without revolutionary polemics, that Mr Chou En-lai represented himself on his visit.

It is clear that the Soviet Union is troubled by this aspect of the Sino-Soviet divergence. The printing in *Pravda* and *Izvestia* of messages from all sorts of women's groups and individuals from Africa after the fracas at the Women's Conference in Moscow in 1963 for weeks after the event, is an illustration of this concern. Throughout the autumn of 1963 official and unofficial support from African and Middle Eastern states for the partial test ban was daily recorded in the press. A much more coherent and forceful picture of the Soviet position is being presented, as contrasted with Mir Zade's, seemingly, off-the-cuff efforts in February 1962. This is built around the thesis that dis-imperialism must be combined with peace rather than violence in the present balance of world forces. Nevertheless, positive support is promised where armed conflict seems imminent or in progress. The Somalia military agreement is a case in point. The article in *Pravda* in May 1963, already referred to, listed decisive situations in which the USSR had intervened on the side of nationalists. A later article discussing the tasks of Communists in new states claimed the best of both worlds.

Communists openly criticise the right wing of the national

bourgeoisie for refusing to solve many cardinal questions affecting the interests of broad masses. It is quite natural that Communists should criticise these representatives of the national bourgeoisie who try to hinder the development of the national-liberation revolution. But Communists not only criticise – they put forward realistic programmes of action which are fully consonant with the specific conditions of their own countries, and they fight for the practical execution of their programmes. They do not fight for sectional interests but for the *whole* nation.[58]

Earlier in this paper it was suggested that Africa was at first both marginal and experimental so far as the USSR was concerned. But with the Chinese intervention the emphasis has changed. The African situation is fluid ideologically, politically and economically. Though African leaders wish to remain outside cold-war groups, they cannot remain aloof from conflicting pulls, whether of ideas or of power structures. To quote President Senghor, Africa is at last free to bring her gifts to the 'rendezvous of history'. But the Soviet Union is already at this rendezvous, and in the last ten years undoubtedly has forced herself into relevance as far as Africa is concerned.

At this particular rendezvous, the Western countries have a flaw in their present image in spite of their immense lead in setting the pattern for the advance to freedom, and in building up the practical ways of this advance. But the Soviet image too is no longer clear. Its earlier ideological positions have been taken over by China, and it has been challenged by China in its ambivalent activities on the side-lines. Soviet repudiation of UN activity antagonises those in Africa seeking stability and strength from the latter. All in all in 1964 the USSR gives an impression of opportunism in its African encounter.

8 LATIN AMERICA

Raymond Carr

In the cold war Latin America has usually been a peripheral and low priority area. Its importance to the USA antedated the cold war. Its significance to the Russians is less as an arena of action than as an area of propaganda. The Latin-American left suddenly saw itself, after a long period of comparative neglect by the USSR, bracketed in importance after the national liberal movements of Asia and Africa, and its long-standing campaign against the imperialism of the United States given world status. The deterioration of Castro's relations with the United States in 1960 gave the Russians an unexpected weapon in the propaganda war which the Americans sharpened by the invasion of 1961. Then, quite unexpectedly, in November 1962, Cuba seemed the very centre of the cold war. But the crisis passed and its passing revealed that Latin-American voices *per se* counted for little. Khrushchev preferred an arrangement with Kennedy, seemingly at the price of neglecting Castro's claims to be an independent sovereign state. This choice gave the Chinese a chance for their sharpest onslaught on a régime which refused to recognise that it was improper to concede to paper tigers. Since then Latin America has reverted to its peripheral position, with the issues somewhat confused by the Sino-Soviet conflict.

The key to Latin America's position in the cold war lies in the difficulties which the USA, as a powerful and highly developed country, finds in establishing a satisfactory relation with a congerie of weak and developing nations. It is not to defend US policy to say that it has been frequently misunderstood and its shortcomings often exaggerated by the Latin American nations, and by the left in particular.

The reasons for this exaggeration are clear. Firstly, nationalism is defined in terms of an enemy; and the enemy is the 'imperialism' of the United States. This factor is particularly acute in those nations with no conceivable historic foundation for nationalism: what was Cuban nationalism other than the struggle first against Spain, and after 1898, against its successor, the USA? Even those nations like Mexico and Peru, with a sort of autochthonous cultural nationalism, cannot resist anti-Americanism. It is a psychological necessity for many Latin Americans, even for those who, *via* the demonstration effects of a 'superior' culture, have adopted in their behaviour as consumers an 'American way of life'. The Mexican bourgeois who eats cornflakes and buys Christmas trees often evinces powerful antagonism to his northern neighbour.

Secondly, the United States has succeeded Great Britain as the dominant economic power south of the Rio Grande. The North Americans regard their position as a natural result of free enterprise. It is not their *fault* that the prosperity of Latin America depends on the price paid for its products by US importers or that its development demands foreign capital. Critics argue that this dependence denies the Latin American nations independence and control of their own natural resources. They are victims of 'monopoly capitalism', dramatically represented by the semi-sovereign status of the great corporations like the United Fruit Company. The paradox is that Latin America needs US investment and a market for her primary products, yet resents the results of this necessity; hence expropriation is a *sine qua non* of extreme nationalism. This imperils the emergence of sensible solutions envisaged by Washington (which in the thirties began to realise the political perils of its economic power in Latin America) and which moderate politicians in Latin America favour.[59]

Communist propaganda can thus be presented as a defence of national independence to be achieved by the elimination of monopoly capitalism. The appeal of this simple solution as a psychological escape mechanism is enormous. In the nineteenth century, Latin Americans explained their political and economic 'backwardness' in terms of national or racial vices which would be cured by imitating the United States. In the twentieth century this passionate self-criticism was turned outwards and replaced by an equally violent criticism of the Yankee who exploits Latin America as a colony, and obstructs both her economic growth and her political progress.[60]

The left, long before such views were publicised in Peace Congresses and the flood of Communist literature, maintained that foreign 'monopoly capitalism' supported domestic oligarchy. All that the Communist propaganda of the cold war does is to put long accepted 'truths' of the Latin American left into an international framework and a rigid ideological mould. Latin America, like the Afro-Asian countries, must seek freedom by alliance with the Socialist camp. The answer to monopoly capitalism and the road to freedom lies in bilateral trade with the Eastern bloc. The Alliance for Progress can only be a blind alley. 'The main hindrance to the development of Latin America is the imperialism of the United States. . . . The defeat of imperialism is the fundamental condition for the development of our peoples. . . . Without economic emancipation there is no political independence.'[61] To approve such utterances, typical of the Communist propaganda line, implied no commitment to the party. They had been uttered by the university youth for a generation.

Finally, and with some reason, Latin Americans cannot easily believe that Washington intends to interpret the doctrines of self-determination and non-intervention in ways acceptable to them. If these doctrines are not respected by the US on the OAS, then that body appears to Latin Americans, not as the bulwark of an

Inter-American system, but as an instrument of the national interests of the most powerful member.

These fears are based on U S action in the Caribbean area where her strategic interests are obvious and her political concern obsessive: the exclusion of 'foreign' influence in the Caribbean is a traditional, not a new feature of US policy. In 1927, Stimson called the Caribbean policy of the US 'perhaps the most sensitive and generally held policy that we have'.[62] The stability and security of the Caribbean are a constant; the area has cast its shadow over US relations with the great Latin American states, where 'intervention' was neither contemplated nor indeed possible. Caribbean policy can therefore get out of step with hemispheric policy as a whole – as has been evident since 1960.

What have not been constant are the means to be adopted to secure stability and security in the Caribbean itself. To understand the fortunes of the cold war we must therefore examine the conflicts and confusions of American policy in the Caribbean, as it veers between Theodore Roosevelt's 'I took Panama' and Franklin Roosevelt's 'good neighbour' policy; between the military concepts of hemispheric defence, paramount after 1945, and the new course of 1960, when the concept of good neighbourliness was expanded into a concern for economic growth and 'democracy' in the under-developed areas of the continent.

Latin American suspicions are rooted in the period of military intervention – on twenty occasions between 1898 and 1920 US forces entered Caribbean states. By 1930 this policy had certainly failed to produce stability: the American experience in trying to create a stable government in Nicaragua was calamitous and the police forces created and trained by the Americans ultimately backed the dictatorship of Somoza. Yet Cuba was to show how difficult it was to abandon intervention. By 1933 the rule of the dictator Machado was intolerable. To 'intervene' against him would be a denial of non-intervention. To refrain from using its

enormous influence opened Washington to the charge of supporting tyranny. Sumner Welles went to Havana to use 'influence' to
hasten Machado's departure, and thus make 'intervention' unnecessary. Yet, in the light of later history, this influence was used
in a disastrous fashion. On the fall of Machado, Sumner Welles
refused to support Grau San Martín's government on the grounds
that it would prove incapable of providing stability. He dismissed
it as 'frankly communistic', as a 'social revolution' supported by
the 'ignorant masses'. The refusal to recognise Grau San Martín
was a 'negative interference', which meant the defeat of a radical
revolution in Cuba. In a very real sense Washington was responsible for Batista and for the 'frustration' of a new departure
which might have made Castro unnecessary.

The 'good neighbour' policy of Roosevelt after 1933 did much
to alter the image of big stick diplomacy and the use of influence
as it had been displayed in Cuba.[63] Apart from the continuing
hostility of Argentina it must be accounted a success. The US not
merely dropped intervention and interference (perhaps an inevitable consequence of her unhappy experiences in Nicaragua
and Cuba); but also began to shed the belief that it was a function
of the State Department to go into battle for the interests of the
corporations. In the end the State Department went a long way
towards accepting the 'nationalist' view of the control of natural
resources (in this case petroleum) in Bolivia and Mexico. In
Venezuela it maintained that the oil companies should share their
profits more generously with the Venezuelan Government, not
merely for the sake of political goodwill, but even, it was hinted,
on the grounds of greater social justice – a view inconceivable in
1930. It took a great deal to persuade the oil companies that
political and defence objectives overrode a narrow defence of
economic interest by international law. Nevertheless, a principle
was established, however feebly. But this negative sensibility
came into operation only when US interests were challenged
effectively, and it could not remove the charge of 'imperialism'.

It was not part of good-neighbourliness to dismantle the great corporations or to change the terms of trade.

Good-neighbourliness, moreover, involved Washington in one of those insoluble dilemmas which put its Latin American policy at the mercy of critics. Paradoxically, given its great influence, the weight of which no administration could escape, non-interference appeared as perilous as intervention. Not using influence appeared as dangerous as using it. The sincere practice of non-interference meant toleration of any régime, since it would be a breach of good-neighbourliness to discriminate. Thus, General Trujillo and General Somoza, dictators respectively of the Dominican Republic and Nicaragua, were entertained at the White House. The Latin American left was never to forget these consequences of the good-neighbour policy, which, after 1938, was increasingly conceived in terms of defence. A great democracy had no right to entertain petty dictators, even in order to get their co-operation in a war against fascism in Europe.

Wartime co-operation tended to emphasise favour to incumbent régimes and the war itself to freeze existing political situations. At the same time, rapid industrialisation with its concomitant social tensions made the growth of a 'populist' left wing inevitable.[64] Thus the goodwill accumulated by good-neighbourliness turned into a liability in the processes of post-war adjustment. The sudden deterioration of the terms of trade after the Korean War, combined with the population explosion, added economic stagnation and inflation to political instability. The fear of an upheaval that would open the way to communism began to obsess Americans. The view that Latin America might 'blow up' replaced the hitherto accepted view that instability was primarily explicable in terms of peculiar political *mores*. To Washington, Latin America become part of the cold war.

It is scarcely surprising that the United States had not been over-exercised by the threat of communism in Latin America, although there had been numerous prophets of doom. The various

Communist parties were weak in most of the countries concerned. They were often discredited by deals with dictators (a process which Communists attempted to insure against by the device of double parties, one legal which collaborated, and a clandestine party which resisted). They were confronted with 'populist' parties like the Peruvian APRA which had attempted to evolve a political doctrine more suited to what its leader, Haya de la Torre, christened 'Ibero America'. Chile, where the party had concentrated on the trade unions, was the only major country with a strong Communist party, and even there the Communists had been pushed aside.[65]

Nor did it seem that Russia sought to fight the cold war seriously in the hemisphere. In the past its interest in Latin America had been sporadic and, in the thirties, areas like India were clearly considered more worthy of effort. The USSR had scarcely attempted to evolve a propaganda line for Latin America. Bolívar was an aristocratic separatist; not till the fifties was he transformed into the leader of a National Liberation movement for the Indian masses. The wartime gains appeared to be in hazard once the peculiar conditions which had made the Communists valued allies of pro-US forces in a common fight against fascism vanished. The strange attempt to back 'pre-conquest' nationalisms against 'progressive' European culture was dead by the fifties.

For both Russia and the United States the terms of battle were altered, not by a victory in one of the great nations, but by events in two small Caribbean countries. In both, a non-Communist revolution was taken over by Communists. In both, the United States sought to overthrow the resultant régime. In Guatemala the effort was a success; in Cuba it was a resounding failure.

In Guatemala the alarming factor was the ease with which Communists succeeded in permeating a non-Communist government. In 1944, General Ubico was overthrown by students waving the Atlantic Charter. O *tempora, o mores!* Ten years later

Communists were a stronger factor in the labour movement and political life of Guatemala than in any other country outside the Iron Curtain.

How is the rapid success of a party which scarcely existed in 1944 to be explained? In part its success was a function of the political vagueness, the lack of hard doctrine under the rule of the Arévalo (1944-50). His 'spiritual socialism' degenerated into the rule of opportunists. To young politicians and students Marxism appeared both systematic and 'pure'. His successor, Arbenz, trusted Communists *faute de mieux*. They gave him trustworthy support when moderate politicians wavered and brought the Labour Unions behind the governments. They pushed agrarian reform and began to bring the *campesinos* into political life. They drew Guatemala *via* extreme nationalism into alliance with the Socialist powers.

Certainly many Guatemalans disliked the alliance with communism and it was of crucial importance that the majority of Army officers increasingly mistrusted the policies of Arbenz and were unwilling to shed blood – either their own or others – in his defence. They were particularly alarmed by the purchase of arms from Eastern Europe – not merely for its diplomatic repercussions, but because the arms might be used to equip a popular militia as a force against an 'unreliable' army. The masses were still loyal if unenthusiastic, but they could not be organised by the Communists against the invasion, from Honduras, of Castillo Armas and his Liberation Army. Arbenz resigned without a real struggle.[66]

In the end the Communists were defeated by the conditions that underpinned their success: a disciplined party could easily dominate formless political groupings and an unsophisticated labour movement. It then used these advantages to draw Guatemala hard and fast towards the Socialist camp and into violent conflict with the United States. Those who objected to this process could overthrow the régime for the simple reason that, although the Communists could *control* hitherto amorphous labour movements and popular parties, they could not make them fight for a Communist controlled state. With greater moderation the Communists could have hoped for a longer stretch of power. And in 1954, no effective gesture of support could be made by the USSR.

The Guatemalan experience is essential for the understanding of the Cuban experience. The United States seems to have deduced that intransigent opposition in the international field and the activities of the CIA could end an undesirable régime: this success might be worth the great unpopularity that the tough line in Guatemala brought throughout Latin America. The US Government failed to get a declaration against Guatemala at the Caracas Conference (March 1954). The fall of Arbenz unleashed an unexpected wave of protest against US 'intervention'; in Chile, the Social Christian leader Eduardo Frei led a protest march on the American Embassy. The Communists deduced that they must organise the masses more effectively into the party so that the national bourgeoisie were effectively kept up to anti-imperialism by pressure from beneath. Otherwise, as in Guatemala, imperialists would play on its 'double character' (half nationalist, half drawn towards international capitalism) and tempt it to desert the democratic revolution: 'The working class and not the national bourgeoisie must be the directing force in national liberation.'[67]

Cuba was, in some respects, an analogue of Guatemala – but only in some respects. As in Guatemala, nationalism was by definition anti-American, and anti-American sentiment was underwritten by powerful US economic interests. The presence of the USA was psychologically oppressive in Cuba as in no other country. No one who has talked to a Cuban can escape the myth of a prostitute economy maintained by, and for, the American tourist.

There the similarities end. Cuba was an island with no hostile Honduras on its borders, offering shelter to a 'Liberation Army'. Whatever Castro is, he is no Arbenz devoid of charisma. Russia's commitment to Cuba was decisive, and by the end of 1960 the hold of Communists in Cuba was probably more secure than it had ever been in Guatemala. Finally, the Cuban revolution had captured the imagination of the Latin American left, as the 'October Revolution' of 1944 in Guatemala had not. Thus the Cuban situation was a more difficult and intolerable problem to the United States, and, by the same token, offered incontestably greater advantage to Russia.

The cold war, as the United States conceived it, had never been a reality to Latin Americans. They were neutralist by inclination, except for those countries whose dictators paid lip-service to the existence of the cold war. It was convenient to label all political opponents Communists – a technique which back-fired by making communism attractive to oppositions,[68] and a crusading posture was profitable in that it eased aid from the US Senate. Cuba made the cold war a reality to Latin Americans because the alternatives were no longer Russia *or* the United States; but the Cuban Revolution *plus* Russia *versus* the United States. The defence of Cuba against 'intervention' *was* meaningful. It involved the sacred principles of self-determination and non-intervention, as first defined at the Buenos Aires Conference in 1936. This had declared that intervention was inadmissible, 'directly or indirectly, and for whatever reason, in the external or internal affairs of any other of the parties'. To Mexico or Brazil, the United States drive against Cuba in the OAS seemed to threaten the inter-American system as they understood it. It was to 'import the cold war into the OAS', which had no concern with the extra-American disputes of the United States.

How did Cuba become a member of the Socialist camp, the first non-aligned state so to do? The Castro revolution was not, in its inception Communist, nor was the policy of the USA of such a character that it must *necessarily* drive Cuba into the arms of the Soviet bloc. The ideology of the revolution derived from Martí, the prophet of the Cuban Independence movement against Spain, rather than from Marx. The doctrine of the 'frustrated' revolution was the key to Castro's thought. Cuba was not a democratic sovereign state, since the War of Independence (1895-98) had been 'captured' by the USA, just as the radicalism of the thirties and the programme of the *Ortodoxo* reformism of the early fifties had been cut short by Batista. Given that Castro saw his task as the 'revindication' of Cuba's sovereignty and given that he accepted the thesis of Martí that a nation which based its economy on one crop sold to one nation had lost its independence, the logic of his position entailed the end of the US sugar quota. The cancellation must, of course, be made to appear an attempt by imperialists to strangle the revolution.

This meant an attack on United States' interests in Cuba. Emotionally the régime must feed on hostility to the United States, on the sensation of a revolution besieged by foes, and Castro's excessive sensibility to criticism in the US press reinforced this tendency. It is very difficult to detect in 1959 a determination by the Eisenhower administration to isolate and 'punish' Cuba. Even if North American statesmen were late in withdrawing support from Batista, if her diplomats lacked imagination and were passive and unenthusiastic about what rapidly became a Socialist revolution, if their view of the defence of US expropriated interests was narrowly legalistic, they did not wish to oust Castro until the 1960 breach; that is, until the drift towards communism in Cuba and the Soviet bloc.

Though few Cubans in 1959 were as politically naïve as most Guatemalans in 1953-54, nevertheless the failure of the Cuban Revolution to evolve a doctrine and a party left a political vacuum and a lack of 'trained' politicians which could be filled by experienced Communists. That this process should be resisted was natural. The Cuban Communists, as in other Latin American countries, had a long history of co-operation with dictatorship when such a course suited their immediate aims. The two leading Cuban Communists – Marinello and Carlos Rafael Rodriguez – had been Batista Ministers during that leader's 'democratic' phase.[69] Blas Roca, the toughest of the Communist leaders, had argued that Castro's guerrilla resistance was misconceived and the party had only patched up an alliance with Castro late in the day.[70] Of course one of the supreme tactical advantages of communism is that its *ultimate* revolutionary credentials are impeccable, whatever tactical contrivances may seem to discredit its struggle against imperialism. Nevertheless, sometimes this argument does not convince. It did not convince some of Castro's original supporters: these protesters were disciplined by the trial of Huber Matos (December 1959).

By spring 1961 Communist influence was probably at its zenith: it had achieved singular triumphs such as the capture, with the aid of the government, of the Trade Union movement. But at the same time Castro's popularity was ebbing away. Russia seemed either unable or unwilling to keep the economy on its feet in the aftermath of agrarian reform and a falsely conceived policy of industrialisation – both of which distorted the economy. It was when this process of political disillusionment with Communist control and discontent at the shortages of food and consumer goods was gathering strength that the US permitted the folly of the April 'invasion'.

This catastrophic failure restored immediately both Castro's domestic position and his prestige throughout Latin America.[71] No one could accept the argument that the invasion was an exile affair, for which no blame attached to the agencies of the US Government. Castro immediately appeared throughout the continent as the symbol of the independence of the Latin American nations. Although he had defeated an ill-conceived invasion by an ill-supplied group of exiles he could present himself as the David who had defeated Goliath in all his might. More

231

significantly, Russia was henceforth clearly committed to the defence of Cuban independence.

The miscalculation of April was particularly disastrous, in that US policy under the new Kennedy administration was making a determined effort to counter the spread of 'Castro-type' revolutions in the continent by accelerating a revision of hemispheric policy which had begun under the Eisenhower administration. Castro posed as the hero of a Pan-American revolution against American imperialism. It was an axiom of the most intelligent policy-makers in Washington that Castro and communism were transitional phenomenona. Latin America was experiencing rapid economic and social change, which created violent situations. These were exploitable by communism only for the limited period before self-sustained growth brought all-round prosperity. Walt Rostow writes:

> Communists know that their time to seize power in under-developed areas is limited. They know that, as momentum takes hold in an under-developed area – and the fundamental social problems inherited from the traditional society are solved – their chances to seize power decline. It is on the weakest nations – facing their most difficult moments – that the Communists concentrate their attention. They are the scavengers of the modernisation process.[72]

Ergo, the optimist conclusion runs, by easing and guiding the modernisation process the threat of communism can be exorcised and Latin America gained for the free world.

American policy in Latin America since 1945 had been conceived in strategic terms and resulted in military missions, equipment standardisation and the Mutual Defence Agreements made from 1952 on.[73] Since in purely military terms the pacts were useless – Latin America could hardly become a field of armed conflict between Russia and the United States – it remained open to question whether such military aid was the best instrument to secure general political support. Was the best way to 'fight communism' internally the formulation of military alliances with incumbent régimes, whatever their political complexion? The political atmosphere of Latin America was undergoing changes which made the Legion of Merit for Perez Jiménez look dangerously like what Castro came to call 'backing the wrong side in the process of historical development'.

Thus on the eve of the Cuban invasion the postulates of US policy were these:

1. Economic aid to the modernisation process was preferable to Mutual Defence Agreements as a means of combating communism and gaining general political support in a cold war. (The votes of the Latin American nations in the United Nations were proportionately diminishing, but they were still significant.)
2. The US must appear as a free society supporting free societies ready to help themselves; only thus could it appear as the champion of a better way of life than that modelled in the Soviet bloc. It must therefore see that aid went to 'progressive' democracies.

These were the premises of President Kennedy's Alliance for Progress.

However, the more negative conception of hemispheric defence (i.e. the use of the OAS to put sanctions on Castro and communism) was not abandoned. It was tested diplomatically at the second Punta del Este meeting in January 1962, where the USA attempted to retrieve some of the losses sustained in April 1961. This conception was based on an interpretation of its fundamental instrument (the Rio Treaty of 1947), which was unacceptable to those Latin American states which enjoyed genuine independence. The Rio treaty laid down that any attack on any American state was to be construed as an attack against all and that collective measures were to be taken to repel such aggression. To states like Mexico and Brazil this meant external attack. To the US the establishment of a Communist régime implied *per se* an attack on national sovereignty, since it mortgaged any states' international freedom to the diplomatic necessities of the Soviet Union. In Castro's case it was argued that the *lider maximo* of the Pan-American left was exporting revolution to other states (e.g. Venezuela) in defiance of the doctrine of non-intervention which protected the independence of members of the OAS. This interpretation was completely unacceptable to Mexico and Brazil. They became the leaders of a neutralist bloc defending the independence of American states against any US attempt to 'interfere' with the nature of the régime of constituent states.

These two mutually irreconcilable interpretations of non-intervention clashed. It was only the support of the smaller states which allowed the US a limited success at Punta del Este. Castro and the Eastern bloc immediately pointed out that only the shameless manipulation of votes of 'imperialist puppets' had allowed the US to escape a major humiliation. The 'peoples' of Latin America had defended Cuba, self-determination and non-intervention.

Once the dust of Punta del Este had settled, the cold war resolved itself into the Alliance for Progress *v.* the Revolution of National Liberation, as conceived by Castro, and the defeat of imperialism, as conceived by the Soviet Union. The Alliance for Progress implied support of economic modernisation within democratic states. What then are the prospects of economic prosperity and of finding respectable democratic states which Washington could support?

Many Latin American observers are pessimistic. The 'structuralist' school (which explains inflation in Brazil, Chile and elsewhere in terms of supply inelasticities and deep societal hindrances) sees growth as possible only after fundamental agrarian reform. This the Alliance for Progress, in spite of good intentions, will not force on recalcitrant governments. Those who explain current difficulties in terms of a deep-seated 'asymmetry' which must result in adverse terms of trade for 'peripheral' primary producers as against the industrial 'centre', see Alliance funds as guilt payments by an 'advanced' country. It fills in with charity the gap which it creates by not paying 'fair' prices for imports from Latin America. Combined with an excess of bureaucratic controls these pessimistic views allow Latin Americans to label the Alliance for Progress, as the Christian Democrat Frei has done, 'already a failure'.

Perhaps this is one more example of the Latin American predilection for external scapegoats. It may reflect an attitude which neglects the self-help principles on which the Alliance is founded and express an over-pessimistic view of the long-term prospects. Nevertheless, there is a case for saying that the West generally must take an attitude to developing countries more dynamic than the mere provision of loans. If it is too much to ask for some mechanism to stabilise the prices on which the economic wellbeing of the Latin America 'periphery' depends, there is a strong case for tariff reductions which would favour Latin American products. Together with free trade in Latin America itself, this might create a more healthy economy which would not stagnate when import substitution had reached the limits of the internal market. Economically, the prospects for the Alliance for Progress, as it is at present conceived, do not look bright, and it is on its efficiency as a promoter of a rate of growth sufficient to keep pace with a population explosion that its utility as a political weapon depends.[74]

It has been argued (by Claudio Veliz) that the political presuppositions of the Alliance are utopian and self-contradictory. Latin American progressive parties are anti-American by definition and yet it is these parties which the Alliance must favour if it is to appear democratic. The 'middle classes', in the thirties reformist, have turned into respectable social climbers aping the aristocratic establishment; the intellectuals have become alienated from this middle class and may take the leadership of a worker-peasant populist revolution. Curiously enough the Communists do not think that the role of the 'national bourgeoisie' is exhausted. Created by the development of native capitalism, and opposed to the 'imperialist' bourgeoisie (natural allies of foreign capitalists who wished to subordinate the internal market on which the 'national bourgeoisie' depends to the conveniences of the foreign monopolies), they may still be useful. 'It is true that in certain periods the bourgeoisie has betrayed the workers and may betray them again. But this does not mean to say that nothing can be done with the bourgeoisie.'[75] Indeed the error of the Chilean Communists, its leaders have argued, was to 'frighten off the lesser bourgeoisie'.[76] It may be that both the United States and the USSR base their policies on a class which does not exist.

If there are limitations on the successful deployment of the Alliance for Progress there are also limitations on Russian interest in Latin America. To exchange students on a large scale is one thing – though even this is often a disillusioning process – but it would be another to land the Soviet Union with the task of underpinning a series of bankrupt revolutionary régimes. Just as US aid has become vital to Bolivia's continued existence, so the aid of the Soviet Union has become necessary to keep a shop window of revolution in Cuba. The spectacle of bearded revolutionaries was not altogether sympathetic to bureaucrats who had not seen a revolution in years. A continental revolution, with Castro as its prophet, might involve Russia in the maintenance of revolutions which reliable local Communists could not control. In Cuba itself the old-style Communists had been edged aside by 'revolutionaries', a process initiated by Castro's denunciation of Escalante in March 1962 for 'sectarianism' – that is, for an attempt by 'old guard' Communists to plant their followers in key posts to the exclusion of devoted followers of Castro. People who had been 'under their beds' in the revolution were not to be permitted to dominate the party organisation of Revolutionary Cuba or threaten the ascendancy of Castro himself. There were frictions with Russian technicians; Cubans felt that the Eastern bloc was not always giving of its best to Cuba, and the Russian technicians that Cubans' economics (e.g. their attitude to petrol rationing) were a little too Bohemian. Given these limitations, how far would Khrushchev go in the defence of Cuban independence? How far would he go in backing 'Castro type' revolutions throughout Latin America?

The missile crisis was the test of the first issue. Was it an attempt to 'force history' in order to get some decisive concession from the West over, say, Berlin? Or was it, as Khrushchev claimed, an action directed against a known plan on the part of the United States to invade Cuba? In either case the crisis was settled between Russia and the USA over Castro's head. The Cuban missiles did not alter the nuclear balance; Kennedy's reaction, just as Khrushchev's action, was political rather than military, and was completely successful. The result was undoubtedly more favourable to Kennedy than to Khrushchev. The actual presence of Soviet missiles alarmed Latin American states: this was proved by the reaction of the OAS. Moreover, the settlement over the head of Castro brought Latin America into the area of the Sino-Soviet dispute.

There had always been the seeds of discord for that dispute in Latin American issues. The Chinese model of revolution, the Chinese view that national liberation had priority over peace, the Chinese advocacy of 'averaging out' aid to national liberation movements rather than concentrating on the demonstration effects of a prosperous Soviet model, – all had attractions for the Latin American left, although China could not here play on anti-White racism as in Africa. The whole Castro thesis of the viability of guerrilla tactics ran against the recent reaffirmation by the CPSU Central Committee that a 'premature' rising was a bourgeois trap: 'under all circumstances let the revolutionary forces grow until the seed is fully ripe'. This concern with what Communists were once in the habit of calling the 'objective conditions' of revolution was clean contrary to the Cuban thesis as expounded by Ché Guevara: that a guerrilla movement in a peasant country would 'induce' its own revolution.

From 1956 the Chinese themselves began to emphasise their sympathy for Latin America, and in 1960 Peking launched a campaign of 'friendship towards Latin America'. By this date invitations to China and the other customary cultural exchanges appeared less as co-operation in a common struggle than as a competitive bid. Nevertheless, the Communist parties of Latin America, though troubled, kept loyal to Moscow. Many of the leaders were ageing party managers who could conceive no other allegiance, whatever doubts the party youth might entertain. The Chilean party (November 1961) went even further in denouncing 'polycentrism' than the CPSU. The Brazilian party was in one of its divisive crises; it nevertheless endorsed the anti-American line after the Twenty Second Congress.

The missile crisis allowed the Chinese to expose Khrushchev. Given his premise that invasion had been prevented and that the US had formally guaranteed Cuban independence, Khrushchev's defence of his policy was convincing.[77] Given the premises of the Chinese his conduct appeared 'cowardice'. 'The principle of peaceful coexistence can apply only to nations with different social systems, not to relations between oppressed and oppressing classes. . . . Those attacking China extend their idea of "peaceful coexistence" to cover relations between the colonial and semi-colonial people on the one hand and the imperialists and colonialists on the other. . . . Doesn't this kind of talk mean that the Chinese people, the Korean people, the Vietnamese people, the Cuban people, the Algerian people, and the people of other countries who rose in revolution have all violated the principle of "peaceful coexistence" and done wrong?'[78] The CCP consistently referred to 'a second Munich'. The weeks after the Cuban crisis saw the most serious bid by the CCP for Latin America. Even Castro himself might be prised away. The behaviour of the

USSR as a great power rather than as a leader of the National Liberation Movement threatened his position as leader of a continental rebellion against imperialism. Thus to save the continental allegiance of Castro by flattery and generous economic aid became a necessity for Khrushchev in the battle against Peking.

It is clear that the Chinese have attracted some support since the October 1962 crisis. This support comes, not from committed Communist leaders, but from the general pool of leftish-revolutionary sentiment whose unifying ideology is a derivative of *Fidelismo* and which finds the long haul of Popular Fronts either intolerable in itself or doomed to failure. Clearly the Chinese view of the primacy of revolution attracts sections of the Venezuelan party. But we can get a different view of the situation in Chile; those who sympathise with China there are a miscellaneous collection of revolutionary Communists, Trotskyists and *Fidelistas*. Nowhere does a Chinese splinter group appear a serious threat although the 'Chinese way' must gain attraction in those countries where a legal existence is denied to the 'official' party; such a denial makes it futile to espouse non-revolutionary courses. Castro himself has remained 'loyal' to the Soviet Union in the sense that he has expressed no support in public for China; the official Cuban attitude is one of distress that the conflict exists and an insistence that Cuba has its 'own position'. The signature of the test-ban treaty was presented as a moral impossibility for a country which was still under attack by one of the signatories (the USA) not as an act of defiance to the USSR – although presumably the line-up with Albania and China was not pleasing to Moscow. Of course the rigid hostility of China to the USA fits the demands of Cuban foreign policy better than peaceful co-existence. If the cold war stopped, Russia would be less useful to Cuba, as long as the revolution is committed against the USA.

Nevertheless China simply cannot replace the Soviet Union as an economic prop. Castro and his government know this and act accordingly. They are, perhaps less concerned with the propagation of revolution than the creation of a viable economy in Cuba as a first priority. The continental revolution cannot be won if the 'model' goes bankrupt. They now realise that the early programmes of diversification and industrialisation were misconceived. Their aim is socialism in one country. Russia is more useful than China, and other countries a useful supplement to Russia; hence the recent purchases of French and British equipment and the revision of the early notions of diversification. In Leninist terms the Cubans must become 'economists'.

In any case it is little short of nonsense for Castro to hope that the 'Cordillera of the Andes' may turn into 'the Sierra Maestra of the American continent'. Cuba is a model for *small* countries: its guerrilla technique of revolution would not work in large countries, where it might well create areas of discontent which would not 'expand' into a national revolution. This is the case in Colombia and Brazil. In Venezuela the activity of terrorists looked as if it might upset the US 'model' of a 'sensible' democracy. In fact it has not, as the victory of the non-revolutionary parties in the December 1962 elections proves. All that Castro could do was to declaim against an 'electoral farce based on bloodshed and terror'. Elsewhere (in Chile and the Argentine, for instance) the Communists were committed to different tactics: the infiltration of labour movements and the utilisation of Popular Fronts.

No large continental country seems in danger of a Communist take-over although an electoral victory for FRAP, which is not impossible, would bring communists peacefully into power in a coalition government. Brazil, in spite of serious political confusion and seemingly insuperable foreign exchange problems, does not appear on the edge of a left-wing extremist revolution. Indeed, since Castro's revolution there has been no example of a comparable left-wing revolution elsewhere. On the contrary, in Castro's own words 'reaction progresses, right-wing military groups progress and the military corps follow one another with amazing speed. . . . So-called democratic institutions clash with military institutions' (speech of 28 September 1962). The danger in Latin America is not a continental revolution, which may drift into communism; but explosions in the *loci classici* of discontent: the Dominican Republic, Panama, Paraguay, Nicaragua. It must nevertheless be remembered that even in 'dangerous' countries like Paraguay, the Communist Party is mistrusted for its ambivalent attitude to revolutions staged by non-Communists.[79]

What, then, is the balance of forces in Latin America?

Firstly, there is a tendency to over-estimate the *short-term* chances of a Castro-type revolution and the opportunities which such a revolution, if successful, would open up for Communist penetration. As we have seen the connection of Castro with Russia and with the Communist party is probably increasingly one of convenience rather than of the convictions expressed in 1961. Conversely, Latin American *Fidelista* revolutionaries feel that the degree of backing they may expect from the USSR is limited by its interests as a great power. Nevertheless it would be a mistake to argue that the USSR would not support another Cuba; it has little option, however expensive the operation may be and however embarrassing for peaceful coexistence. The US rightly sees long-term economic stability as the only permanent solution to Communist chances. The success of this depends on too many variables for prediction to be possible – above all, on a rate of economic growth sufficient to outstrip population pressures. Certainly Marxist-Leninism, especially in its Chinese form, attracts revolutionary intellectuals: and one of the odd features of the Latin American system is that yesterday's intellectuals may be tomorrow's ministers. Nevertheless, the indications are that they may well have to wait some time.

Secondly, the Cold War does not seem to Latin Americans an issue which directly concerns them: anti-communism within their own borders does not imply for them support of the United States against the USSR. Though Latin American statesmen may be sceptical where Castro's Cuba is concerned and determined to have no Castros at home, they do not share the great-power, Caribbean obsessions of the United States, and these – where they are not psychological reactions to the apparently successful rejection of the US way of life – are based on a sea-power situation which is losing its significance. The US determination to isolate Cuba may well merely isolate the US; though her allies may understand her Cuban policy they find it hard to pardon. The Latin Americans are natural neutralists, who must welcome any loosening of the situation which gives them some freedom of action. For example, if de Gaulle had not existed it would have been necessary for them to invent him. The US may be saved the strain of making up its mind in public as to the fundamentals of its Latin American policy if FRAP fails to win the 1964 elections in Chile. If, however, it is confronted with an legally elected left-wing government which includes communists, then it must decide whether it prefers 'influence' based on respect for Latin American self-determination, to defence of immediate economic interest and to the maintenance of a cold war ideology in a sub-continent that rejects its relevance.

9 THE POLARISATION OF THE COMMUNIST WORLD

Edward Crankshaw

Once there was one Communist world, based on Moscow. Now there are two, one based on Moscow, the other on Peking. Here, then, at first sight, is the polarisation the title of this chapter implies. And the obvious and immediate questions would seem to be: what do these two opposed Romes stand for? What sort of a following can the two Popes, temporarily Khrushchev and Mao Tse-tung, aspire to, and why? Which will win, and why? If neither wins, if we are in for a period of uneasy coexistence between the two rival authorities, what effect will this have on what we think of as the Communist movement and the West's relations with it?

All those questions, and more besides, are fair enough. But they are not perhaps the most important questions. They arise only if we take the Sino-Soviet conflict at its face value as an essentially ideological struggle. But we should not take this conflict at its face value. And the more we contemplate the problem the more we shall find that what we are watching is not the polarisation of the Communist world, but its fragmentation. I shall suggest that far from being two Romes, in fact there is no Rome at all.

There is only one way of organising a world-wide ideological movement, whether secular or spiritual, and that is on the basis of a universally recognised central authority. If this authority is effectively challenged from any quarter, one of two things can happen. Either the original authority falls and is replaced by the challenger, or else the movement splits and, dissipating much of

243

its energies in internecine strife, ceases to be a coherent global force. Peking has not yet superseded Moscow, and shows no signs of doing so. This means that the world Communist movement is split and, axiomatically, is more concerned with its own divisions than with the world outside the Communist party.

This would be true even if the Russians and the Chinese Communists were in fact quarrelling about doctrine, as they insist that they are. Then one would expect an ideological line-up among the fraternal parties, each individually split, each side passionately convinced that it stood for the truth and anathemising heresy in the other.

In fact the situation is much more complicated than that. Although the quarrel was first stated in ideological terms and was debated, if that is the word, in those terms by the assembled comrades of the eighty-one Communist parties at the secret Moscow meeting in December 1960, it was apparent even then to the simplest of the comrades that there was a good deal more behind it than interpretations of Lenin. Many of the delegates on that occasion reproached the Chinese for 'great-power chauvinism' and others criticised Peking sharply for importing questions of state relations (seen as a matter for private negotiation between Moscow and Peking) into what should have been an intra-party ideological discussion. The Chinese reproached the Russians with the same offences. Both were right. Mao and Khrushchev were quarrelling about state power rather than ideology, and both sides knew it. This meant, among other things, that the role of the other Communist parties of the world was strictly limited. Although both Moscow and Peking demonstratively appealed to them for support in what was presented as a doctrinal quarrel, what was in fact going on, and the Communist leaders knew it, was bidding and counter-bidding for support in an inter-state quarrel.

The implications of this, though it is very doubtful if any of the participants were fully aware of it at the time, was that the fraternal parties were being invited to vote on a matter from which they were, in effect, excluded. The Moscow Conference of 1960 was not an intra-party discussion about the party line: it was a duel between Moscow and Peking, with both sides demanding the unconditional support of the Communist parties of the world in a quarrel having very little to do with communism.

Moscow won, hands down. Only a very few South-East Asian parties, plus, queerly, the New Zealand party, stood up for Peking. And it seems to me that one of the best ways of enquiring into the nature of what is still flatteringly called the Communist movement as it is today is to ask why Moscow then won so easily. Because, on the face of it, China had the better case. Practically all the charges flung by Peking at Moscow were true. Practically all the charges flung by Moscow at Peking were untrue. Further, the Chinese argument, taken at its face value (which we may do for a moment) was a good Leninist argument. The Russian argument (again taken at its face value) was not – for its Leninism was perfunctory in the extreme.

But before considering the behaviour of the fraternal parties, perhaps we should run over the ground which lay between the assumption of power, in 1949, of the Chinese Communist Party and the formal denunciation before the assembled Communist leaders in 1960 of the thought and manners of the Chinese Communist Party.[80]

It is not at all clear to me in what light the accession of China to the Communist camp in 1948 was regarded by the Communist parties outside the Soviet Union. Had I been a Communist I should have viewed this climacteric with the greatest unease. But I suspect that most Communist officials in most Communist parties are, to put it politely, no more intelligent than most American officials in most American departments of state. Why should they be? No doubt the fraternal parties, just as most worthy Americans, and many Englishmen, regarded the Chinese revolution as a tremendous accession of strength to the

Communist cause, instead of as a drastic dilution of Muscovite authority. They probably had no clearer idea of what the Communist cause was than, for example, Mr Dulles.

The man who had a clear idea was Stalin, who knew exactly what it was: it was anything in this world that could be turned to the greater glory of Great Russia, or the Soviet Union as he liked to call it. Stalin was alarmed by the Chinese revolution. He knew he could not manage the Chinese.

I hope it will not be thought that in stressing the power aspects of the Sino-Soviet conflict I am ignoring the force of ideology. I am very well aware of the force of ideology. I know a little – though luckily from observation, not from participation – of the overweening dynamic of those happy enough, individually or in groups, to be seized of the conviction that to them has been vouchsafed the vision of ultimate truth. I can guess, a little forlornly, as it were from the outside, something of the intoxication of those among them who, having read some difficult books, feel that they can fortify this vision with rational argument. How can anybody in the world who was born early enough to receive baptism at the hands of British imperialism and who in one short span has felt the impact of Lenin, Mussolini, Hitler, the Spanish Civil War and the American Way of Life *not* believe in the power of ideology? If I speak of the Soviet Union, and now China, more in terms of *Realpolitik* than in terms of Marxist and Leninist ideology it is because I think we have had too much ideology. As long as there are ex-Communists, (as I hope and believe there always will be), they may be trusted to keep us informed of the ideas which were betrayed. As long as there are government officials in the West who come, generation after generation of them, with minds fresh, open, and ready to be shocked by the duplicities of Lenin (and I hope and am sure there will always be such), we shall be kept fully informed of the intricacies of the great conspiracy. But I feel we should also remember people; and man does not live by ideas alone.

Stalin knew, then, he could not manage the Chinese. Between the wars he had discouraged the Chinese Communists because he needed, or thought he needed, a reasonably coherent China to be used as an ally in face of the Japanese, the Germans, the British or whoever. Kuomintang China seemed more likely to fill this bill than any other China. After the war Stalin indicated to Mao Tsetung that the time was not ripe for a Communist revolution in China. He may or may not still have had hopes of Chiang Kaishek. He certainly wanted to have his way in Manchuria in a manner inimical to any Chinese state. And he certainly knew that he had no hope of controlling China in the way in which he was able to control the East European satellites – by his army and police, or by the threat of their intervention. Throughout his lifetime Stalin was always quite clear that the only Communists he wanted in power anywhere were those to whom he could dictate absolutely.

This equivocal, inward-looking Russian attitude, cannot have escaped the Chinese, who themselves had no intention of being controlled by anyone. In the early days of the Chinese revolution, with Chinese publicists glorifying Mao's way, there was some speculation as to whether China might one day 'do a Tito' and assert her independence. It escaped the notice of the speculators that by the very act of carrying through her revolution, China had already 'done a Tito'. The Communists had seized power in Stalin's despite, though in the name of Leninism, and without any help from Russia.

The situation being as it was, it was clearly in the interests of the Soviet Union to make the best of a good job by pretending that China was the greatest accession to their cause and a colossal ally *vis à vis* the West, and of China to embroider on a good job by obtaining as much material help from the Soviet Union as she could get without a sacrifice of sovereignty. The task of each was made so much easier by the conduct of the West, above all the United States, whose main object in life appeared to be to magnify

the Communist menace and insist that all peoples calling themselves Communist must be clamped ever more firmly into each
other's arms by outside pressure. It took the greatest determination on the part of Marshal Tito to bring Yugoslavia out of the
Communist camp in the teeth of Western disapproval – he
just managed. The Chinese were content to stay where they
were, so long as they could do so with no apparent sacrifice of
honour.

The great alliance persisted through the Korean War and until
after the death of Stalin. Nobody questioned it. The Chinese
Communists, as novices in the game of government, evidently
felt they could accept Moscow's supremacy without loss of face
in return for a great deal of vital Soviet aid. The language held by
Stalin during the worst period of the cold war was the sort of
language they liked to hold themselves. Stalin was a great man, a
man of exceptional stature, universally recognised as such, and he
had decades of practical experience behind him. It was becoming
for the proudest Chinese to recognise him as the father-figure and
to keep his reservations to himself. It was also expedient.

When Stalin had gone it was another matter. The senior revolutionary figure in the world was now Mao Tse-tung. The Russians
could not decide whether they wanted Malenkov or Khrushchev
to rule them, and neither of these when it came to prestige and
grandeur could hold a candle to Mao. All the same, as far as we
can gather, the Chinese for the time being were content to let
things ride. No matter how much they may have distrusted
Stalin's heirs, as they manœuvred for position, it was very much
in their interests for the Soviet Union to re-establish itself under a
strong leadership. The only visible sign of independent thinking
on the part of Mao at this stage was the difference of tone he
permitted himself when speaking of Stalin. The Russians, though
still three years from the Twentieth Party Congress, began to
play down Stalin's role immediately after his death: the Chinese

did not join in this game and continued to pay homage to the great genius and leader of mankind.

In 1956 came the Twentieth Party Congress in Moscow, and Khrushchev for the first time emerged as a serious revisionist. His new role was at first concealed from all but the most attentive by the heat and excitement engendered by his notorious secret speech, with its selective denunciation of Stalin's ways. More important in the long run, however, was his amendment of the Leninist canon: war was no longer 'fatally inevitable'; in some countries revolution might be achieved without violence; it was necessary for all Communists to recognise that there were different paths to socialism. This amendment was a climacteric. It brought Moscow communism into the mid-twentieth century. It recognised by implication the facts of nuclear warfare and was doubtless forced upon Khrushchev by the knowledge that in the atomic age the simple, belligerent certitudes of Lenin (who thought of wars in terms of guns and bullets and mud and slogging death) would no longer do. What was the good of seeking revolution through war, when modern war would destroy the very raw material of a new society?

Later the Chinese were to reproach Khrushchev bitterly both for his disrespectful attitude towards Stalin and for his amendment to the canon. But at the time, as far as we know, they allowed themselves to subscribe to the new doctrine. It was not until the autumn of that same year of 1956 that, for the first time since the 1949 revolution, Peking began to make itself felt as a powerful and independent voice, though still harmonising with Moscow. Then, as we know, under the impact of the de-Stalinisation, the European Empire of Muscovy started going up in flames. We knew at the time that Chou En-lai made a flying visit to Warsaw, and other places, to lend, to all appearances, his moral support to Khrushchev, who badly needed it. But it was not until 1960, certainly at Moscow in November, perhaps at Bucharest in July, that the Chinese claimed that it had been they who had persuaded the Russians not to put down the Polish revolt in blood and, a little later, to move troops and tanks into Budapest in order to smash the Hungarian revolt. We do not know the truth of these claims: we only know what the Chinese have said. But there is no essential contradiction in Communist eyes between the policy of restraint in Warsaw and violence in Budapest. Had Russian troops tried to put down Gomulka, the Soviet Union would have found itself with a war on its hands, the whole Polish nation, Communist and non-Communist, united against them under a powerful Communist leader. In Budapest the situation was sadly different. Here was a divided people; here the party and the people were irreconcilable. Had the revolt triumphed, communism would have been swept away and Hungary would have been free to turn its back on the Soviet Union and make friends with the West. Unlike the Poles, the Hungarians were not hemmed in by East Germans and Czechs.

Be that as it may, Khrushchev, under heavy domestic fire for the consequences of his policies, was under a deep debt of obligation to the Chinese for sustaining him. He, in his turn, had committed the revolutionary act of bringing China, for the first time in history, into Europe – a most extraordinary performance for a patriotic Russian statesman.

At this stage the Chinese must have begun to feel that the time had come to claim equality with the Soviet Union. But they did not apparently press this claim with arrogance. Their great moment came in the autumn of 1957 at the celebrated Moscow Conference of Communist parties which culminated in the publication of the first Moscow Declaration, a policy statement setting down the party line, which was to be binding on all parties. Although this Moscow declaration did not deny the thinking of the Twentieth Party Congress it was essentially the outcome of a fence-mending operation, a new assertion of revolutionary vigour, and some of the language used was a great deal more belligerent and uncompromising than anything that had been heard from Moscow for some time. We know now that the Chinese were invited, to their very great joy, to assist in the drafting of the declaration, which was simply put before the other party leaders for their signature. We know that some of the other party leaders, above all Gomulka, were reluctant to sign. We know that the Poles relied on Mao Tse-tung personally to act as a moderating influence, as Chou En-lai had acted as a moderating influence in their favour a year before – and that they were deeply shocked and disappointed when Mao showed himself tough and uncompromising. We know now that it was at this meeting that Mao developed his notion of the East Wind prevailing over the West Wind and made his famous observation, which the Russians were later to throw in his teeth, to the effect that nuclear warfare might be a dreadful thing, but that good Communists would not flinch if faced with it, because, even if 300,000,000 Chinese died in it there would still be 300,000,000 left to build the earthly paradise in a world from which capitalism had been blasted away in blood and fire.

It seems possible, in the light of subsequent events, that Mao went away from this meeting well content. He had put some stiffening into the Russians, into Khrushchev in particular; he had helped to re-define the objects of the Communist movement in sufficiently dynamic terms; above all he had at last been admitted as an equal on policy-forming occasions by the Soviet leadership. China had arrived. Henceforward Peking and Moscow would march forward in step, consulting each other in all matters requiring fresh initiatives, and, between them, laying down the line for the lesser parties to follow. Given all this, Mao was perfectly content to concede public recognition of the Soviet party as the leading party. He showed himself very keen on the concept of a leading party at a time when some of the more sophisticated Western parties were trying to get it done away with – substituting a concept of equality between all parties, best defined by Togliatti in his thesis about polycentrism. Was this keenness due to the fact that Mao looked forward to the day when the Chinese party would become the leading party? We do not know. But by 1960 he was clearly thinking along these lines.

I do not propose to move step by step through the events of the next two years, from the end of 1957 to the end of 1959. But it was during this period that various things happened to show Mao that he had over-rated his influence on Khrushchev, and to show Khrushchev that Mao was very much determined to follow a path of his own at home (this was most manifest in the affair of the communes and the Great Leap Forward); to recommend the Chinese path, as opposed to the Soviet, to other unsophisticated peoples seeking to make their own revolutions; and to exploit, and persuade the Russians to exploit, in the interests of the East Wind, the vaunted supremacy of the Soviet Union in the matter of rockets and nuclear bombs. It was during this time that the Russians refused to support Mao in the matter of the offshore islands; refused to exploit their military supremacy at the time of the Iraq crisis – instead of threatening, Khrushchev made a desperate appeal to President Eisenhower to meet and talk ('the guns are almost firing') in order to stave off disaster – while the Chinese were breathing fire. It was during this period that the Russians refused to give the Chinese atomic weapons and nuclear know-how. There was clearly a basic misunderstanding on the part of the Chinese of the realities of armed might. They believed genuinely that the Soviet Union had achieved overwhelming superiority in long-range missiles. They were not alone in this! They were outraged by what they took to be Khrushchev's pusillanimous (or treacherous?) refusal to exploit this superiority.

But appearances were kept up until the autumn of 1959, when Khrushchev achieved his heart's desire, visited the United States, talked as an equal with an American President in Washington, and came back praising the good sense, peace-loving character and statesmanlike wisdom of President Eisenhower. Later, in Bucharest and Moscow, the Chinese were to single out this attitude to Eisenhower as the supreme iniquity, the supreme betrayal of the revolutionary cause. At the time, it was only clear that there was a great difference of opinion between Moscow and Peking. Khrushchev's visit to Peking and to Mao after his American trip produced no heart-warming declarations of solidarity and unity. There was no adequate reception of the Soviet leader, and no communiqué was issued when he left. Instead, the Chinese went on condemning Eisenhower as the arch-fiend, while Khrushchev went on referring to him in amiable terms. From now on, too, Khrushchev used every possible occasion to stress his preoccupation with securing the prosperity and material progress of the Soviet Union, with no more than the most perfunctory reference to assistance to other less happily situated Communist lands, or to the struggling masses still outside the pale. References, implicit or explicit, to the presumption of the Chinese in thinking that they had found a special road to communism through the communes and the Great Leap Forward became increasingly frequent and contemptuous.

It is clear now that the end of 1959 marked a turning-point. The Chinese were ready to accept the supremacy of the Soviet Communist party so long as this party acted as a trustee and a mainstay for the Communist movement everywhere, above all in China, and provided that they had a voice in decisions of high policy. They were not, however, prepared to accept a subordinate position to a Russia interested above all in achieving physical security by unilateral deals with the enemy and material prosperity of an increasingly bourgeois kind at the expense of aid to the faithful – again especially the Chinese. There were other elements in the situation. I have not, for example, mentioned Russia's betrayal of China in the Indian border dispute; I have not mentioned the material cost to China of the immense expenditure the Russians were compelled to make in order to set the European satellites on their feet after the stormy period at the end of 1956;

I have not mentioned Russia's equivocal attitude to national liberation movements, which it ought to have been whole-heartedly supporting. It is enough now to say that by the turn of the year 1959-60 the scene was set for a heavy confrontation, and it came.

The Chinese prepared the ground, and they made the decision to challenge the Soviet Union in the field of ideology. This was easy for them. All they had to do was to remind the comrades of the true essence of Lenin's teaching – above all those elements of it which had been jettisoned by Khrushchev at the Twentieth Party Congress – and to denounce those who departed from it in a revisionist sense. They were helped in this in that revisionism, as opposed to dogmatism, had been pin-pointed as the main immediate danger at the 1957 Moscow Conference. The Yugoslavs were the arch-revisionists, and all the Chinese had to do was to attack the Yugoslavs and attribute to them Khrushchev's sins as well as their own. They had all the holy texts on their side. When the first broadside was fired in the article 'Long Live Leninism' in April 1960, they could make a cast-iron case for their attitude, based entirely on a conventional reading of Leninist texts.

For the Russians it was harder. They had departed from the texts. Furthermore, they knew very well that this ideological dispute was not the real essence of the quarrel, which was already clearly a power contest. They replied in kind, but their replies were ideologically inferior, and often perfunctory to a degree. In straight doctrinal argument they were the losers – although they could and should have done much better.

Evidently Khrushchev was not particularly interested. He had another card up his sleeve, which he proceeded to play for all he was worth. He played it for the first time at the Bucharest Conference, before a limited audience of Communist leaders, in July 1960, after the Paris Summit fiasco, when he decided to expose the iniquity of Peking in simple terms. He did not reply to Chinese ideological arguments. He had observed that the Chinese

how much they tell themselves that Lenin was the supreme opportunist, reading themselves to sleep over the relevant passages in
Left Wing Communism – an Infantile Disorder and elsewhere, they
must ask themselves where it is all going to end – at what point
if any, is the Soviet leadership going to feel that its own country
is sufficiently invulnerable, its own people sufficiently prosperous,
to permit it to pay more attention to the needs of the global
revolution? At what stage will it feel ready to give more full and
active assistance to despairing revolutionaries all over the world
instead of using its resources to bribe the uncommitted and the
bourgeois neutralists into staying neutral? And so on.

There is little doubt that had the Chinese shown less arrogance
and more sense and flexibility in presenting their case, they would
have won more adherents. If their speeches had been less warlike
and provocative; if they had attacked the Russians more in
sorrow than in anger; if they had not made it so clear that it was
Khrushchev's head they were after; if, later they had limited
themselves to preaching the pure doctrine of Leninism, instead of
injecting matters closely connected with inter-state rivalry, having
nothing to do with ideology – border claims, betrayal of military
pacts, charges of racialism, etc. – if they had conducted themselves
in this way and confirmed the popular, but apparently erroneous,
image of the Chinese as a people worldly wise, tolerant, subtle,
flexible and gentle, whiter than white and wiser than wise, they
could have made a better effect.

But they did not so conduct themselves. Instead, they went on
attacking all along the line, until a new climax was reached with
the Cuban crisis of October 1962. This gave the Chinese a first-
class opportunity to develop a personal attack on Khrushchev.
By retreating before President Kennedy, they said, he had not
saved the peace, as he claimed, he had only made war more likely.
But the edge of their attack was blunted by their own conduct in
staging at this moment a massive invasion of Indian territory.
Nevertheless, some of the things they had to say about Khrushchev

were near enough to the truth to be awkward, and there were many earnest comrades all over the world who were inclined to agree with the Chinese when they likened Cuba to Munich and charged Khrushchev with 'irresponsible adventurism' followed by 'capitulationism'.

It was against this background that the Russians decided that the time had come to drop all camouflage and pursue their quarrel with Peking openly. The first man to come out into the open, to say 'When we mean China we have no need to say Albania', was Signor Pajetta, speaking at the Rome Congress of the Italian Communist party in December 1962. He was soon echoed by others. But still the hard political facts behind the quarrel were largely concealed: it was not generally known, for example, that the trade between Russia and China had dwindled to practically nothing, and that Moscow had made no move at all to help the Chinese in their fight against famine arising from fearful agricultural disasters.

On 1 March 1963, Peking made what seems to have been its last bid to keep the quarrel on a high ideological level. *People's Daily* published a long and definitive article which was a direct challenge to the ideological leadership of Moscow. It contrasted the revolutionary purity of the Chinese with the opportunist manœuvring of the Russians. In a most striking passage attacking Khrushchev directly (though still not by name), it paraphrased the opening words of the *Communist Manifesto* in terms calculated to send a shiver of appalled recognition down the spine of every devout Communist: 'A spectre is haunting the world – the spectre of true Marxist-Leninism, and it threatens you. You have no faith in the people, and the people have no faith in you. You are divorced from the masses. That is why you fear the truth.'

In an attempt to draw the Russians, the Chinese printed in its own press the translations of a number of Soviet attacks on China, and dared Moscow to reciprocate. But Moscow was unmoved. After a good deal of manœuvring for position a Chinese delegation arrived in Moscow in June 1963, supposedly to discuss differences in a calm and friendly atmosphere. But the atmosphere was neither calm nor friendly, nor was there any discussion. The talks took place only because, despite intensive mutual provocation, neither side was prepared to take the blame for cancelling them.

Then in August 1963, came the signing of the test-ban treaty. At this point the Chinese seem to have decided that there was no longer any point in pretending that the great quarrel was ideological in origin. By signing the treaty, they said, the Russians had not only betrayed the revolutionary cause, but had also entered into what was nothing less than an alliance with the imperialists, directed against China. Then grievance after grievance came tumbling out. On 14 August Peking announced to the whole world that in the summer of 1959 the Russians had refused to give them technical know-how in the matter of nuclear arms and to let them have samples of atom bombs. This, they said, amounted to the unilateral denunciation of a treaty of mutual technological assistance signed in October 1957 – i.e. just before the Moscow Conference, which represented the high peak of Sino-Soviet co-operation. To make matters worse, they said, the Russians had confided the terms of this treaty to the Americans. Finally, and in a way which showed how mutual suspicion and rival ambitions as between two neighbouring sovereign powers completely dominated the quarrel, in September 1963 Peking accused the Soviet Union of 'provoking frontier incidents' in general as far back as 1960, and in particular, of engaging in 'large-scale subversive activities' in Sinkiang.

As time went by it became increasingly apparent to all interested observers that there was a very marked discrepancy between Chinese revolutionary theory, as propagated in the great debate with Moscow, and Chinese political practice. This discrepancy was particularly marked in the matter of support for national liberation movements in the backward areas and for oppressed Communist parties in bourgeois states. While reproving the

Russians for inactivity in these matters, China in fact showed very little activity herself. And when she did show activity, as in the matter of the Indian border dispute, what had this to do with communism? Again, with all their talk of paper tigers, the Chinese seemed no more anxious to invite an armed collision with the West, with America, than Khrushchev himself. They, too, for reasons of *Realpolitik*, could engage in agreements with a hostile state, Pakistan, of a kind which they would have denounced with righteous indignation had they been entered into by the Russians.

In a word, China, with all her talk about the sacred trust of Leninism, seemed to be behaving in the international field scarcely less obviously as a great power as such, with an eye to her own state interests, than the Soviet Union. Even in Indonesia she seemed more anxious to lend comfort and support to the Chinese entrepreneurs, Communist or not, than to the strong indigenous Communist party.

Finally, by her arrogant, exclusive and excluding, touch-me-not aspect, she has reminded many Communists all over the world that, throughout her history, China has not shown the faintest comprehension of what it means to play a part in an alliance – or even of what is meant by diplomacy.

It is because of all this that, at the beginning of this chapter, I queried the conception of polarisation. Where are the poles? We can discover no clear-cut ideological division. On examination, the great schism presents itself as a conflict between two powerful and unfriendly neighbour states, each trying to exploit the once apparently monolithic Communist movement in its own material and territorial interests.

One of these states, moreover, belongs to Europe, the other to Asia (some of us may like to think of the Russians as a quasi-oriental people, closer to Asia than to Europe, but this view is shared by extremely few Russians and by no Chinese: certainly the Soviet Union comprehends a number of Asian peoples, but these are clearly seen as such by the dominant Russians, and they play no effective part in the evolution of Soviet Government attitudes towards the outside world). Already, as we have lately seen, attempts have been made by each side to present the other in the most damaging light imaginable – as seeking to divide the world on racial lines and to organise conflict between East and West – or, more accurately nowadays, North and South. The less developed peoples of Asia, Africa and Latin America are supposed to be rallying round China, in opposition to the more fortunate 'have' peoples of North America and Europe, including the Soviet Union from Minsk to Vladivostock.

In fact there are no clear demarcation lines. Far from representing a polarisation of the Communist world, the Sino-Soviet conflict seems to be well on the way to releasing movements and forces which cut, and will almost certainly increasingly cut, across all the familiar groupings which, since shortly after the last war, we have accepted, foolishly I think, as virtually immutable. Thus, already General de Gaulle is profiting by the conflict in order to further what he takes to be, perhaps rightly, perhaps not, the interests of France, putting new strains on the Western alliance. There will be other strains arising from the different attitudes, different approaches, different expedients assumed and resorted to by individual Western governments *vis-à-vis* individual Communist states or parties seeking to profit from the breakdown of Moscow's absolute control of their destinies, or thrown into confusion by the terrible necessity of making a choice: the whole point of becoming a Communist is that by making one choice one is liberated from the responsibility of ever choosing again – how fearful, how calamitous to be expelled into the rough light of day from the dark and cavernous certitudes of a universal womb – and just because a Chinese had to quarrel with a Russian.

The Communists of Eastern Europe see a new freedom of manœuvre. The challenge to the West is to meet them half-way – and the West will quarrel about it. The West is already quarrelling about Cuba, about British Guiana: Castro, owing so much to Mr

Khrushchev, flirts with China, assumes Chinese attitudes, makes it up to Russia, buys omnibuses from the British, whose willingness to sell is an affront to the United States. Canada sells wheat to Russia and China, America only to Russia – to deplete her gold reserves, according to Washington. America puts pressure on the British to stay in British Guiana to keep it from going Communist, but wants British troops out of Borneo, cost what it may to Malaysia (small) in order to appease Indonesia (large), because Indonesia has a powerful Communist Party. Pakistan makes deals with China: India makes deals with Russia. Nearer home the new mood among the great European Communist parties will soon lead to startling changes in the domestic political arrangements of a number of countries, above all Italy, where, by the look of things, the flexibility of Togliatti and other Communist leaders will shortly make it hard for the Italians to reconcile domestic harmony and perfect loyalty to NATO.

Behind it all lies the very long-term threat of ultimate physical conflict between the Soviet Union and China, which could embrace us all.

10 POLYCENTRISM IN THE WEST

Max Beloff

It is customary and correct to talk of a crisis within the Western Alliance; and much thought has recently been devoted to ascertaining the reasons for it, and to suggesting possible cures; more in the United States than in Britain; more perhaps in Britain than in most continental countries; but all in all this is not a subject where our problem is the paucity of materials.[81]

In the period when the institutions of the Alliance were created, it was possible to disagree over the form they should take, and it was understandable that people should be worried as to whether they would be set up in time to meet the urgent needs of European recovery and defence; but only a few people on either side of the Altantic were prepared to deny the need for them altogether. The United States had twice gone to war to redress the shattered balance of power in Europe and in the world; it had hoped that the new international institutions of the United Nations would make a third such experience unnecessary, but the conduct of the Soviet Union between 1944 and 1947 was such as to suggest that the rapid withdrawal of American power from Europe would expose the rest of Germany together with Austria and the countries of Western Europe to incorporation within a Soviet-controlled bloc on the model of what was happening in Eastern Europe.

In these circumstances the essential element in the Marshall Plan, in the North Atlantic Treaty and in the organisations to which they gave rise was the bringing to bear of American economic and military power to redress the imbalance created in Europe by economic dislocation, and by the apparent predominance of Soviet military power on the ground. In that sense the whole operation must be regarded as one of the most successful in the annals of diplomacy. The decline of the Western European economy was halted and reversed; and political stability established to the west of the military line of demarcation. By the peace treaty for Austria of 1955, the limit of Soviet control was actually moved a step back at the price of that country's neutralisation.

Why then do we speak of crisis? What has gone wrong? The immediate answers to these questions are simple enough. The Atlantic Alliance as extended in 1954, included as a partner and not simply as an area under guarantee, the Federal Republic of Germany. The Federal Government claims to be the only legitimate political authority in Germany – a claim accepted by its partners – and regards the so-called German Democratic Republic as merely a cover for the fact that Soviet military power prevents the reunification of Germany; nor does it accept, formally at least, as final the loss of territories east of the Oder-Neisse line. The Western Alliance (while uncommitted on Germany's future Eastern frontiers) has repeatedly proclaimed the ultimate reunification of Germany to be an object of its policy, and maintains itself in West Berlin both as a protection for the people of that city and as an additional guarantee of its fidelity to this further goal. In other words, the Atlantic Alliance is not merely a defensive alliance, but is also an alliance dedicated to achieving an alteration in the *status quo*. Since any attempt to change the *status quo* involves an element of risk, and since there are differences on the degree of risk that should be run, and since finally, among the peoples if not among the governments, there are strong differences of view about the priority, if any, that should be given to German reunification, there is in the German situation an inherent ambiguity which has become ever more apparent with the passage of time.

The next most obvious reason for discontent with the way in which the affairs of the Alliance have been run has arisen from the fact that its very success in stabilising Europe has helped to focus attention on other areas of the world where political stability has been even harder to obtain, and where the challenge of militant communism has been even more striking. And here again the fact that some members of the Alliance have or have had deep commitments outside Europe has involved a different assessment of the relative importance of these overseas developments as compared with the original challenge in Europe itself. For some members of the Alliance their entire security needs can be assured by its success; for others it can at best only meet them in part.

Such ambiguities were not the only ones inherent in the original creation of NATO. For many of those who accepted, and indeed welcomed, the Alliance did so while feeling that its purely military aspects might be regarded as a transient phenomenon. What they were really concerned to bring about was an Atlantic Community – some form of organic and permanent link between the countries of Western Europe and North America based upon their common dedication to a particular set of social and political beliefs. But here again the desire to bring about such a Community, and ideas as to how an objective could be achieved, were very unevenly distributed between the countries of the Alliance, and appealed even within them only to very limited groups even among the politically active elements of the population. And the fact that this objective remained in the realm of aspiration created in some quarters a degree of discontent which helped to obliterate the very real achievements of the Alliance as such.

One cause for the failure of the Atlantic Community idea to make much headway in the first fifteen years of the Alliance's existence was to be found in the fact that it did not, in itself, by any means account for the entire range of long-term political thinking in the period. In continental Europe it had from the first to face a competitor already occupying some entrenched positions – the European idea itself. For some people the two ideas were complementary – an Atlantic Community could well be thought of as a partnership between a European and a North American entity. But for others they were rivals, in that the unity of Europe was thought of as a method of avoiding what some people saw as an excessive degree of dependence upon the United States in the economic, military and cultural fields alike.

It is understandable that confusions of this kind should have arisen, because the notion of Europe itself was so unclear. In practice the scope of European integration narrowed as the years passed; the lesser Europe of the Six replaced the wider Europe that had still been envisaged at the time of the Hague Congress of 1948 and of the creation of the Council of Europe. But this was not to say that wider notions ever disappeared entirely; and clearly some conceptions of Europe lent themselves much more readily than others to schemes in which the United States would be an active, not to say the leading, participant. But even at a more concrete level, the lists of the various European organisations were never exactly the same as the list of the European members of the Alliance. And except for Western European Union – which it is sensible to regard as an ancillary organ of NATO itself – all the European organisations, other than the three Communities of the Six, contain countries whose neutral status precludes membership in the Alliance, or any closer union that might grow out of it. Nor – as has been shown in its relations with Spain – does the United States regard itself as being limited in its European connections to countries which are active participants in the European institutions themselves. The characteristic feature of the Western side in the 'cold war' was thus a proliferation of institutions, either general or designed for more specific purposes, but none of them unmistakably marked out to be the final focus of political decision-making at the highest level.[82]

It was not inside Europe or the Atlantic Community alone that the countries of the West found themselves involved in the working of international institutions. Almost all of them were members of the whole range of organisations set up at the end of the war on a global basis – the United Nations. But their common membership of the United Nations was itself a source of division rather than of unity. For whereas the co-operation of the Soviet bloc under Russian leadership extended to the UN as well, the countries of the West did not regard themselves as under any such obligation to support each other's point of view and rarely voted together except in the face of a direct Communist challenge. In part, this arose from the fact that the principal members of the Alliance had from the beginning very different views of what the United Nations might achieve and what principles should govern the working of the Charter. But, alongside this, there was the more specific factor of discord arising from the fact that while the League of Nations had been preponderantly concerned with Europe, the main weight of UN activities came to lie in the field of the problems thrown up by the retreat from Asia and Africa of the former European colonial powers. And these in their turn were not at one with each other as to the policies to be pursued within this framework; nor could any of them normally rely upon the support of the United States which demanded full freedom to present itself as a champion of 'anti-colonialism'.[83]

But all these elements in the position of the West are in a sense secondary; the real reason for polycentrism, for the failure to develop a single sense of purpose, and a single set of organs for such a purpose, must be sought elsewhere. It is to be found not in the relatively static aspects of the situation which have so far been sketched, but in certain dynamic factors which could not so readily have been forseen in the early stages of the creation of the new institutions of the West. And there is the added difficulty that arises from the fact that the two principal developments whose interaction has produced the present confused situation are developments of a quite incommensurate kind: on the one hand, the development of nuclear weapons and its consequences for basic strategy, and, on the other hand, the unexpected recovery in the vitality of the European nation-state, or if one prefers it, the discovery that the confident announcements of its obsequies that echoed through the political speeches of the late 1940s were, to say the least of it, premature.

One could therefore bring the whole thing down to the rather simple proposition that the ordinary problems that have faced all alliances are rendered much harder to solve, perhaps impossible to solve, when weapon technology is such that the actual outbreak of conflict could mean national obliteration. To allow the decisions of peace and war to rest in hands other than those of the leaders of one's own nation has always been a difficult thing to accept; it becomes doubly difficult when the price of error is so high. For at this point it is natural for the members of one political society – one nation – to be uncertain whether members of another political society – a different nation – are prepared to take the risks inherent in the use of nuclear deterrence in order to preserve a foreign country's interests or territory. In this respect the decisive change since the Alliance came into being has been in the technological, not the political, field. Originally the assumption was that the United States itself was invulnerable to nuclear attack, and would long retain if not a monopoly at least a decisive superiority in nuclear weapons. The logic of the treaty was that it would assure the European members of the Alliance that American nuclear power would be used to make up for their seeming weakness on the ground. For the Russians to challenge the territorial *status quo* would be to risk for their cities the fate of Hiroshima and Nagasaki. In as far as there were anxieties in Europe about this basic strategy they arose from the desire to make certain that American deterrent power was called in swiftly enough to prevent any advance by the Soviet armies before it came into play.

Otherwise Europe might risk becoming a battlefield between the two great Powers. Western Europe wished to be defended, not 'liberated' again.

But although the debates provoked by such considerations still have their echoes – for public discussion in such matters is likely to be in arrears of the actual state of technological development – the contemporary problem is quite a different one. Since 1957 the vulnerability of the United States to direct Soviet attack has become increasingly manifest and with both sides able to do mortal damage to each other, America's European allies may understandably ask the question as to whether, in this situation, the deterrent is still credible. For what European objective would the United States risk the total destruction of New York or Chicago? And once such questions are asked the answer will tend to be that greater safety lies in making one's decisions for oneself. As an acute analyst of these things has put it: 'the disarray of the Atlantic alliance has been due to an attempt to substitute for one national formula – the absolute guarantee by an invulnerable United States – another national formula – the ultimate guarantee of each vulnerable state by itself.'[84]

The supporters of this line of argument can point to certain aspects of the history of the past fifteen years which appear to lend credence to it. In spite of brave talk about 'roll-back', the United States did not use the period when its armed superiority was unquestionable in order to alter the position in Europe, for instance by bringing about German reunification: not even when apparent opportunities of intervention were provided by the armed risings in East Germany in 1953 and Hungary in 1956. The whole concept of 'negotiation from strength' proved to conceal an underlying willingness to accept a state of affairs which, while clearly compatible with America's interests as a world power, was for different reasons unacceptable to many of its allies. If the European countries had reflected on their own conduct as critically as they assessed America's, they might also have noted their own reluctance to see the strategic dispositions of the Alliance altered in such a way as to increase their risks when, for a period after 1957, its need for more 'diversified means of delivery' made the United States somewhat more a 'consumer' of security *vis-à-vis* the European members of NATO.[85]

At a later stage, the Cuban crisis of 1962 could also be used to fortify the claim that the European members of the Alliance were excessively dependent upon the United States. The immediate reaction of the United States (without consultation with its NATO allies, though not without informing them) to the strategic threat implied in the presence of Soviet missiles on the island took a form which was bound to raise certain questions in European minds. American policy as it developed presented a twofold character. In the first place America's local naval superiority was made use of by agreement with the OAS to prevent further weapons from reaching Cuba. In the second place communications were kept open with the Soviet Government, both directly and through the Secretary-General of the United Nations, so as to make it clear what the minimum objectives of American policy were, and what risks the Soviet Union would run if it endeavoured to thwart them.

Since these objectives were obtained without war – through the removal of the missiles – the Cuban affair must be regarded as an American success. But its reactions upon the cohesion of the Alliance were equivocal. Those who feared that the United States might impetuously involve the world in war without regard for its allies' wishes expressed concern at the risks that had been taken. And even if they admitted that the diminution of American security, and so of the credibility of the deterrent, inherent in the placing of the missiles in Cuba was a threat to all the allies, they could argue that the Castro régime might not have lent itself to the Soviet manœuvre but for the apparent American determination to bring about its overthrow in the name of an anti-Communist crusade. On the other hand those, like General de Gaulle, whose policies rested on the alleged possibility that the Americans might reach an agreement with the Russians over the heads of their European allies, could also claim confirmation for their views from the way in which the crisis was actually solved. Finally, it could be suggested by analogy, that the Russians' decision to override any wishes Castro might himself have in the matter rather than run the risk of nuclear war on his behalf, was a warning of what might be the fate of junior partners even in alliances less centrally controlled than the Communist bloc.

In the light of these developments in strategy the reactions of the different members of the Alliance have followed along different lines as new facets of the position have presented themselves to governments. In the nature of things the initiative has rested throughout with the Americans – as not only the strongest partner, but as the only totally indispensable one. Indeed Americans have been known to complain since the end of 1962 that the Europeans are usually ready to criticise proposals put forward from Washington – such as the 'multilateral' seaborne nuclear force – without suggesting clear alternatives. The Europeans could be accused of as much parsimony in mental effort as they have shown in men and money. Indeed the very language in which this strange and horrifying new world of nuclear strategy is discussed is wholly American in provenance. It was therefore in the wake of the Americans that NATO strategy altered from its early confidence that all that was required was a 'trip-wire' to bring American nuclear superiority into play as soon as aggression was confirmed; to the post-1950 belief in the necessity to be ready actually to fight a war; from this to the short-lived reliance on tactical nuclear weapons as an economical way of providing a balancing factor against Russian superiority in mobilised manpower; and then to the reluctant abandonment of this view in favour of the idea of the need for a wide spectrum of available military 'options' with the corollary that large-scale 'conventional reinforcements would be required'.[86]

While the successive American-inspired strategies can in each case be explained (if not always accepted) on the basis of the then existing stage in weapon-technology, it is hard to resist the feeling that the policies of many of the European countries were based upon a rather simpler set of reactions to their own position. These policies ranged from the determination of a country like Norway to be involved as little as possible in overt preparations for nuclear war, in the hope that a minimum of provocation to the enemy camp might stand it in good stead, to the precisely contrary view of the French that the only safeguard for a country in France's position was to have at its own command means of deterrence so powerful that it would not be worth while an aggressor striking at it, since no possible gains could outweigh the losses that it could by itself inflict upon the adversary. A very special position has been occupied by Germany – the country that would provide the battlefield if there were ever to be a battle; a country barred by treaty from manufacturing nuclear weapons; a country that for itself and for its neighbours cannot but evoke grievous memories as its armed forces increase, and yet cannot help becoming, as far as conventional forces are concerned, by far the most important element in the total power of the West.[87] There are also some feelings that all the European members of the Alliance share to a greater or lesser degree: against the weighty arguments that it would be more efficient and more economical if forces and equipment were provided on a specialised basis which would mean leaving advanced nuclear technology to the Americans, there is to be set the widespread feeling that for Europe to fall in with this role would be to accept a state of technological inferiority not only unacceptable from the military and political point of view, but also carrying disturbing implications for the industrial and economic future of the countries concerned. If one partner supplies space-ships and the others 'boots and barbed-wire' this will have, it is said, the effect of turning an alliance of equals into a relationship between a dominant power and a group of satellites more like that prevailing, at least until very recently, in the Soviet bloc itself.

One suspects, however, that the divergences in public sentiment on strategic questions run at an even deeper level as between the United States and its European partners. American public opinion, while never as bellicose as left-wing demonology in Europe would have it, has nevertheless hitherto been unconvinced that nuclear war is literally 'unthinkable'. The considerations of the great space available for the deployment of weapons or the dispersal of population in North America as compared with Western Europe may have given some degree of strength to the view that the United States could still fight such a war and survive. But whatever its plausibility, it is true that its prevalence enabled the American Government and American military leaders to plan not merely for deterrence but for war itself; to argue indeed that deterrence makes no sense unless one plans for war in the event of its failure. In a relatively recent period one can see the effect of this difference in underlying sentiment in the European reaction to the apparent American move towards a 'counter-force' instead of a 'counter-city' strategy. For a 'counter-force' strategy makes sense primarily in terms of actual conflict; for deterrence, so the Europeans argue, the threat to the Russians' cities should be enough. And in any event, of course, the technical demands of a 'counter-force' strategy are such that no one of the European allies could reckon upon meeting them.

It is possible to exaggerate here: and many of Europe's anxieties arise from a failure to follow the course of the strategic debate in the United States, so much of which is carried out on the public forum.[88] But the impression that more people in America are likely to criticise their government's policy as being too conciliatory rather than as too tough, is certainly a correct one, as the role of the Cuban affair in United States internal politics amply illustrates.

But this fact is not simply the outcome of a different assessment as to the extent to which the advent of nuclear weapons had altered all the assumptions upon which relations between sovereign States had been conducted throughout recorded history. It is also the product of a very real difference in the appreciation of the nature and significance of the 'cold war' itself. For while European observers sometimes attributed the toughness of America's responses to the increasing part played by the professional military in the country's leadership, it has been pointed out that this is to reverse cause and effect. As a recent British commentator has observed:

> the influx of military personnel into government was not the cause but rather the outcome of the American 'wartime' approach to foreign policy in the contest with the Soviet Union. The ebullience of the military and the character of the policy of containment were two hand-in-hand results of the fact that America pictured itself as being at war with the Soviet Union.[89]

Differences about the assessment of the nature of the Soviet challenge, and about the best methods of dealing with it, would not in themselves necessarily promote disintegration within the Western Alliance, any more than national communities are disrupted by divisions over policy between different political parties. Nor indeed is it clear that the differences are necessarily permanent in the form they have taken since 1947. For while it is probably true that 'anti-Communism' will continue to evoke a greater emotional support in the United States than anywhere else in the Alliance, except, perhaps, West Germany, it is also true that the Americans may prove more ready than some others to accept the differentiation between 'international communism' and the Soviet Union as a great power – a differentiation that came so easily to President Roosevelt – should further possibilities of an East-West *détente* present themselves. In a similar fashion, it is unlikely that the causes of disruption are to be found in other issues – economic issues, for instance – where differences of policy or emphasis may be found. No doubt there are great and continuing difficulties in the differences in productivity between North America and Europe; and differences in matters of tariff policy that in part flow from them. The Alliance itself, which imposes expenditure on troops abroad upon some of its members, while others are in receipt of payments derived from this source, helps to complicate the always delicate questions of the financial relations between advanced countries. But the problems that present themselves under both of these heads are again quite clearly capable of solution. Even the issue of anti-colonialism and its successor, the disagreement over the treatment of newly independent and economically under-developed countries look less formidable now than they did a few years ago when the French feeling about the American 'take-over' in Indo-China and the failure of its Allies to support France in North Africa were responsible for strongly anti-American trends in French public opinion, and for a high degree of scepticism about the reality of the Atlantic Community and the utility of the Atlantic Alliance.[90]

What has changed has been not so much the advent of new problems (apart from those of the new strategic situation) as a growing confidence in the ability of individual states to solve them, and consequently an increasing failure to adapt the institutions of the Alliance in order to solve them collectively. One could of course say that the retreat back towards nationalism is on the part of the Europeans no more than an acceptance of the inevitable. If the Communist challenge is still a serious one – in the military sense as well – it could be argued that the common danger should drive the nations of the West into a full-scale merger of sovereignty. It would mean treating Atlantic Alliance, and whatever is understood by the 'Atlantic Community', as the basis for an Atlantic federation. Such an idea has had its advocates throughout the period among public-spirited persons, particularly in Britain and America. But it has also been clear that no government in the United States could contemplate asking for the necessary constitutional changes in the United States itself, for the simple and conclusive reason that such an initiative would make no sense in a country where national self-confidence has never suffered a serious eclipse. And if there is no question of the United States surrendering any part of its sovereignty, then the best that can be hoped for is an improvement in the machinery for consultation which it is difficult for some people to regard as of the first importance.[91]

What makes it difficult to assess the degree to which the alternative solution of national self-sufficiency has now reasserted itself is in part the problem raised by a certain progress towards integration within a Western European rather than an Atlantic framework. Indeed one element of the Gaullist 'myth' is the belief that Europe as a whole should achieve greater independence of America and could become, in effect, a new world power on a par with the Soviet Union and the United States. Such a view could of course be reconciled with the view of the Atlantic Alliance as a partnership between two equal halves, but only if the Americans were willing to abandon their standing attitude of hostility towards the further diffusion of nuclear weapons. And in any event such a conception would presumably not satisfy those who talk about the need for Western Europe to have a foreign policy of its own.

It would be out of place to argue in detail why both weapons technology and Western European attitudes towards the proper disposal of the increments accruing from greater productivity make this conception of a European 'great power' so fanciful to those who do not share the ideology upon which it is based. But it can be pointed out that the development to date of the European Communities themselves – despite the genuinely dramatic innovations which they embody – does not in fact suggest that the community spirit is so dominant within them that their member-states are on the verge of sinking their political identities. Indeed, on the logic by which the credibility of the American deterrent is questioned, it is somewhat difficult to see why a joint European one should be thought more reliable from the point of view of each national entity.

The history of the Communities could most easily be seen as the outcome of a continuous dialogue between those two highly asymmetrical partners, France and West Germany. Each has sought to achieve certain national objectives within this framework. But the objectives are not identical and the Franco-German treaty of 22 January 1963 could be regarded as the culmination of one period of *rapprochement* rather than as the prelude to a further one. For as a penetrating and experienced French observer has remarked:

> Without clearly stating it, General de Gaulle seems to favour a sort of division of forces in Europe: France would handle atomic weapons and Germany conventional weapons. To those who challenge this idea he would doubtless reply that such a shared responsibility corresponds to that which has existed between Americans and Europeans since 1949. He seems not, however, to understand that West Germany will always prefer, if it has to choose, American protection, even at the price of political dependence, to protection by a hypothetical French force, even with political equality.[92]

Similarly, within the Common Market itself, the interests of the Germans in keeping the lines to Britain and Scandinavia as open as possible, and in supporting American initiatives towards a freer world-trading system are, with the departure of Dr Adenauer, likely to be pressed more firmly, as against the French preference for a more tightly knit economic community, building up its own preferential position in certain areas outside Europe.

It would be slightly paradoxical for anyone looking at these developments from a British point of view to indulge in moralistic pronouncements about the failure of continental statesmen to live up fully to the conception of a higher interest, and for refusing to disregard the special position of their respective countries. The

Atlantic Alliance was entered into by Britain under a Socialist government, and its basic assumptions were fully accepted by its Conservative successors. Similarly – despite the application for admission to the Common Market – the limits within which Britain can see herself in a purely European role are fairly well understood. Only a lunatic fringe on the left believes that the defence of Britain can be assured without the protection of the American deterrent; only a lunatic fringe on the right can believe that Britain could afford to act as though the economic integration of Europe was a matter of no concern. On the other hand, of the countries within the Atlantic Community, Britain is one of those that has shown the most consistent determination to follow along its own lines, and to measure the new institutions that have been created primarily by their impact on Britain's own national interests.

It is of course possible to regard some of the policies that have been pursued as foolish, and some of the arguments by which they have been sustained as resting on illusions. On the military side most though not all of the criticisms that can be levied against the Gaullist *force de frappe* might equally well be made against Britain's claim to be in possession of, or to retain, an independent strategic nuclear force. On the political side, Britain's confidence, arising very largely from the special wartime arrangements between Churchill and Roosevelt, that a similar 'special relationship' between Britain and America could be taken as a permanent feature of the international scene survived the suspension of collaboration in the nuclear field with its resultant burdens, the highly equivocal attitude of Mr John Foster Dulles to Britain's security requirements in the Middle East, the more recent American failure to co-operate in ensuring the safe launching of the Malaysian federation by using its economic pull to curb Indonesia, and many other differences. And while one could argue that Britain as a much weaker partner has had little option in this respect, a case could be made out for saying that it has been fidelity to the idea of the 'special relationship' that has made Britain less interested in developing the general machinery for consultation and common planning within the Alliance than it would otherwise have been natural to expect.

But wise or foolish, Britain's policies have reflected a general truth that is at the core of the whole tendency towards polycentrism in the West; and *mutatis mutandis*, probably in the East as well. One need not accept the more exaggerated theories of earlier 'organic' schools of jurisprudence or political science, in order to be aware of the fact that a political community is more closely analogous to a living thing than to a mechanical construction. It can function effectively only in certain ways, dictated by its evolution to its existing form, and it will always devote itself primarily to enhancing its own command over its environment. Other things being equal, a political community will show most activity in those spheres in which it can itself act to the greatest effect. So far from foreign policy always having a prime place in the affairs of a state, foreign policy and defence will always be marginal to the dominant interests of the mass of the people; and therefore the more democratic a state, the more compelling the crisis that is needed if the people are to cease to give priority to their own concerns, and to assent to curtailing their freedom within the confines of a tight alliance or other political system transcending the national group.

Britain during the fifteen years of the Alliance's existence has been engaged both in reconciling itself to a much diminished status in terms of world power, and in making the changes that are needed if this fact is not to have untoward repercussions upon the standard of living of its people and their hopes of social betterment. Much of what requires to be done can only be done by a goverment able to wield considerable authority within the economic field, and this fact prevents any very ready acceptance of supra-national authorities whose priorities might be different. In addition Britain as the centre of the greatest and most populous of the European empires has been the country most closely affected by the process of decolonisation; and because Britain's interests in former imperial possessions naturally outlived the period of political control, the need to secure a peaceful and orderly transition to new stable political arrangements for the post-colonial era has been a call of the first magnitude upon Britain's resources both physical and intellectual.

When so many vital decisions about vast areas in Asia and Africa have been made in London, or through processes of consultation of which London has been the natural and inevitable centre, it would be absurd to pretend that the special position of Britain in the world (quite apart from the special position of Europe) is not a perfectly valid reason for a high degree of polycentrism in the West, or that the viability of the Commonwealth system with all its limitations is not an important Western interest in the broadest sense.[93]

Polycentrism in the West is not, then, in itself a sign of morbidity, though it may take on morbid forms, as in the Gaullist repudiation of the whole idea of a necessary solidarity between the Atlantic countries. It is the natural outcome of the fact that although the countries of the West have much in common, and share many joint interests including their overriding interest in global defence against the Soviet challenge, they are at the same time individual communities, facing tasks both at home and abroad, which they can best perform (perhaps only perform) on their own.

The future does not lie in obliterating diversity, nor in repudiating the steps that have been made towards a more rational order in Europe or in the Atlantic Community; but in finding the correct balance between two sets of needs and sentiments which are equally compelling and equally legitimate.

11 THE CONDITIONS OF COEXISTENCE

Evan Luard

Almost the only unmistakable content of the phrase 'cold war' is its pejorative flavour. Implicit is the belief that while a situation of cold war is infinitely preferable to its warmer counterpart, it is one that, in a better-ordered world, would no longer exist. In considering the conditions for a viable international coexistence, it is necessary to analyse the basis of this supposition. Political struggle is an inevitable feature of all communities. Even in the most homogeneous and compact society, there exist radical, sometimes violent, differences of view concerning how that society, or individual sections of it, should be ordered. There are differing opinions concerning the type of change, the degree of change, and the rapidity of change that is desirable. If this is true even of uniform and long-established political communities, how much more is it likely to be true of an international community, barely yet conceived as a single entity, formed of largely independent units, having totally different cultural backgrounds and political preconceptions? Are there, therefore, good grounds for expecting a condition of coexistence significantly different from that which prevails today? Can cold war ever find conclusion in an armistice?

There are, of course, many fundamental differences between the forms of political struggle undertaken within states and that which takes place between them. The struggle on the international scene, because of the close identification of divergent political viewpoints with existing national states and governments, has a

281

more clearly defined *geographical* basis than most political contests that take place within states. In the wider sphere, too, the ideological, and the political, struggle (the struggle to win adherents, and the struggle to win power, respectively) becomes infected with those loyalties and prides that are already clustered around national entities; and becomes thus in part an *inter-state* contest. Finally, because national states are the ultimate repositories of military power, a political contest in which these may be the protagonists involves dangers and apprehensions of a purely *military* nature, not normally encountered, except in a few unruly states, in other forms of political competition.

All of these, however, are differences of degree, rather than of kind. Even within states, political struggle is at least partly on a regional basis: for example, in the political differences between north and south in the United States, between the various regions of federal states, such as Nigeria, or between more and less developed areas, such as the north and the other regions of Italy. Nor do national loyalties entirely condition ideological affiliations within the international scene: in every country of the world, there exist substantial bodies of opinion whose ideological predilections do not conform to those upheld by their government in confrontations elsewhere. Finally, while the control of central governments over the instruments of power is more complete than that of individuals within them, the numerous civil wars of political origin over the last twenty or thirty years suggest that this is not a difference in kind. For some at least, today, the loyalties imposed by ideology are as powerful as those instilled by national identity. The international community has become already a political structure as compact as most within national states 200 or 300 years ago: and must therefore inevitably form the arena for a single integrated ideological contest.

In analysing therefore how far the desire for 'an end to the cold war' represents a reasonable, or even a meaningful, hope, it is necessary to distinguish between the different elements of meaning implicit in that term. That is, what are those components of the struggle in which it could reasonably be hoped, or expected, that modifications might be brought about? and which are those that represent the inevitable and legitimate expression of political differences within a shrinking international community?

There are two kinds of distinction to be made here. The first is that between the different *types of struggle* comprehended in the term 'cold war'. That expression is used largely indiscriminately, to denote the competition between the contesting governments involved; between the contesting political parties, or other forces, supporting those governments and their views; or between the divergent beliefs with which both governments and parties may be identified. Different considerations may apply to each of these.

The second distinction concerns the different *types of expectation* bound up with the general, vague, and ill-defined desire for 'an end to the cold war'. Though not all of these can profitably be disentangled, it is possible to distinguish two beliefs that are most commonly implicit in such assumptions. The first is the sense that, even if a condition of intense political struggle is an inevitable feature of contemporary international existence, its present form requires modification, if only because of the perpetual threat that its existing comfortable frigidity will be replaced by something warmer and more perilous: this hope, therefore, concerns the *dangers* of the existing struggle. The second is the feeling that, even if there were no military dangers inherent in the type of struggle conducted over the past fifteen years, that contest has assumed a violence and unscrupulousness in style that is insupportable in a world technically at peace: this apprehension therefore concerns the *intensity* of the struggle.

It is necessary to consider each of the three forms of coexistence in relation to these two apprehensions.

What, first, are the conditions under which an acceptable coexistence between different *governments*, ruling sovereign but closely interacting states, and closely identified with conflicting and intensely evangelistic ideologies, may be possible?

It is clearly conceivable that forms of state practice, or principles of international conduct, might exist that were formally incompatible with the possibility of peaceful coexistence. A programme of systematic territorial aggrandisement by one state at the expense of others, for example, would (if one may assume the unwillingness of other states to accept voluntary annexation) in itself be sufficient to destroy that possibility. The decision by more powerful states, that, in any dispute in which they may become engaged, a solution should be sought solely on the basis of armed force is another practice which (assuming the unwillingness of weaker states to accept such a principle) would alone preclude a state of peaceful coexistence. This effect would be the same whether those practices were adopted by one, or by all, members of the international community.

It was to regulate some of those forms of behaviour that were, *in principle*, incompatible with a condition of peaceful coexistence that some of the principles of international law were developed. In its most elementary form this process is to be seen in the increasingly explicit prohibition of 'aggression'. In the early days of international law, writers, such as Grotius, regarded an armed attack on another state as legitimate if its intention was 'anticipatory self-defence', that is to forestall an attack which that state was believed to be preparing. Even if the law proclaimed were formally accepted and obeyed, states were thus enabled to claim justification for an assault, if they could plead a belief that the other power was itself preparing for armed attack. Similarly, international law, until very recent times, and still today according to some authorities, regarded 'self-preservation', including sometimes the protection of 'vital national interests', as adequate justification for attack: and acceptance of the jurisdiction of international courts for the settlement of disputes has often specifically excluded such cases. Thirdly, the right to use force to protect national citizens, in hot pursuit and other forms of armed action in times of emergency have, even until the last few years, often been regarded by international law-courts as a legitimate use of armed force.

But the application of each of these principles (exceptions to the general rule that the initiation of armed force against another state cannot be justified) depends on *subjective* assessments of the qualifying conditions. For this reason they may be in themselves incompatible with a condition of peaceful coexistence. For it is arguable that nation-states wielding a superiority of armed force are likely always to find conditions which, using subjective assessments, they will claim make the use of that force justifiable. And it is partly for these reasons that many international lawyers, and even some governments today, no longer accept many traditional justifications as legitimate.

But in conditions of cold war new justifications have arisen that may be equally incompatible with a state of peaceful coexistence. The justification, still occasionally heard, of 'preventive war', an allowable use of force to forestall a war planned by opponents, is as open to subjective interpretation as the right of 'anticipatory self-defence' long upheld by international lawyers. The continued assertion by some that certain types of war, for example against 'imperialism', or wars of 'national liberation', represent 'just wars', which are permissible, as opposed to 'imperialistic' or other forms of war, that are illegitimate, may equally demand arbitrary assessments of whether a war falls into one or other of these categories. Similarly, the characterisation of certain actions of foreign states, such as the use of violent propaganda, espionage, subversion and others, as 'indirect aggression', has the effect of providing a rationalised excuse, sanctified by international law, for armed action in retaliation. These all therefore represent modern forms of exception to the general principle that the initiation of war cannot be justified. Their dissemination does not necessarily imply their adoption in practice by governments, but it can be argued that it may well, in times of crisis, increase the capacity of governments to find convincing reasons to justify aggressive action.

Such examples are concerned only with the more blatant forms of warlike action. But, even if no principles of international conduct existed to deter them, it is doubtful whether, in the conditions of modern war, such overt assaults would be those most likely to be indulged in by governments. New activities have emerged today even less clearly defined by the traditional concepts of international law. A new class of ambivalent cases has arisen, where the legitimacy or otherwise of government activity remains unclear or disputed.

The vast majority of the cases of armed conflict that have occurred during the period of the cold war have taken place within the boundaries of a single state. Civil wars, colonial conflicts, *coups d'état*, and other internal disputes have been the prime instruments of ideological struggle. On the rights and duties of states in such situations there exists little consensus, either in international law or international practice. On the permissible limits of assistance that may be given to one side or the other in cases of civil war (as in Greece, China, Indo-China, Laos or the Belgian Congo); whether those limits differ in the case of a legitimate and recognised government defending itself against rebellion, and of their opponents (as in the Lebanon and the Congo); whether the limits differ in the case of assistance offered in the form of 'volunteers' (as offered to Korea and Egypt); whether they differ in the case of assistance to a people fighting for the right of self-determination (as in Algeria, Tibet, Goa, Nagaland or South Africa); what are the limits of support that may be given to the dissident nationals of another state outside their own country (as in the case of refugees from Spain, China, Algeria and Cuba); at what point propaganda in favour of a change of political belief becomes subversion in favour of a change of political régime (for example in the propaganda sent by Egypt to Jordan, by the

United States to East Europe, and by China and the Soviet Union to many other parts of the world); whether the situation is different in the case of propaganda by 'private' agencies (as in the case of Radio Free Europe, and other comparable organisations) or assistance by non-government personnel (as in Indonesia or Katanga): on these and other points international law courts provide no guidance. Yet they are those most crucial in effect in the conditions of modern international and political inter-relationships.

Over such problems two questions arise. One is whether or not a particular type, or principle, of behaviour (such as military assistance by governments to revolutionaries in other states) is *in itself* incompatible with a state of peaceful coexistence. The other is whether *differences* on these matters (as over the degree of assistance that may be given to refugees from other states) may themselves carry with them the risk of armed conflict. Where differences exist, an initiative that one party regards as legitimate may be resisted by another which does not. A form of escalation may result, such as has once or twice occurred in Berlin, Laos and elsewhere, by which each move by one party, determined of its own rights, is followed by another from the other, contesting its legitimacy and determined to counter it. Even if a particular class of actions is accepted by both sides as undesirable, it may none the less be felt that certain actions of the other side have given sufficient pretext for their use. Finally, such divergent views of the rights and duties of states may be the cause of miscalculations of the reactions of others.

Thus, though today there exists in certain respects a greater consensus than at earlier times concerning the more blatant types of international transgression, there remain a large number of other forms of activity, on which no understanding exists but which may yet threaten coexistence almost equally seriously. One condition of stable coexistence, therefore, may be the formulation of clearer, more specific, and more detailed, principles regulating the conditions of coexistence than any that exist at present. Every society is dependent, explicitly or implicitly, on agreed principles of interaction. This is as true of the international community as of any other. The *common* elements implicit in that title need not include agreed principles and values governing the internal government of the community's constituent parts. But they must include the general principles to regulate relationships between those parts. And an important condition of an effective international order may be the deliberate and conscious discussion among its members of the principles necessary to sustain it.

The principles evolved may be clear-cut and explicit; or they may be tacit and unwritten. They may be publicly formulated: or privately negotiated. They may be a result of unilateral initiatives; of bilateral understandings (for example between the two major powers today) which are subsequently extended; or of multilateral discussions in the United Nations. They may emerge, almost unnoticed, through the gradual institutionalisation of existing practices; or be deliberately and self-consciously formulated to meet particular needs.

Whatever the institutional framework, the formulation must be the work of nation-states themselves. One of the principal weaknesses of traditional international law, and perhaps the main reason for its lack of influence on governments, is the fact that it was largely devised by international lawyers, working in isolation from governments, and compiling a theoretical framework of law that was not necessarily closely related to the views and attitudes prevailing among the governments of their day. At the same time, because it was always conceived as closely analogous to the law applying within sovereign states, especially the elaborate written statutes of Roman Law, it has never possessed the flexibility to adapt itself to the rapidly changing conditions and aspirations of a fluid international society. Political procedures may be better equipped for the task of building up an acceptable and flexible body of conventions than those of international lawyers could ever become.

Quite apart from the difficulties inherent in the formulation of a code governing inter-governmental relations among representatives of competing and widely diverse ideologies, separate problems arise concerning its detailed application. Some of these may be illustrated from the conduct of the cold war during the last few years.

The first problem is to define principles in such clear-cut terms that no dispute concerning their interpretation arises in specific cases. These difficulties may be exemplified in the situations arising over Berlin in the past years. Here the fluidity of the political situation and the divergence of views are such that the basis of interaction may be perpetually threatened by new developments. Innumerable problems of administration and interaction arise, and each move to meet these may arouse disputes on how far a violation of the existing *modus vivendi* has been committed. Was the building of the Berlin wall in 1961 the stabilisation of an already existing situation, or the injection of a new and dangerous provocation? Is a small alteration in the procedure for the inspection of traffic on the Autobahns, not affecting the numbers involved, a procedural matter within the jurisdiction of the police authority, or an illegitimate interference in freedom of access? Yet in many cases there is reason to believe that, if acceptable conventions could be defined, both sides would be ready to avert the dangers of a major conflict. The first conclusion from such examples is the necessity of detailed and precise understandings and definitions, even on matters of detail. The second is the importance of rapid communication, or formalised procedures for discussion, where differences over such conventions arise.

The next difficulty arises over determining disputed questions of fact. In many cases, where the situation is obscure, action may be taken to counter *believed* initiatives by the other side, or to anticipate action on their part *thought* to be imminent. In Laos in

1960-61, because the country remained remote and little known, there was perpetual doubt about the degree of involvement of either side. None knew in any exact terms whether, or how much, assistance was being afforded by the other to the faction it favoured. Thus, even if there were any definition of the degree, or type, of aid regarded as legitimate, questions might have arisen over what in fact was being afforded. Each increased its own help in one field or another, and the process was only finally broken by the Vienna meeting of the United States and Soviet leaders. Such examples demonstrate the importance of accurate and impartial sources of information to verify the accusations of both sides. UN missions of enquiry may sometimes serve to secure this, and to publicise the results among international organs.

The third difficulty is that of defining which principles among those that sustain the existing coexistence are relevant in particular situations. This may be illustrated from the Cuba crisis of 1962. Here the Soviet Union believed, or claimed, that her action in establishing missiles in Cuba represented no violation of the existing conventions, since it merely balanced earlier action by the US in stationing missiles on her own borders: in these circumstances, the 'violation of norms' (in Mr Khrushchev's own words) occurred through the US declaration of a blockade and the searching of vessels on the high seas. To the United States, it was the Soviet Union, by its provocative installation of new missiles on the US border, which deliberately overturned the existing equilibrium, and so justified violent counter-action. Here both parties could finally be satisfied by mutual withdrawal of missiles from the other's borders. But there cannot be assurance that at moments of crisis understandings of that nature will always be easy to achieve. Once again the conclusion seems to be the need for clearer definitions of equilibrium, and of the conventions required to maintain it, in time of peace as well as of rapid and secret communication at times of crisis.

A fourth and even deeper difficulty concerns agreed *definitions* of the *status quo*. Here the situation in Germany is characteristic. For there both sides seek to sustain the *status quo* in certain areas, but to subvert it elsewhere. The Soviet Union seeks to see the position of the East German Government confirmed and its borders recognised; while it would like to bring about alterations in the status of Berlin. The West would like to see the situation in Berlin maintained; and that in East Germany transformed. This example suggests the importance of the principle that attempts to bring about change shall at least not be exerted against existing administrative boundaries. While the political *status quo* must be inevitably always subject to challenge, the territorial *status quo* may be more readily respected.

A final problem, and perhaps the most complex of all, is that of securing *compliance* in time of violation. Even when powers have accepted a given principle of conduct, where emotions are strongly aroused they may refuse to accept its relevance to their own situation. In such conditions the rational faculty, that of applying general principles to particular situations, is inhibited. For example, many British, French and Israelis, in periods of calm might accept that the invasion of Egypt by their forces in 1956, however provoked, represented a violation of international law as commonly interpreted. But the emotions of each party were so violently aroused by the separate provocations each had received from Egypt that in the moment of crisis the relevance of that principle was not acknowledged. Subjective interpretations provided them with home-made justifications. Here perhaps only the influence of respected outsiders, less influenced by the passions that inspire those most interested, can help in enforcing the principles of international order adopted. It is perhaps significant that even over Egypt all parties involved were finally induced to accept the necessity for withdrawal rather by the weight of opinion and influence raised against them, than of the armed force available to eject them.

It is sometimes asserted that precisely because in times of crisis they will often remain unregarded (as international law has so often been in the past) attempts to create recognised principles of international behaviour are unrealistic and Utopian. But this is to ignore the function that such a code may be expected to perform. There will, no doubt, continue to be occasions, especially when emotions of security are powerfully aroused, when the code appears powerless to influence the behaviour of principal actors effectively. This does not mean that it is without value. Even of international law it might be maintained that, while on many occasions it has been flouted, it has on innumerable others provided a perceptible, and often unconscious, influence on the conduct of nations. Today, especially, when national governments are more concerned with winning adherents and goodwill abroad than in acquiring control of patches of foreign territory, their actions may be conditioned by the norms that are widely accepted elsewhere. The function of a code of coexistence is not to enforce totally new standards of conduct on unwilling governments, but to establish recognised conventions, standard forms, negotiable and adjustable, that may serve as *ad hoc* guide-lines to conduct, often unconscious influences; and so obviate many of those disagreements, often the most violent, arising from rival interpretations of the 'rights' or 'duties' of nations, and of what constitute intolerable violations of accepted standards.

When we turn to consider the relationship between political parties and ideologies, it is rather with the problems that concern the *intensity* than the dangers of the cold war that we are confronted. This results automatically from the fact that it is only governments that control the instruments of power, while the pamphlets and manifestoes with which parties contend arouse less fearsome dangers.

The distinction is not an absolute one, however. Governments are themselves usually controlled by parties. It is not always easy to distinguish between action that derives from the one and from the other. If the Soviet Communist party promotes the recruitment of volunteers to engage in some distant conflict, it is little different from the same action being undertaken by the Soviet Government. If a particular party or group in the United States encourage refugee revolutionaries from a foreign state against their home government, it may be similar in effect to the same action undertaken by the US Government.

Where the actions concerned are those that come easily under the control of governments, the principles of coexistence between ideologies may thus be fairly easily deduced from those that apply to governments. Clearly in such cases it is a condition of coexistence that the commitments arrived at between governments should be extended to cover equally the actions of parties and individuals within their borders. If this were not so governments might merely continue to pursue unmodified policies under cover of party organisations. It is open to question whether this is not already done in some cases. Governments need, therefore, in many cases, not only to undertake not themselves to engage in particular forms of action (for example to supply arms or armed men to a particular country or faction); but to ensure that no individual or organisation within their borders does this. Agreements that prevented action by US armed forces, but tolerated them by the CIA; that limited incitement to rebellion by Soviet Government organs, but tolerated it by Soviet CP organs, would be of little value. Both may equally undermine the basis of coexistence.

In some cases, however, the types of activity undertaken by parties, or other supporters of an ideology, derive specifically from their sources. Where, for example, they concern the attempts by a party member to convert members of other states to the ideology which they favour, or to win power for a faction they support, new considerations arise. Activity by or between parties may be less easily identified and defined than that undertaken by states. Secondly, political contacts may be less justifiably restricted between parties than between governments and others. Finally, difficulties of definition concerning the legitimate limits of intervention arise: at what point does co-operation between parties of similar political faith (as in the Socialist International) become illegitimate interference in the internal affairs of other countries (as by the Comintern)?

It would be tempting to believe it might be possible to solve such problems on the basis of the principle used at the end of the last great ideological struggle in Europe, that of *cujus regio, ejus religio*. It might seem at first sight, that this principle had been to some extent already applied: in the relatively stable political configuration of most European states since 1948, in the readiness of the West to accept the *status quo* in East Europe, the increasing readiness of the Soviet Union to accept the durability of non-Communist régimes, both in the West and among the uncommitted, and in the toleration, by both sides, of partition settlements in Germany, Korea and Indo-China.

Such accommodations, however, perhaps derive more from the mutual strategic apprehensions and interests of the two sides than from the application by them of any consistent principle of political non-intervention. Political and ideological proselytism has been practised more vigorously in some of the opponents' buffer-states than almost anywhere else. And events surrounding the one total exception to ideological stability in the past fifteen years, that of Cuba, reveal the dangers that exist in the twilight areas where political competition remains severe. It might indeed be maintained that, far from any acceptance of long-term political partition, attempts at political subversion have increasingly replaced the more blatant direct assaults of previous ages.

It is certainly totally unrealistic to hope for some form of ideological live-and-let-live. A hundred, even fifty years ago, political parties and political régimes might have been expected to remain indifferent to the political complexion of regions in other parts of the world. The convention of non-intervention in internal affairs rested partly on this assumption. While it might still, if suitably defined, be applied to the actions of governments, it cannot today reasonably be applied to those of political parties. Political aspirations are directed almost as much towards bringing about changes in neighbouring states as at home. Because knowledge of neighbouring states is so much clearer, because their allegiance may be so important to great powers in both military and prestige terms, the political complexions of each state must today often be of importance to others. New means of communications and political organisation and persuasion make efforts at conversion an attractive alternative to military action. Within a closely interacting international community, inter-state political activity by parties is inherent in the process of change.

Nor is it easy to find any solution in the principle that political activity be confined to those recognised as 'constitutional' under the existing system. For in many cases the very basis of political dissension concerns the constitutional system itself. For Western parties to accept the principle of restriction of speech and publication in other parts of the world is to ask them to abandon one of the foundations of their political faith. For Communist parties to accept the principles implicit in the constitutions of some Western countries involves a negation of their *raison d'être*. In both cases attempts to subvert the existing system derive from the deepest levels of political conviction.

But the fact that political disputes will continue to be conducted across the borders of national states is not to say that understandings concerning the conduct of those disputes are impossible. They may be less easy to achieve than those that concern government activity. Because the dangers of provoking a holocaust are here less intense, the incentives to understanding are smaller. Because sometimes the practices in question derive from fundamental political convictions, they may be less easily influenced. Yet it may be no more impossible to find the basis of principles governing relations between parties than between governments.

The states of Africa have recently agreed on the proscription of propaganda designed to incite to the assassination of political leaders and 'subversive activities on the part of neighbouring states on other states'. The Latin-American countries have formulated charters designed to lay down the limits of political activity between states. Even between East and West, discussions have been held on the content of foreign broadcasts and their jamming, and the legitimate limits of propaganda. Cultural agreements on the number of films, books, newspapers, students or scientists exchanged, on the circulation level of foreign magazines, serve in a crude form to define the terms on which political dialogue takes place between states. All of these represent embryonic attempts to arrive at an agreed basis of political interaction.

In some cases the problem is to define the boundary between legitimate political persuasion and illegitimate political subversion. In so far as the subject of concern is related to *mood*, no understandings can be effective. Moral fervour is one of the few conditions it is by definition impossible to legislate against. In this sense there will always be cold wars on some topic or another within the world's political arena. All that may be done is to denote the specific *actions* that may result from those moods, whether by nations or parties or individuals, that may be made the subject of taboos. These may condemn specific activities: for example the explicit exhortation to war or assassination. Or they may define the limits of action; clandestine radio stations of *emigré* revolutionaries may be forbidden, while propaganda in the form of books, films or newspapers, is permitted.

But conversely, given that freedom of information and persuasion is a widely accepted value within the modern world, certain understandings may relate to positive levels of communication, as well as negative: of this type are agreements on the prohibition of radio-jamming, limiting censorship, encouraging tourist and student exchanges. Attempts to dam up the flow of opinion may be almost as dangerous and provocative as attempts to influence it by threat or abuse. And the free flow of news and views may indeed be the condition of achieving the mutual tolerance and understanding on which coexistence might ultimately be based (the intellectual isolation of China today may well be a factor in promoting her present unco-operative mood).

There exists one factor within the modern world that may slightly reduce the difficulties in finding a basis for political coexistence. This is the readiness of all, among Western powers as among Communist, among Latin-American oligarchies as among Middle-Eastern dictatorships, to pay lip-service to the principle, if not the practice, of 'democracy'. Interpretations of that term vary so widely that it is open to question whether the same word can legitimately be employed to cover all. But it remains true that in the final resort all accept the principle, widely challenged until modern times, that authority is dependent on the expressed will of the people governed. And it is an observed fact that violent conflicts concerning legitimate political authority take place today primarily in countries where there has been, for whatever reason, legitimate reasons to doubt how far existing authorities could claim to enjoy popular support, (as in Laos and the Belgium Congo, Algeria and Cyprus, Greece and the Lebanon, Hungary and Cuba). They rarely take violent form in states where the existing government has been elected by democratic procedures. In such states even revolutionary parties, such as the Communist Party, increasingly become converted to the parliamentary road.

If, therefore governments under challenge by violence were to invite international inspectors to supervise or confirm their election (as has been done already, for example, in Greece, the Lebanon and Malaysia, the Cameroons, and in plebiscites elsewhere) they might serve to relieve some of the pressures raised against their authority. If governments with long traditions of democratic procedures, as in West Europe and North America, were to invite UN supervision as a normal practice, it might be more commonly adopted elsewhere. The nominal allegiance to democracy provides, indeed, almost the only available basis for the type of consensus that may, ultimately, be the condition of harmonious co-existence in the purely political sphere. For, in the final resort, it is only agreement on the means of effecting change that can resolve those disputes that surround basic political principles and values.

But certain of the problems concerning political coexistence are especially intractable. These are those that derive, not merely from differences concerning the *methods* of political activity; but from those surrounding the *matter* of political belief.

At first sight it might seem absurd even to consider the problem of coexistence between beliefs. A contest of beliefs is a fundamental human condition that cannot sensibly be influenced. Only those who share the preconceptions of the inquisition can reasonably wish to abolish it. Many would hold, indeed, that it is precisely the lack of a sufficiently vigorous competition in belief in certain areas, on both sides of the Iron Curtain, that exacerbates existing differences. If, in East Europe, all political faiths received everywhere the same rights of expression, and all parties the same rights of activity, some of the actions that now originate elsewhere would no longer be felt necessary. If Communist parties were everywhere allowed a place within the existing political framework, they might be more ready to conduct their activities within prescribed constitutional limits.

Yet this does not alter the possibility that there may exist classes of belief that in themselves affect the chance of lasting coexistence. While coexistence between conflicting, even contradictory, beliefs must be regarded as inevitable, some beliefs may themselves inhibit, even preclude, coexistence between governments or parties. While it is the behaviour of governments and parties that is ultimately at issue, this may derive directly from the beliefs they hold. A recognition that this is so may prove useful if only for purely analytic purposes. It may even, in time, help to modify the basis of belief itself.

The beliefs here concerned are only those fundamental elements of the faiths of each side that represent a relatively stable element within their world-view. It does not include those of less deep-lying character, which are unlikely to modify the possibilities of inter-state or inter-party coexistence, which have been already considered.

A fundamental belief of this type, clearly precluding peaceful coexistence between states, is that held among many early Moslems in the fundamental duty of the faithful to prosecute a jehad, or holy war, against all infidels wherever situated. In any universe where all are not of a single faith, any belief of this character must preclude the possibility of peaceful coexistence. Virtually none today uphold such a principle of faith. But the claim, briefly put forward in parts of the West during the fifties, to the right of 'liberation' of certain territories, held to be enslaved by unrepresentative rulers, would be similar in effect if actively put into practice. It is perhaps unlikely that even the most ardent protagonists of that doctrine ever intended that it should be fulfilled in action. But, as in other cases to be considered, the dissemination of the belief alone may be disturbing in its effects. For once more the justifying accusations, resting largely on subjective assertions, could readily be made by any government as the pretext for attacking almost any other.

A second basic belief that could, if widely held and consistently practised, threaten the basis of coexistence is one which seeks to revive the ancient concept of 'just wars'. This too, as already seen, opens the way to subjective assessments of whether or not the conditions for the initiation of such wars exist.

Both China and the Soviet Union at present uphold the concept of the 'just war', though with varying degrees of intensity and conviction. The Chinese Government have expressed their view as follows:

> As Marxist-Leninists see it, war is the continuation of politics by other means, and every war is inseparable from the political system and the political struggles which give rise to it . . . Lumping just wars and unjust wars together and opposing all of them indiscriminately is a bourgeois pacifist, and not a Marxist-Leninist approach. . . .[94]

The Soviet Government do not deny that there can be just wars. In their reply to this Chinese letter they quoted earlier words of Mr Khrushchev:

> There will be wars of liberation as long as imperialism exists, as long as colonialism exists. These are revolutionary wars. Such wars are not only permissible, but even unavoidable, since the colonialists do not grant independence to people voluntarily.[95]

This statement seems to identify revolutionary wars with wars against imperialism, and so by implication excludes other forms of revolutionary war. The Soviet leaders have also reaffirmed earlier statements that 'a real possibility to exclude world wars from the life of society will appear even before the complete victory of socialism on earth, while capitalism still remains in parts of the world'.[96] They have pointed repeatedly to the dangers of nuclear war, 'because the nuclear bomb does not adhere to the class principle and destroys everything within the range of its devastating force'.[97] And, more recently, they have denounced the Chinese leaders for 'trying to impose on the international working-class and the national liberation movement the theory of spreading revolution by means of "revolutionary wars".'[98] They nevertheless maintain, at least in some of their statements, the thesis that there may be just wars, for example, against colonialism.

Neither side specifically justifies the *initiation* of 'just wars'.

Often inherent in the context is the premise that these are a response to warlike actions on the part of 'imperialists', or to support armed action already undertaken. They do not explicitly uphold support for just wars in the form of arms, men or other assistance, by outside governments, though this implication is likely to be drawn elsewhere. There is, too, a marked distinction to be drawn between words and actions (it is striking that at the very moment when Chinese revolutionary militancy was at its height, in action China has remained indifferent to the colonies on China's own doorstep, was largely inactive in Laos, and allows the Vietcong guerrillas to remain dependent on the arms they are able to capture). Yet once again the theoretical position upheld may be an important influence on action at moments of crisis. It may affect the acts of other governments. And the attempt to distinguish generally between just and unjust wars tends to create the presumption that this applies to the initiation of such wars, and therefore to serve as a pretext for virtually any armed action desired.

Finally, there is a third belief, related to this but perhaps more fundamental in nature, whose propagation must equally serve to endanger a condition of peaceful coexistence. This is the belief that it is the duty of parties and governments to promote and support revolution all over the world. External support for revolutions could indeed, in a world as closely inter-related as today's, merely become an alternative method of aggression. With modern means of communication it becomes as much an international activity as military invasion. It is equally one involving violence. And it becomes an especial danger to international peace when publicly advocated by governments themselves.

Such advocacy was once a fundamental element in Communist doctrine in all countries. In the days of the Comintern it represented an important component of Soviet foreign policy. For a considerable period today, however, the Soviet leaders appear to have recognised its dangers. They have denounced the 'export of revolutions'. The Comintern and its successor have been disbanded. In August 1963, at the time of the signing of the test-ban treaty in Moscow, Mr Khrushchev declared:

> No treaties and agreements between states can overcome the radical contradictions which exist between the two coexisting social systems. But we, the Soviet people, firmly stand by the principle that social and class questions, the questions of internal, social and political systems, should be settled not through or between states, but by the people of every country without any interference from outside.

In their letter to the Central Committee of the Chinese Communist Party of 16 July 1963, the Central Committee of the Soviet Party declared that 'the working-class and its vanguard, the Marxist-Leninist parties, endeavour to carry out the socialist revolution in a peaceful way, without civil war', while the Chinese, by identifying revolution with armed uprising, denied 'the possibility of using peaceful forms of struggle for the victory of the Socialist revolution' . . . The Soviet Union itself, and many Communist parties elsewhere, have recognised the legitimacy of 'the parliamentary road to Socialism'.

Even today the attitude of the Soviet Union is not totally unequivocal. Soviet statements declare that 'It is the task of the working-class and the Communist parties to make the maximum use of the opportunities now available for the peaceful road of a Socialist revolution not involving civil war; and at the same time to be ready for the non-peaceful method, for armed suppression of the resistance of the bourgeoisie.'[95] Similarly, some Western powers in certain of their broadcasts and other propaganda to East Europe, for example, especially at the time of the Hungarian uprising, or in British propaganda to Egypt during the Suez invasion, have sometimes advocated revolution by foreign populations. The Egyptian Government have made similar calls in broadcasts to other parts of the Middle East and Africa. The Nationalist Chinese Government have made such policies a basic element of foreign policy.

The Chinese Communist party have declared more emphatically:

> ... The people still living under the imperialist and capitalist systems, who comprise two-thirds of the world's population need to make revolution. .... In the imperialist and the capitalist countries, the proletarian revolution and the dictatorship of the proletariat are essential to the thorough resolution of the contradictions of capitalist society. ... The proletarian party and the revolutionary people must learn to master all forms of struggle, including armed struggle. They must defeat counter-revolutionary armed force with revolutionary armed force wherever imperialism and its lackeys resort to armed suppression.[99]

The view of the Soviet party and of many European parties that accept the possibility of a 'peaceful transition' or even a 'parliamentary transition' to socialism is contested.

> Communists will always prefer to bring about the transition to socialism by peaceful means. But there is no historical precedent for peaceful transition from capitalism to socialism. .... The vanguard of the proletariat will remain unconquerable in all circumstances, only if it masters all forms of struggle—peaceful and armed, open and secret, legal and illegal, parliamentary struggle and mass struggle. ...[99]

Yet even here there is not a complete absence of consensus. For, as the quotations here clearly reveal, the contest is not in fact over what is the most desirable means of change. All parties agree that peaceful change is preferable, where it is available. All agree, similarly, in the equally fundamental principle that, however chosen, governments should be representative of their people. If it could be shown, therefore, that other processes of change are not only more peaceful, but better capable of securing representative government, the rationale supporting revolutionary theories is destroyed. Belief in revolution dates from an age, above all the first half of the nineteenth century, when most governments were not, nor even claimed to be, representative. The object of revolution was, in the words of the *Communist Manifesto*, 'to win the battle for democracy'. Revolutions have in practice (like civil wars) occurred in the past overwhelmingly in countries that did not possess representative governments. Where such a situation persists today it is not easy to show persuasively that belief in revolution is untenable. But where systems that can clearly be seen to be better equipped to provide representative government exist, this may cease to be true.

It is not difficult to demonstrate that governments established by revolution are not *necessarily* representative. It might even be shown that they may be less likely to be representative than those chosen by electoral methods. It can be shown how arbitrarily, unpredictably and inefficiently revolution functions as a selector of governments. Certainly governments themselves have a vested interest against revolution as a method of change. Sometimes their people may share this interest. Only a very widespread and profound degree of dissatisfaction with existing régimes is likely therefore to assure popular support for revolutionary dogmas. But so long as no evidence exists that governments are based on popular consent, there can be no finally persuasive argument that revolution is immoral. Once more only the introduction of a system by which elections, or referenda, are held, perhaps under UN supervision, could render revolutionary appeals finally unconvincing and unprofitable. Where these are refused, revolution may continue to be advocated, at least by parties if not by governments.

Any of these three beliefs would appear therefore to endanger the basis of coexistence. It is true that such dogmas may give little guidance to the policy of governments in concrete situations. The existence, and the active dissemination, of attitudes of this type serve to influence the total environment within which decisions are reached. They may always become an influence on action tomorrow, if not today. They may affect reactions in times of crisis or indecision. They may be quoted as justification or encouragement by interested parties or factions when policy is disputed. If the fundamental beliefs on which conduct is based are unfavourable to a harmonious coexistence between states, it becomes even less likely that their day-to-day actions, with all the pressures and passions to which these are subject, will remain co-operative. Precept remains a perpetual incitement to practice.

Possibly a clearer understanding of the implications of particular beliefs may finally induce some modification of belief itself; as, already, recognition of the dangers of nuclear war, or of any major conflict, has apparently induced some adjustment of Soviet attitudes to revolution and war. The understanding and encouragement of such recognition by third parties (as in the recent declaration by African states) may act as an important influence. Above all, it is possible that the practice and precept of the United Nations may serve to encourage a clearer awareness of the implications of particular beliefs, and to build a consensus concerning the conditions of ideological coexistence between political dogmas, as well as national states and parties, within the modern international community.

It is sometimes asserted that there can be no basis for a stable order within the existing international community because of the widely varying systems of valuation that prevail within it. The term 'valuation' is one that may cover a broad variety of meanings. If used to refer to attitudes towards specific and limited principles of international behaviour, the statement merely represents an alternative formulation of what has here been suggested. But if used, as is normally the case, to denote attitudes on far more fundamental points of ethical and political principle, it is most doubtful whether (except in the few specific cases here considered, none of which relate to the most fundamental levels of belief) this

12 THE COLD WAR AND THE FUTURE

Sir William Hayter

What do we mean by the expression 'cold war'? Obviously it means different things to different people. In Soviet terminology it denotes something which other people, the capitalist governments, do. In Moscow, the expression 'cold war' is used to describe attacks upon, or criticisms of, Communist achievements or policies. The Soviet Government itself, in its own view, does not take an active part in the cold war, but is the victim of it. It is in this sense that we must read Soviet appeals for the end of the cold war. These appeals mean that other people ought to change their existing policies; they do not necessarily imply any change in present Soviet policy.

The Western definition of the cold war is rather different, and perhaps less one-sided. It would include the Western activities which, to the Russians, are its sum total. But it would also include various Soviet activities which the Russians would exclude, and which, if they acknowledged them at all, they would describe under other headings – 'the international class struggle', for instance, or 'competitive peaceful coexistence'.

Indeed the last term, as used in Moscow, comes very close to coinciding with what most people in the West mean by the cold war. They mean, by and large, a state of affairs in which nations, while renouncing the methods of hot war as a means of settling their disputes, nevertheless pursue these disputes by all other means open to them, with a view, not to the ultimate settlement of the disputes or to a general reconciliation, but to a victory of one side over the other. Mr Khrushchev has summed up the mentality of the cold war, as those in the West understand it, in his speech to the Central Committee of the Soviet Communist party on 21 June 1963. 'Hatred of class enemies', he said, 'is necessary, because it is not possible to become a good fighter for your people, or for communism, if one does not know how to hate enemies. . . . Yes, comrades, a harsh class struggle is now in progress throughout the world.' He reverted to this theme during the ceremony at the signature of the test-ban treaty, when he spoke of 'the unquestionable historical fact that two opposite social systems exist in the contemporary world. No treaties or agreements between states can overcome the radical contradiction which exist between the two social systems.'

Again, speaking to journalists who attended the Third World Meeting of Journalists, he said, as reported in *Pravda* on 27 October 1963:

> Peaceful coexistence between states with different social orders is necessary and possible. But this does not in any way mean that there should be peaceful coexistence between oppressed peoples and their foreign enslavers, or between the workers and their exploiters. Here, there can be no understanding, there can be no reconciliation, since each people has the sacred right to wage a struggle of liberation for the expulsion of the foreign enslavers, to overthrow the rule of internal enslavers. We are in favour of peaceful coexistence between states with different social and political systems, but, on the other hand we render support to the people who are fighting for their independence, for their liberation.

In June, 1964, during his visit to Denmark, Mr Khrushchev was asked by a journalist when he expected ideological coexistence would be possible. He replied 'under communism'. Mr Khrushchev could hardly have said more explicitly that in his view the cold war must continue until communism is established everywhere.

It should be emphasised that these are four recent personal pronouncements by the present Soviet leader, the man whom many people outside Russia believe to be the strongest partisan there of some kind of reconciliation with the West. These quotations make it plain that though he is anxious to avoid war he, like all the other Soviet leaders of whose views we have any knowledge, is in fact a convinced believer in the permanence of the ideological struggle.

It is here that an essential difference appears between the attitudes of the two sides to this phenomenon which the West calls the cold war, but for which the Russians have other names. We believe that this struggle ought to end, and could end, without the defeat and destruction of the other side. Indeed some people who should have known better recently proclaimed that it had ended, or had even been 'won', when the test-ban treaty was signed. We in the West think there is no reason why the two parties to this dispute should not recognise its futility and settle down to live peacefully side by side, respecting each other's rights, ideas and institutions and accepting the reality of ideological coexistence.

This is not the Soviet idea at all. Ideological coexistence is fiercely repudiated. When the Chinese accuse the Russians of favouring it, the vile charge is indignantly denied in Moscow. The Moscow Declaration of 1960, still accepted as authoritative by both sides to the dispute, lays down that 'peaceful coexistence of countries with differing social systems does not mean reconciliation of Socialist and bourgeois ideologies. On the contrary, it implies intensification of the struggle of the working class, of all the Communist parties, for the triumph of Socialist ideas.'

This distinction is important. The West is full enough, now, of cold warriors, and in their various ways the Western countries pursue the cold war with varying degrees of vigour. But nothing in our doctrine or our outlook on life requires us to regard it as permanent, or as bound to continue until one side or the other collapses. On the contrary, we often try to persuade ourselves that it is over, with the forces on both sides intact. This is an inconceivable solution to the Russians. For them one side, presumably theirs, must win in the end; the reconciliation of communism and capitalism is a logical absurdity which cannot occur; one will always seek to destroy the other and will, in the end, succeed in doing so; unconditional surrender is the only possible conclusion.

If this is so, and as long as this is so, it does not seem likely that the future of the cold war will be very different from its past. The struggle will continue indefinitely, though it may take different forms. It can presumably only end either when one system does effectively destroy the other, or when the side that believes in the inevitability of such destruction abandons this belief and accepts the view of the other side that reconciliation is possible. There is no sign that the present rulers of the Soviet Union are likely to abandon this belief, which they have indeed recently reiterated with obvious sincerity and passion, and which is an essential element in the way of thought on which their whole system is based. Pressure of opinion, or economic developments, within the Soviet Union could conceivably modify their attitude, or the present rulers might be replaced by others with different ideas. But there is no easily demonstrable reason to expect this, and it is probably better to continue to act on the assumption that it will not occur, at any rate within any period for which reasonable plans can be made.

Assuming, then, that the Soviet leaders will continue to act in the way in which they say they are going to act, and in which their most cherished beliefs indeed require them to act, what forms can we expect this struggle to take from now on? Since, for reasons which will emerge subsequently, the Soviet side generally has the initiative in this struggle, it is perhaps best first to attempt some analysis of probable Soviet strategy, before trying to plot the course of Western policy.

First of all, it is obvious, so obvious as hardly to need stating, that the Soviet leaders wish the cold war to remain cold. They do not want major hostilities to break out between the major Powers. There are, presumably, certain interests which they would not surrender even if their defence involved a serious risk of major hostilities. But they are firm believers in the deterrent and believe their own to be effective. Furthermore, they have now apparently convinced themselves that this desire to avoid major war is shared by the capitalist West, and that it is therefore possible to work out with us practical technical arrangements to reduce the risk of such war, of which the test-ban treaty is the first example. Others may follow.

It is here of course that they differ most from the Chinese. The Chinese put the avoidance of major war lower in their priority list, and are entirely unconvinced that the 'imperialists' have made up their minds to avoid it or that one can make agreements with them about it. They differ, too, from the Russians about the next category, minor wars. On this the Russians have been ambivalent; they deny the possibility of 'limited war', but they also say that 'just wars', mainly wars of liberation of colonial areas, are possible. What they seem to mean here is that wars may be all right provided that the forces of the major Powers are not directly involved. The Chinese would of course go much further. But this hardly matters, for the time being. The Chinese are obviously quite incapable of waging a major war at present, and even the kind of minor war against their immediate neighbours in which they have indulged themselves in the past will become increasingly risky for them as their lack of Soviet backing becomes more obvious.

The Russians, at any rate, seem to have abandoned hot war as a means of achieving national aims. They must sometimes regret this. It will be remembered how Stalin explained to the Yugoslav leaders, before the breach, that it had been impossible to establish communism in France and Italy, despite the massive Communist

311

parties in those two countries, because unfortunately the Soviet armies had been unable to advance so far. But these good old days are over, and other methods must be sought.

The first and most avowable of these is what is commonly described as 'economic competitive coexistence'. This is the process by which the Soviet Union or China, or other communist countries, are expected to 'catch up and overtake' this or that capitalist country by this or that date in this or that sphere of production. When this occurs, capitalism will presumably throw up the sponge, humiliated by its defeat. Communism will then be established everywhere and the millennium will start. If this were all, we should not have much to worry about, for a number of reasons. First, no one who has had recent experience of living standards in Communist and capitalist countries would expect that the moment when the latter will have to hang their heads in shame at the contrast with Communist opulence is particularly imminent. Secondly, even if Communist economic standards do eventually catch up or even overtake those of the West, there is no particular reason why this alone should induce us to change our whole way of life and succumb to communism; we might think that certain other factors, other, that is, than the strictly economic, might still favour our system. Finally, Soviet economic progress ought to be a matter for encouragement, and not alarm, to sensible people in the West. Russia ought always, on the basis of her natural resources and population, to have been one of the prosperous countries of the world. She has been held back from this in the past by incompetence of one kind or another, and if she does really overcome this incompetence and manages to ensure a high standard of living for her people this should make her a better, not a worse, neighbour to the rest of us, and might even enable her to spare more than she now does to help the less developed areas of the world.

So if economic competition were Russia's only weapon in the cold war we should not have much to fear. But of course it is not.

What else is there? There is no doubt that the process of decolonisation offers great opportunities to Moscow. The Soviet leaders' detestation of colonialism is deep and perfectly sincere, and is quite untempered by the fact that they themselves now control the largest colonial empire remaining in the world. To them the countries of Central Asia and the Caucasus, which look so like colonies to us, are merely slightly backward countries which they are 'leading forward to socialism'. So their consciences are untroubled, and they can indulge their genuine distaste for other people's colonialism in all-out attacks on it in the United Nations and elsewhere and in unreserved support for all the most extreme demands of Asian and African nationalism. This naturally gains them much popularity in colonial and ex-colonial territories, and there is no doubt that they are able now to exert influence in places which, even a decade ago, were right outside their sphere of action. But this influence, though wide in extent, is limited in depth; the void left by retreating Western imperialism has been filled not by Communist control but by local control. The former colonies, as they progress to independence, have with the solitary exception so far of North Vietnam remained independent of Moscow or Pekin and have evolved forms of government that are not Marxist. So the question whether the newly emergent countries will or will not adopt communism really merges into the larger question of the ability of communism to come to power in the rest of the non-Communist world.

This brings us back to the 'harsh class struggle' which Mr Khrushchev assured us is now in progress 'throughout the world'. What are the prospects of Communist success in this struggle, and what can the Soviet Union do, what is she doing, to contribute to this success? The public Soviet view is that this struggle is entirely a matter for the working class within each country, and officially the Soviet leaders have repeatedly asserted the necessity for non-interference in the internal affairs of other countries. It is indeed obviously true that communism can only succeed in a given country if the internal conditions there are propitious, and that it cannot be imported wholesale by any method other than Soviet military occupation, which however successful in the past is unlikely to be feasible in the future. But it is equally obvious that if favourable conditions exist in a country for a Communist success its 'working class', a specialised term in this context, can count on Soviet assistance in a number of forms, and that if a Communist régime is successfully established open Soviet support will be forthcoming. *Kommunist*, the leading theoretical journal of the Soviet Communist Party, in its fourteenth issue for 1963 clearly defined the party's role in this context. We are here told that the Communist Party of the Soviet Union, sees its international duty not in working out or in imposing ready-made schemes of revolutionary struggle on our foreign comrades, but in passing on to them its experience, in giving them the fullest possible help and active support for the realisation of the policy they had themselves chosen.

It is worth considering where situations of this kind are likely to develop. Europe is the least probable area, even though it contains two of the largest Communist parties outside the Communist world. There was a time when a massive spread of communism in Europe seemed likely. When the Second World War ended the Communists found themselves disposing, for the first time, of genuine popular support in Europe. They profited by the prestige which the USSR had won in the war, by the discredit into which the old-established régimes and parties had fallen in many countries, by the shattered state of most European economies and by the impression of irresistible advance which the Soviet Union created. In France and Italy especially, the mass Communist parties which appeared with the end of hostilities soon found themselves participating, often in key positions, in the government of their countries. But Stalin's post-war policies soon alienated the sympathies of all but the inner core of the faithful, the build-up of the Western alliances and the Western economies destroyed the myth of Soviet irresistibility, and the older parties and régimes regained their prestige and their powers and managed to extrude the Communists from the Governments. Since then the European Communist parties have seemed stagnant or declining, still useful no doubt to the Soviet Government for the purpose of espionage or sabotage, but increasingly remote from power or the prospect of it, a situation which the Soviet Government has had little or no power to alter and which seems likely to persist.

In other parts of the world the situation is very different. Mass parties, with the important exception of Indonesia, are still rare. But the kind of conditions that could lead to Communist success can be found in many places. It used to be Communist doctrine that communism could only come to power by revolutionary means involving the violent overthrow of the existing régime. This doctrine was modified by the Twentieth Congress of the Soviet Communist party, and access to power by parliamentary process is now accepted as possible. It is not perhaps, in the present state of the world, very likely. But there are many other roads to power, not all of them involving violence or even illegality, though the latter are by no means ruled out; the gradual penetration of key organs of government, for instance, or the penetration of other parties, or the capture of the leadership of popular movements whose original or ostensible aims had nothing to do with communism, or, eventually, the support of guerrilla forces. All these grow out of internal conditions which the Soviet Union cannot itself create. But once they begin to grow they can undoubtedly count on all the aid that the Soviet Union can furnish, in money, advice, personnel, the support of front organisations and, where appropriate, arms; and once power is achieved, as in Cuba, full-scale and open backing will be given, to the extent that conditions permit. That this is so is confirmed by *Kommunist*'s previously quoted summary of the party's role and by Mr Khrushchev's remark ('we render support') to the World Meeting of Journalists.

Cuba is of course the classic example of an operation of this kind. But there are other countries where similar conditions prevail, which could lead to similar results, more particularly in Latin America and South-East Asia, and perhaps in Africa. Stalin used to be relatively reluctant to encourage the establishment of Communist régimes in areas remote from his military perimeter; he thought they could not be sustained, and so, though he pushed out his empire as far as his armies could reach, he seldom attempted serious operations in remote areas. Khrushchev is perhaps both more and less inhibited. He realises that the days when he could hope to establish communism by force or violent subversion in countries on his own borders, as Stalin tried to do in South Korea or Greece for instance, are over; the régimes in these countries are under American protection, and so too dangerous to attack. But he also realises that Communist régimes in areas remote from the Soviet borders, once they are firmly established, come under his protection and so may be too dangerous for the Americans to attack, as perhaps Cuba is.

It looks, therefore, as if we may be in for a period of some adventurism in Soviet policy, with Cubas or attempted Cubas an essential element in it. It certainly seems that a considerable number of successful Cubas might lead to a real and dangerous change in the balance of power in the world. A slight doubt could persist here because it is no longer necessary to take it for granted that a newly established Communist régime would in all circumstances remain loyal to Moscow. In Stalin's time it was certain that all Communist régimes and all Communist parties not in open schism were faithful allies. Events in Albania and in Cuba itself, quite apart from China, have of course made this more uncertain. But on the whole it is probably safer to assume that a Communist party which achieved power now, particularly in an area normally under American or Western influence, would tend to lean heavily on Moscow.

The situation which such Communist achievements of power

would create for the West would be all the more disagreeable through being, on most calculations, irreversible. Communist governments are almost never overthrown from within, however unpopular they may become and however slight the popular backing they may originally have had. The only example to the contrary is Hungary in 1956, and this was a very special case, arising in circumstances very unlikely to be repeated elsewhere. Thus the West must assume that a Communist régime, once established in a country where other institutions and other international relationships used to prevail, is virtually certain to remain in power in perpetuity unless attacked and overthrown from without.

So to sum up the Soviet side of the cold war, it looks likely that what the Moscow Declaration called 'the intensified struggle of the working class', what Mr Khrushchev has called 'the harsh class struggle', will continue indefinitely. It will not have much effect within the industrialised countries of the West, though these countries will be its principal targets and will be the object of constant verbal attack in the United Nations and elsewhere. These attacks will vary in volume and intensity in accordance with the particular tactical situation, but they will be unlikely to cease. Meanwhile, opportunities for the establishment of Communist régimes in less developed countries may well occur, and will be taken if they do. Such régimes will probably be irremovable by internal forces. They are likely, but not quite certain, to be loyal to Moscow.

We must now consider what the Western reaction to this Soviet policy is likely to be. As has been suggested earlier, it is more likely to be reaction than initiative. There are people in the West, more particularly in the United States, who believe that the destruction of communism everywhere, and the overthrow of the Communist régime in the Soviet Union itself and of course in China, are legitimate objectives of Western policy. This belief is in itself a reaction. Nothing in American history or political thought before the rise of communism in Russia ever suggested that the overthrow of a particular political system or régime, at any rate in a country outside the Western hemisphere, would or could become an American governmental objective. But the Soviet doctrine of the incompatibility of communism and capitalism and of the inevitable destruction of one by the other inevitably produced its rather crude counterpart in American thinking. This thinking is so far, luckily, minority thinking; it has never entered into governmental doctrine, even in the Dulles era. There are good reasons for this. The first is the already mentioned incompatibility of such ideas with normal American political attitudes. The second is the obvious impossibility of achieving any such objective in modern conditions.

It seems unlikely that this minority view could ever become dominant in American politics. Even if Republicanism of the Goldwater stamp came to power its objective would seem to be more the withdrawal of American political activity abroad than its intensification. And certainly no such ideas are likely to be entertained in any other Western country. Thus it seems very improbable that the overthrow of communism in Russia and China will ever take its place among the objectives of Western policy in the cold war. In fact, the West is, and is likely to remain, on the defensive.

There is nothing unnatural or even necessarily disadvantageous about this. Generally speaking, Western feelings about communism in Russia and China are that, distasteful as it is to most of us, it is not, in what it does within its own borders, our affair. Its policy and behaviour there are no more objectionable, in themselves, to Western opinion than were those of Tsarism in Russia or the Kuomintang in China. Both of them were in many ways repugnant to liberal opinion in Europe and the United States; but no one in London or Washington ever thought seriously of trying to overthrow them. The same would be true of communism in those two countries if it were not for its universalist pretensions, and Western objection is primarily to these pretensions and not to Communist rule in its home bases.

This clear distinction is somewhat blurred by the situation of the satellites. It is one thing to accept with equanimity the continuance of communism in Russia and China where its establishment, however rough and violent, was an indigenous phenomenon. It is another to acquiesce in the perpetuation of communism in countries into which it has been imported on the bayonets of the Soviet Army. But Western objections to communism in the satellites are primarily moral rather than political, and there is little that can effectively be done to sustain them. We may look upon Russian insistence on a glacis of subservient states on her Western borders as rather old-fashioned in conditions of modern warfare, and wonder whether the expense and odium of propping up these unpopular régimes are repaid by any sufficient military or political advantages to the USSR. No doubt the disappearance of Communist régimes in countries where they have long been established would be a temporary blow to Communist prestige, but this would seem, to outside observers, to be more than compensated for by the credit Russia would gain from liberating what everyone outside the bloc regards as captive nations. But the Soviet Government sees this otherwise, and as long as this remains so there is nothing that the West can do, as events in Hungary in 1956 convincingly demonstrated. Thus our continuing objections to Soviet control of the satellite countries, since we can in fact do nothing about them, do not invalidate the contention that our position in the cold war is essentially defensive.

There is a general dislike of conducting purely defensive operations in warfare. But military metaphors are often misleading. Cold war is not war. It cannot be won, it can only be sustained. And there is no inherent reason why it should not be sustained indefinitely, or as long as both sides want it to go on. In these conditions there is nothing wrong with a defensive position. It remains to consider what this Western defensive position could be.

It is, in a way, more difficult to come to a conclusion about this than about Soviet policy. It is useless for us to tell the Russians what they ought to do; we can only try to guess what they will do, basing this guess on what we know of their past behaviour and their doctrines, which are more precise and more immutable than the shifting political sands on which Western policy is built. When we come to consider Western policy in the cold war there are two lines we can follow; we can consider either what the Western powers are likely to do or what we think they ought to do, and these two strands are quite likely to become entangled. Perhaps it is best to start with the first; if a little of the second, a little moral admonition, creeps in later that cannot be helped.

It seems unlikely, then, that the Western powers will seek to carry the war into the enemy's camp. The reasons for this have already been examined. No doubt we shall try to keep open as many lines as possible to the Soviet people. This will be resisted by the Soviet authorities, as recent events have shown, and with more complete success by the Chinese. Both are closed societies, with very nearly complete control over the communications media in their territories. This control is exercised with ruthless absolutism by the Chinese; but the more awakened Soviet public, encouraged by the post-Stalin liberalisation, fluctuating though it has been, is beginning to demand and is occasionally permitted to receive little shafts of light from outside the ring-fence. Curiosity about Western ideas is of course enormous and is fed by the difficulties placed in the way of its gratification. These difficulties, incidentally, are in themselves a refutation of the belief that the West, as contrasted with communism, lacks a dynamic creed. The Communist authorities would not go to all that trouble to keep out powerless ideas, and in fact the West has a set of beliefs which seem to strike the Soviet and Chinese leaders as highly dangerous, judging by the precautions they take to keep them away from their people. It is not difficult to see why. In the stifling atmosphere of Communist conformism there is something wickedly attractive about ideas, so banal to us, such as legalised opposition, possibilities of an alternative government, free criticism of the men in power. Again, if you live in a state of personal insecurity, the rule of law can be a seductive concept.

The very charm of such notions is a sufficient guarantee that the Communist leaders will make great efforts to keep their peoples immunised from them. Nevertheless, there are still ways in which some Western ideas can get through the barriers. The most effective is no doubt broadcasting, now unjammed at last. Another is worth brief consideration. The Soviet Government seems to attach great importance to the free circulation of the information bulletins put out by its Embassies and other official organisations. It is a little hard to see why this should be so, since all the information contained in them is freely available to the Western public from other sources. But in fact they do seem to pin great faith to them, and this fact is exploitable. A strict insistence on reciprocal rights can ensure that, in return for permitting the circulation of Soviet official publications in the West, at least some official Western publications can circulate in the Soviet Union; and since these official Western bulletins are the only source of information about the West available to the Soviet public the balance of advantage is in this instance clearly on the Western side. To use these channels for attempts to weaken the Soviet régime would of course be as unprofitable as it would certainly be short-lived. On the contrary, the picture conveyed should be one showing the Western countries as stable, prosperous and friendly, only anxious to live in peace with the Communist countries if the latter would agree.

This is as far as the cold war within the Communist countries is likely to go. Within the Western countries, where communism is stagnant or regressive and is likely to continue so as long as the present favourable economic conditions persist, official action is likely to be confined to the control of Communist espionage and of its preparations for sabotage; the rest can be safely left to public opinion, which by now knows the form. From time to time real questions about which people in Western countries have genuine feelings, such as nuclear disarmament in Great Britain or reunification in Germany, will be worked up and distorted by various forms of Communist insinuation. Externally, alarming crises such as those which periodically affect Berlin can be created by Soviet governmental action. But these crises, internal and external, tend to become routine; the internal ones usually die down when the Communists show their hand, and the external ones are beginning to fall into an accepted pattern; the recurrent Berlin crises, for instance, are assuming a more and more formalised air. The real battlefield is likely to be in the uncommitted countries.

It is here, as has been suggested earlier, that the main Communist effort in the cold war will be deployed, and it is here that Communist successes are most likely. The Communist Powers have certain real advantages in this field. Almost all the uncommitted countries are either, in Asia or Africa, former colonies of the Western powers or, in Latin America, resentful of what they regard as Western economic imperialism. They are thus inclined to regard the West with a suspicion which does not extend to Russia or China. Aid from the West, infinitely more bountiful than any received from any Communist source, is apt to be regarded as simply the righting of an ancient wrong and thus engenders neither gratitude nor sympathy for Western ideas.

This is of course no reason for not giving aid. Indeed, the winning of gratitude and sympathy ought not to be the reason for giving aid. Aid should be given because it is needed, and because the present division of the world into the increasingly enriched and the increasingly impoverished is intolerable, immoral and incompatible with the principles upon which Western civilisation is supposed to be based. It may be that generous Western aid, by halting the slide into the abyss of poverty, may remove the feeling of despair that sometimes breeds communism. It may also be that this kind of aid will, by promoting industrialisation, create the seed-beds in which communism is supposed to grow best. These considerations are really irrelevant. Aid to the under-developed nations ought not be considered as a cold-war operation at all, but as an imperative moral necessity. But it is of course true that the withholding of Western economic aid would be likely to have a disastrous effect on the Western situation in the cold war, and that to this rather negative extent a generous aid programme from the West is a contribution to its cold-war activities.

Is there any more positive action that the West can take in relation to the uncommitted countries, which are of course roughly coterminous with the under-developed countries? We have seen that the Communist powers are likely to take any available opportunities to win allies among them, subservient allies if possible. Ought the Western powers to do the same?

Here we come to the question of neutrality. Foster Dulles used to treat neutrality as a form of juvenile delinquency, a dangerous and immoral phase through which a new country would pass before it saw the light and allied itself with the forces of righteousness. In this as in so many respects Dulles's thinking was a mirror-image of that of his Communist opponents. Moscow Radio for instance, broadcasting a year or two ago to the Arab world, told its listeners that 'between the policy of the West and that of the Socialist countries there is a gap which cannot be narrowed or bridged by any theory. The theory "Neither East nor West" is one which serves the interest of imperialism and aims at depriving the young States of the East of the strong support of the Socialist countries'. Since Dulles's day the West has moved forward, and now is ready to accept neutralism or non-alignment as a valid position in international affairs, while the Russians and still more the Chinese remain intransigent about this. The West might be well advised to do more than tolerate neutrality; they could well advocate it. They have enough allies. Their interests do not require that the uncommitted countries should follow their policies or support their strategic plans, nor is the form of government or economic organisation within these countries of any particular interest to them. All that they need is that these countries should remain independent of Moscow or Peking and should not subserve the strategic requirements of these capitals. On this basis neutrality should suit them very well, and they have a strong common interest with the uncommitted countries in promoting this, in sustaining their non-commitment.

One of the more positive ways in which this can be done is through the United Nations. To the uncommitted countries, the United Nations represent a channel through which they can receive aid and still be without commitment, not only economic aid, but technical, military and administrative aid. It is therefore immensely important to them that the United Nations should remain financially sound, efficiently run and detached from the power struggle. It is also very much in the interests of the West that this should continue to be the case.

The United States Government, to judge by the Congo affair, seems to see this more clearly than the British Government. The Soviet Government does not see it at all. They have made frequent proposals that would disrupt the organisation of the United Nations, they are largely responsible for its financial difficulties, and they do not at all like it as a channel for aid: 'We prefer to render assistance on a bilateral basis,'Mr Khrushchev told the General Assembly in October 1960, and this has been regular Soviet policy. An all-out attempt to sustain the autonomy, the independence and the powers of the United Nations would be a programme by which the West could gain much credit among the uncommitted countries, and in which the Communist powers are unlikely to outbid them.

However, it is probably true that, for all the West may do to establish its general credit with the uncommitted countries, by not withholding aid, by defending neutralism, by supporting the United Nations, situations may yet arise in individual countries in which a Communist take-over occurs or appears imminent. Such a take-over, as has been said, is likely, if not halted, to become permanent. Cuba is a good example of this. A revolutionary régime which on the face of it appears both shaky and incompetent has been able, owing to its Communist stiffening, to survive not only a rather ineffective attempt at counter-revolution from without, with half-hearted American support, but also the public humiliation and withdrawal of its Soviet champion. It owes its persistence very largely to the efficient Communist techniques of seizing and maintaining State power, which can operate, if necessary, quite independently of popular support. The Castro régime of course has such support now, but if it should lose it there is no reason to suppose that it will lose power as well. The West has to reckon with this factor of permanency, once Communist control is established, and it therefore becomes relevant to consider whether there are any circumstances in which the West is likely to consider itself justified in intervening to prevent the establishment, or the consolidation, of Communist power in a country where it does not now exist.

This somewhat embarrassing question is probably unanswerable. Certainly no general answer can be given; one can only say that it will depend on the circumstances of each individual case, on the degree of popular support communism seems to possess, on the importance of the country concerned, on the prospects of subservience or otherwise of the new régime to Moscow. The precedents are confusing. In Cuba, after the first fiasco, the Americans confined themselves to preventing the installation of Soviet nuclear weapons, leaving the pro-Communist régime intact. In Guatemala they went rather further, but no forces intervened. In Jordan and the Lebanon, in the summer of 1958, British and American armed forces were sent in at the request of the local governments to deal with threats that were partly internal and partly external. The threats in these cases were of course not Communist, but the action taken perhaps provides a useful guide to the probable limits of Western reactions to comparable cases of threatened Communist take-over. These limits are likely to fall well short of the Soviet action in Hungary in 1956, where Soviet forces were openly sent in to overthrow a legitimate government that was still Communist, but slipping, and to replace it by a more subservient Communist régime, the members of the former government being subsequently arrested and executed. Similar action was threatened in Poland but not in the end taken, because it proved unnecessary.

It seems very unlikely that we shall see the United States Government, or any other Western government, taking action of this degree of ruthlessness. Their own public opinion would prevent them. Probably the furthest they are likely to go is to support with armed forces a legal government still in power, or at any rate in being, which asked for such support. The actions taken by the Americans in South Vietnam and South Korea, and by the British and American Governments successively in Greece, provide precedents for this. In Cuba the difficulty was that there was no indigenous government, before the Castro revolution, sufficiently respectable to earn the support of the United States Government. The position might well be different in, say, Venezuela.

To sum up the Western side of the cold war, then, the probabilities are that the West will remain on the defensive and that no serious attempt will be made to carry this war into the Communist camp, though channels for communication of a non-subversive type will if possible be kept open to the Soviet people. The Western powers will not have too much to worry about in their own territories, and can deal according to established procedures with such crises as the Communists may manufacture there. The real struggle will come over the uncommitted countries. There the West possesses, with some liabilities, some valuable assets, and can win much credit by fostering neutrality and the

United Nations. But with all this, further Cubas may occur. Not all may be preventable, and the West will have to decide in each individual case how far it can and should intervene.

It is always difficult, in writing about the future, not to see it in terms of the present, as a mere extrapolation of existing factors. This difficulty is not less in dealing with the cold war than it is elsewhere. Reasons have been given for thinking that the present will, in fact, continue into the future, the chief of these being the nature of existing Communist régimes and the character of Communist doctrine. The Soviet régime, at least, is certainly evolving. But nothing in its evolution so far has given Western observers any real excuse for the optimism some of them sometimes display about the future of the cold war. That the régime is, in certain internal respects, notably more liberal than it was ten years ago is undeniable. But there is no reason to believe, and every reason to doubt, from the utterances of the existing Soviet leaders themselves, that this liberalising tendency will have any effect on their view of the relationship of communism and capitalism. Till this changes, the cold war will go on.

New and unforeseen factors may appear to alter all this. A change of leadership in Moscow might have this effect. But this is highly speculative. No one knows who will succeed Mr Khrushchev or in which direction, backwards or forwards, the régime will move when the change of guard has taken place. The only safe basis for calculation about Soviet policy is what we see and hear in Moscow now, and this gives no great basis for optimism.

Another new and unpredictable factor is the ultimate effect of the Sino-Soviet dispute. Some people in the West believe this to be so profound and fundamental that it will in the end drive the Russians into the arms of the capitalists. Mr Khrushchev, in spite of the abuse showered on him from Peking, does not agree, and nothing in the course of the dispute so far bears it out. China will no doubt seek to outbid Moscow in championing

327

the cause of the under-developed countries, and may even seek to set herself up as the champion of these countries in opposition to the Soviet Union. But to suppose that this will induce the Russians to ally themselves with the West is to misunderstand both the motivation of the Soviet leaders and the nature of the dispute. When Mr Khrushchev and his colleagues contemplate the world scene (and of course for the greater part of their time their gaze is elsewhere, on their own internal problems) they do not regard the Third World, or even the Chinese, as enemies against whom they need allies in the West, but as their own natural allies against the capitalists who have somehow gone astray and must be brought back into the fold. Indeed, their dispute with China is about means, not ends. Moscow and Peking agree that capitalism and imperialism must be destroyed and that communism must triumph; they disagree mainly about how this is to be accomplished. The dispute is bitter and far-reaching, but none of its developments until now gives any reason to suppose that it could have any fundamental effect on the continuance of the cold war between the Communist countries and the West.

After so many quotations from Mr Khrushchev perhaps it is not inappropriate to conclude with one from the other side. Reporting to the American people on his discussions with Mr Khrushchev in Vienna, President Kennedy said:

> We have wholly different views of right and wrong, of what is an internal affair and what is aggression, and, above all, we have wholly different concepts of where the world is and where it is going. . . . We believe in a system of national freedom and independence. He believes in an expanding and dynamic concept of world communism. The question is whether these two systems can ever hope to live in peace, without permitting any loss of security or any denial of freedom to our friends. However difficult it may seem to answer this question in the affirmative as we approach so many tests, I think we owe it to all mankind to make every possible effort.

NOTES

2 THE RISE OF COMMUNIST POWER IN THE FAR EAST

1. *See* Vladimir Dedijer, *Tito Speaks* (Weidenfeld & Nicolson, London, 1953, p. 331; Simon & Schuster, New York, 1953).

3 GERMANY

2. *See* the suggestive and provocative work of Lionel Kochan, *The Struggle for Germany 1918-1945*, (Edinburgh University Press, 1963; Aldine Publishing Company, Chicago, 1963).

3. Address to the American Historical Association, 30 December 1962 (XLVI, *Department of State Bulletin*, No. 1175, 15 January 1962, pp. 83-88).

4. Kochan, *op. cit.*, p. 93-94. According to the former German Communist, Wolfgang Leonhard, these negotiations actually got to the stage where laudatory articles were prepared for the Free German press in Moscow; W. Leonhard, *A Child of the Revolution*, (Collins, London, 1957; Regnery, Chicago, 1958), pp. 254-56; I am unable to accept Dr Kochan's thesis that this episode was mainly intended as a means of pressure on the West, despite the cogent arguments he advances to support it.

5. Sir Llewellyn Woodward, *British Foreign Policy in the Second World War*, (HMSO, London, 1961), pp. 524-27.

6. The actual circumstances are still obscure. At the crucial meeting of the European Advisory Commission on 26 March 1945, the British delegate introduced discussion of the dismemberment of Germany with the remark that the British Government regarded this not as a binding commitment, but rather as a last resort to be adopted if other means of restraining a revival of German strength should seem insufficient. This led the Soviet delegate to make a statement which the British and American delegates apparently interpreted as indicating that the Soviet Government had abandoned the idea. With that theory they were able to convince their governments that any further discussion of dismemberment was pointless. Stalin later told Hopkins that Soviet abandonment of the idea, made public in his Victory Address on 9 May, was influenced by his conviction that British and the United States had abandoned

the idea – on his version of the vital meeting of 26 March, the Soviet representative had protested the British view, but had been driven to accept it by the American failure to follow his lead. *See* Herbert Feis, *Between War and Peace, The Potsdam Conference,* (Oxford University Press, London; Princeton, New Jersey, 1960), pp. 237-38; Woodward, *op, cit.,* p. 527.

7. *See* F. Roy Wilks, *The French in Germany, 1945-1949,* (Stanford, 1962), p. 21.

8. *See* Hugh Dalton, *High Tide and After, Memoirs 1945-1960,* (Frederick Muller, London, 1962), p. 115.

9. *See* Bevin's views on Germany: 'the Germans were more dangerous than the Russians and soon everyone will be courting them'; recorded in Dalton, *ibid.,* p. 189, diary entry of 4 January 1947.

10. Leonhard, *op. cit.,* p. 359.

11. This was virtually admitted by Lord Pakenham, the British minister responsible for German issues, in his speech of 24 September 1947, when he said that the Potsdam conception of a united Germany 'had foundered on the reluctance of the Soviet Government to honour the postulates on which it is based and above all to honour its obligations to operate Germany as an economic unit'.

12. It is a comment on the way in which world opinion was shortly to change, that by 1954 of these five powers only Brazil would be regarded as 'neutral', Iceland and the Netherlands being members of NATO, Pakistan of CENTO and SEATO, and Poland of the Warsaw Pact.

13. In his speech to the Socialist Congress, 30 March 1946, Wilks, *op. cit.,* p. 39. Similar proposals had been advanced at various times by Mr Bevin.

14. *See* Sir Anthony Eden (Lord Avon), *The Eden Memoirs, Full Circle,* (Cassell, London, 1960; Houghton Mifflin, Boston, 1960), pp. 59, 61, 75.

15. Eden, *ibid.,* p. 59.

16. *See* Marshal Bulganin's remarks to Eden at Geneva, Eden, *ibid.,* p. 301.

5 THE MIDDLE EAST

17. Winston Churchill, *The Second World War,* Vol. VI (Cassell, London, 1954, p. 579; Houghton Mifflin, Boston, 1960).

18. For his theories, *see* A. Benninger in W. Z. Laqueur, *The Middle East in Transition* (Routledge, London, 1958, p. 398; Praeger, New York, 1959).

19. For development between 1919 and 1955 *see* W. Z. Laqueur, *Communism and Nationalism in the Middle East* (Routledge, London, 1956; Praeger, New York, 1957).

20. At the end of the World War, Persia was by far the largest Middle Eastern producer (16 m. tons in 1945). By 1947 Saudi Arabia, and by 1948 also Kuwait were approaching this figure. Production for 1950 was: Persia 31·7 m. tons; Saudi Arabia, 25·9 m. tons; Kuwait, 17 m. tons; largely owing to the Palestine War and consequent transit difficulties, Iraq did not begin production of similar dimensions until 1952.

21. Harry S. Truman, *Memoirs*, Vol. I (Doubleday Edition, 1955, p. 552; Hodder & Stoughton, London, 1955).

22. For an account of all these negotiations *see* Elizabeth Monroe, 'Mr Bevin's "Arab Policy" ' in *St Antony's Papers, No. 11*, 1961, pp. 12 ff., or, in greater detail, George Kirk, *The Middle East, 1945-50* in the Chatham House Survey Series.

23. Conversation of 9 December 1950, as recorded in the *Egyptian Green Book* on the negotiations of 1950-51.

24. When Egypt's case for the evacuation of British troops was heard (and lost) in 1947.

25. *Al Misri*, 5 July 1950.

26. *Al Sarkhat*, 14 February 1952, quoted in François Laurent, 'L'URSS et le Moyen Orient' in *Orient* (Paris), July, 1957, p. 30.

27. Text in *BBC Summary of World Broadcasts*, No. 431, January 1954.

28. For a fuller summary *see* Geoffrey Wheeler, 'Russia and the Middle East' in *International Affairs*, July 1959.

29. For the consistency of British disdain for Egypt, *see* Elizabeth Monroe, *Britain's Moment in the Middle East: 1914-1956*, particularly Chapters 3 and 8 (Chatto & Windus, London, 1963; John Hopkins Press, Baltimore, 1963). Also Sir Anthony Eden, *Full Circle*, (Cassell, London, 1960), p. 437.

30. Speech at Iowa State College, 9 June 1956.

31. *Full Circle, op. cit.*, p. 422.

32. Text of his letter to Eden of 5 November 1956, reprinted in Chatham House Documents volume, 1956, pp. 288-89.

33. Speech of 22 March 1959.

34. *See, e.g.*, Eisenhower's letter to Neguib of 15 July 1954. Quoted in Charles D. Cremeans, *The Arabs and the World*, (Praeger, New York, 1963), p. 299.

35. Percentage of Egypt's trade with the Soviet bloc (value figures) 1955: imports, 7%; exports, 22%; 1959: imports, 32%; exports, 54%; 1959 was the peak year.

36. US Senate Hearings (85th Congress, First Session) Jan.-Feb. 1957, Vol. I, p. 168.

37. Text as approved on 9 March 1957, in *Documents on US Foreign Relations*, (Harper for the Council on Foreign Relations, 1958), p. 201.

38. White House statement of 29 October 1956.

39. Cairo Radio Home Service, 9 June 1961. Quoted in the *BBC Summary of World Broadcasts*, Part IV, No. 662, 12 June 1961.

6 SOUTH-EAST ASIA

40. For a full account of the Philippine situation, and indeed of all Communist developments in the area, *see* J. H. Brimmell, *Communism in South-East Asia* (Oxford for Royal Institute of International Affairs, 1959; Oxford University Press, New York, 1959).

41. *See* Jeanne S. Mintz's chapter on 'Marxism in Indonesia' in the symposium, *Marxism in South East-Asia*, ed. Frank N. Trager (Oxford University Press, 1960; Stanford, 1960); and Arnold C. Brackman, *Indonesian Communism* (Praeger, New York, 1963).

42. The most circumstantial account of the MCP's activities is contained in Harry Miller's *Menace in Malaya* (Harrap, London, 1954; Praeger, New York, 1954).

43. For an account of Communist insurrections in the context of other post-war rebellions, *see* Brian Crozier, *The Rebels* (Chatto & Windus, London, 1960; Beacon, Boston, 1960).

44. Perhaps the best account of these battles is given by Bernard Fall in *Street without Joy* (Pall Mall Press, third revised edition, London, 1963; Stackpole, Harrisburg, Pa., 1963).

45. *See* A. Doak Barnett, *Communist China and Asia*, (Oxford University Press, 1960; Harper, New York, 1960), pp. 291 ff.

46. *See* Donald Lancaster, *The Emancipation of French Indo-china* (Oxford University Press for Chatham House, 1961, p. 326; Oxford University Press, New York).

47. *See* Brian Crozier, *Peking and the Laotian Crisis: an Interim Appraisal*, and *A Further Appraisal*, in China Quarterly of July-September 1961, and July-September 1962, respectively.

48. *See* Ellen J. Hammer: *The Struggle for Indo-china*, (Oxford University Press, London; Stanford University Press, 1953), p. 271.

49. *See* Allan B. Cole *et al.*, *Conflict in Indochina and International Repercussions* (Oxford University Press, London, 1957; Cornell, New York, 1956) the most complete documentation of the cold war in Indo-China yet compiled.

50. The Vietnam Lao Dong (Workers') party, which was set up in February 1951, in effect filled the gap left by the tactical dissolution of the Communist Party of Indo-China in 1945.

51. In a speech in the United Nations General Assembly on 27 September 1963.

7 AFRICA

52. *Narody Afriki*, ed. Potekhin, 1. 1. Ol'denigge, D. A., Moscow, 1956.

53. i.e. President de Gaulle's referendum to French West Africa and French Equatorial Africa on independent status within the community, in September 1958. Guinea opted out of the community.

54. On 28 November 1963, the ninety members of staff of the Soviet Embassy in Leopoldville were declared *personae non gratae* and two members were evicted on charges of active subversion allegedly carried on from Brazzaville.

55. *West Africa*, 9 November 1963, p. 1257.

56. Problems of communism, December 1962.

57. 'We do not carry on what is in many cases a long and bitter fight for freedom just in order that we may become jumping jackasses, which wait to

see what a western or eastern power will say about an affair before automatically doing likewise or taking an opposite line. We must treat ourselves with the same respect that we demand from others.' President Nyerere, Moshi, 2 February 1963. Reported in the *Guardian*, 12 February 1963.

58. *Pravda*, 14 June 1963.

8 LATIN AMERICA

59. *See* the conflict in Brazil over the buying out of American interests. Leonel Brizola challenged a 'moderate' solution by a doctrine of expropriation based on the right of the 'people' to any industry aided by government concessions, e.g. the automobile industry and the press, because both enjoyed tariff advantages (*Hispanic American Report*, XVI, No. 6, August 1963, 627).

60. *See* the brilliant remarks of A. O. Hirschman in *Latin American Issues*, (Twentieth Century, New York, 1961), pp. 33 ff.

61. For a collection of essays characteristic of the Communist line, *see* 'Gegenwartsprobleme Lateinamerikas' in *Deutsche Aussenpolitik* (Sonderheft 11/1961.) Its day-to-day applications can be studied in the Mexican periodical *Política*.

62. *See* his classic statement of U S strategic and political interests in the Caribbean, in Henry L. Stimson, *American Policy in Nicaragua* (Scribner, New York, 1927).

63. For a brilliant description of the successes and failure of U S Latin American policy in these years, *see* Bryce Wood's *The Making of the Good Neighbour Policy* (Columbia University Press, New York, 1961).

64. The roots of these 'populist' parties lay in the radicalism of the thirties; in the forties it was represented by the quasi-radicalism of Perón in Argentina or Vargas in Brazil.

65. For the history of communism in the sub-continent *see* R. J. Alexander, *Communism in Latin America* (Rutgers University Press, New Brunswick, N. J., 1957).

66. For an account of the Arbenz régime, *see* R. M. Schneider, *Communism in Guatemala 1944–1954* (Praeger, New York, 1959).

67. C. del Campo, 'La revolucíon guatemalteca' in *El movimiento contemporánea de liberación national y la burguesia national*, ed. A. Rumianstev (Prague, 1961).

68. For instance in Guatemala the Communists may have gained in attraction when Ubico classed all opponents of his dictatorship as Communists.

69. The Communist Party was still a legal party when Castro made his first revolutionary *coup*: the attack on the Santiago barracks in July 1953.

70. Blas Roca's evolution from his position in the fifties can be traced in the later editions of his *Los Fundamentos del Socialismo en Cuba*, (Havana, 1960).

71. For a critical examination of the invasion, *see* Ted Szulc and Karl E. Meyer, *The Cuban Invasion* (Praeger, New York, 1962).

72. W. Rostow in *Modern Guerilla Warfare*, ed. F. M. Osanka (Collier Macmillan, London, 1962; Free Press of Glencoe, New York, 1962).

73. For these agreements and their consequences, *see* E. Lieuwen, *Arms and Politics in Latin America*, 1961. Chapters 8 and 9 (Oxford University Press, London; Praeger, New York).

74. For a characteristic piece of left-wing pessimism see R. Ramírez Gomez 'El informe Prebisch y la realidad Latinoamericana' *Cuadernos Americanos* XXII (1963), pp. 7-72. For a balanced view, see Sir George Bolton 'Problems of Economic Development in Latin America' in *International Affairs*, vol. 39, no. 2 (1963), pp. 184 ff.

75. Claudio Veliz, 'Obstacles to Reform in Latin America' in *World Today* (January 1963, 19, No. 1).

76. Galo Gonzalez in the Tenth Congress of Chilean Communist Party.

77. *See* Khrushchev's Report to the Supreme Soviet of the USSR, 12 December 1962, in *Diversity in International Communism*, ed. A. Dallin, (New York, 1963), pp. 670 ff. Paper tigers, Khrushchev insisted, now had atomic teeth.

78. 'The Differences between Comrade Togliatti and Us', editorial in *Jen-min jih-pao*, 31 December 1962.

79. Hence the Communists are accused of 'betraying' the invasion of December 1959 to Stroessner once its offer to join the movement was rejected. The CP nevertheless has a strong following among the exiles in Argentina.

9 THE POLARISATION OF THE COMMUNIST WORLD

80. The facts on which this account is based are documented partly in '*The Sino-Soviet Conflict*' by Donald S. Zagonia (Princeton and Oxford, 1962); in 'The Sino-Soviet Dispute', documented and analysed by G. F. Hudson, Richard Loewenthal and Roderick MacFarquhar (published by *China Quarterly*, London, 1962); in *China Quarterly*, No. 11, 1962 (*The November 1960 Moscow Meeting; A Preliminary Reconstruction*, by William E. Griffith; and in my own Penguin Special: *The New Cold War: Moscow v. Peking*, London, 1963).

10 POLYCENTRISM IN THE WEST

81. For a recent symposium of views on the subject, see the special number (Vol. XVII, No. 3) of *International Organisation*, entitled 'The Atlantic Community: Progress and Prospects', and edited by Francis O. Wilcox and H. Field Haviland, Jr. It is also available as an independent book (Praeger, New York, 1963).

82. The above paragraphs represent only the barest summary of views which the present author has developed further in a number of books: *Europe and the Europeans: an International Discussion* (Chatto & Windus, London, 1957); *The Great Powers* (Allen & Unwin, London, 1958; Macmillan, New York, 1959); *New Dimensions in Foreign Policy* (Allen & Unwin, London, 1961; Macmillan, New York, 1961); *The United States and the Unity of Europe* (Faber & Faber, London, 1963; Brookings Institution, Washington, DC, 1963).

83. The literature on the United Nations is distinguished for quantity rather than quality; an exception must be made for the brief but admirable study by H. G. Nicholas, *The United Nations as a Political Institution* (Oxford University Press, London, 1959; Oxford University Press, New York, 1959).

84. George Liska, *Nations in Alliance* (Oxford University Press, London, 1962; John Hopkins Press, Baltimore, 1962, p. 283).

85. Coral Bell, *Negotiation from Strength* (Chatto & Windus, London, 1962, p. 173; Knopf, New York, 1963).

86. For a thoughtful analysis of these developments, *see*, e.g., R. E. Osgood, *NATO, The Entangling Alliance* (Chicago University Press, 1962).

87. For an informed view of NATO's problems by a leading German of the opposition, *see* Helmut Schmidt, *Defence or Retaliation* (Oliver & Boyd, Edinburgh and London, 1962; Praeger, New York, 1962).

88. For an admirable and suggestive summary of this debate, *see* Robert A. Levine, *The Arms Debate* (Oxford University Press, London; Harvard University Press, Cambridge, Mass., 1963). For a sample of the conflicting attitudes, *see* the symposium *Arms and Arms Control*, edited by Ernest W. Lefever (Thames & Hudson, London, 1962; Praeger, New York, 1962). For a recent European assessment of the situation, *see* the report of an Anglo-German-French study group presented in A. Buchan and P. Windsor. *Arms and Stability in Europe* (Chatto & Windus, London, 1963; Praeger, New York, 1963).

89. Michael Donelan, *The Ideas of American Foreign Policy*, Chapman & Hall, London, 1963, p. 100.

90. *See* on this highly illuminating essay by Alfred Grosser 'France and Germany in the Atlantic Community' in the special number of *International Organisation* referred to (Vol. XVII, No. 3).

91. For a recent discussion of a possible approach to a greater degree of integrated planning and production within the NATO framework, *see* the second edition of Alastair Buchan, *NATO in the 1960's* (Chatto & Windus, London, 1963; Praeger, New York, 1963).

92. Grosser, A., *op. cit.*, p. 568.

93. *See* the present author's article 'Britain, Europe and the Atlantic Community' in the special number of *International Organisation*, already referred to.

II THE CONDITIONS OF COEXISTENCE

94. Letter of the Central Committee of the CCP to the Central Committee of CPSU of 14 June 1963.

95. Open letter from the Central Committee of CPSU to party organisations and all Communists of the Soviet Union, 14 July 1963.

96. Statement of aims by world Communist parties of November 1960.

97. Letter of CPSU, 14 July 1963.

98. Statement by Soviet Government, 21 September 1963.

99. Letter of Central Committee of the CCP of 14 June 1963.

INDEX

Abbas, Ferhat, 207
Abboud, General, 206
Accra: Soviet cultural centre in, 200; African heads of state conference (1958), 215
Acheson, Dean, 73, 74, 79
Addis Ababa, 198; conference of African heads of state (1963), 207, 213, 215
Aden, 157, 161
Adenauer, Dr, 105-7, 109, 110, 114-16, 118, 132, 137, 277
Adoula, Mr, 209, 210
Aflaq, Michel, 149
African Communist, 212
African Institute of the Academy of Sciences, Moscow, 193, 194, 204
African National Congress, 194
African Unity Organisation, 211, 215
Afro-Asian grouping, 213, 214
Afro-Asian Journalists' Association, 182
Afro-Asian Solidarity Conferences, 216; (1955), 151-2, 173, 182, 195, 213; (1958, 1960, 1963), 213, 216-17
Afro-Asian writers' conferences: Tashkent (1958), 214; Cairo (1962), 216
Afro-Shirazi party (Zanzibar), 204
Ahidjo, President, 207, 218
Aidit, D. N., 181, 182
Albania, 239, 256, 316
Alexandria, 154
Algeria, 286, 297; and USSR, 207-8; Communist party in, 212; trade agreement with China, 217
Alimin (Indonesian politician), 168
Alliance for Progress (OAS), 222, 229, 233-7, 270

Allied Control Commission, Germany, 89, 95
Allied Control Council, 103, 126, 219
Andrade, Mario d', 210
Angola, 203; Angolan freedom fighters, 209
Anti-Fascist People's Freedom League (Burma), 167, 168
'Appeal of the Fifty Generals', 87
APRA party (Peru), 226
Arbenz (Guatemalan dictator), 227-9
Ardahan, 141
Arévalo (Guatemalan dictator), 227
Argentina, 224, 240
Armas, Castillo, 227
Aswan dam, 153
Atlantic Supreme Council, 110
Atomic bomb, 63-4, 142
Attlee, C. R., 142
Attlee-Nu agreement (1947), 170
Australia, 178; joins SEATO, 176
Austria, 55, 263; occupation of, 59; peace treaty for, 264
Azerbaijan, 141, 142

Baath party (Syria), 149, 151, 156
Babu, Abdul Rahman, 204
Baghdad Pact (later CENTO; 1955), 152-5, 159, 198, 214
Bakdash, Khaled, 147
Bandung, Afro-Asian conference in (1955), 151-2, 173, 182, 195, 213
Bangkok, 178
Bao Dai, 166, 175, 176
Barisan Socialis party (Singapore), 184
Basutoland, 212
Batista (Cuban dictator), 224, 230
Bayerische Partei, 113

337

Belgium, 215

Benelux, 102

Benes, Eduard, 55, 61

Bereitschaften, the, 106, 109

Berlin, 46, 287, 289, 322; the Social Democrat City Council, 100; Soviet claim it as part of their Zone, 107, 128; in relation to the German problem, 120-2; Soviet pressure on, 122-6; Inter-Allied Kommandatura, 123, 124, 126; the Magistrat, 124, 126, 130; split into two, 126-31; blockade of, 128-31 (other references, 54-9, 97, 98, 103-4, 107); lessening of tension, 131-3; ultimatum of 1958, and the crisis of the next three years, 133-7; hope of a solution, 137-9

Berlin conference (1954), 115-16

Bessarabia, 51

Bevin, Ernest, 96, 142, 146, 152

Bidault, Georges, 101, 110

Bismarck, 101

Bizonia, 100-3, 128; Economic Council, 100, 103

Bolívar, Simón, 226

Bolivia, 224, 236

Bonn, 107

Borneo, 184, 262

Brazil, 109, 240; anti-Americanism in, 229, 233-4, 238

Brazzaville conference (1946), 196

British Cameroons, 207

British East Africa, 203

British Guiana, 261, 262

Brussels Treaties, 54, 104, 116

Bucharest, 249; Conference, 254

Budapest, 250

Buenos Aires Conference (1936), 229

Bulganin, Marshal, 153

Bulgaria, 50

Bundestag, 109

Burma, 164, 185, 186; nominal independence under Japan, 165; Communist schism in, 167-8; Attlee-Nu agreement, 170; NeWin's *coup d'état*, 186

Byrnes, J. F., 73, 142, 145; on Germany, 48, 100

Cairo, 210; Conference (1943), 73; Afro-Asian writers' conference (1962), 216

Calcutta youth conference, 169-70

Cambodia, 173; American intervention, 175; leanings towards China, 186-7

Cameroun, 207, 210, 217, 297

Camp David Meeting (1959), 135, 252-3

Canada, 262; Canada Act (1867), 196

Caracas Conference (1954), 228

Castro, Fidel, 220, 224, 230, 233, 239, 270, 271; popularity ebbs, 231; symbol of independence, 231; theory of revolution, 234, 237, 240-1; denounces Escalante, 236; and the Sino-Soviet dispute, 239-40, 261-2

Castro, Pedro, 166, 167

CDIN (Comité pour la Défense des Intérêts Nationaux; Laos), 177

CENTO (formerly Baghdad Pact, *q.v.*), 159

Central Africa, 203, 204

Central Intelligence Agency (CIA), American, 177, 228, 293

CGT, 206

Chiang Kai-shek, 62-4, 67-72, 80, 81, 144

Chile, 226, 228, 242; Communists in, 226, 236, 238, 240

China: Kuomintang - Communist struggle, 62-3; treaties with USA and USSR, 64, 72-3; and the Communist occupation of Manchuria, 65-8; the civil war, 68-71, 171; Communist victory in, 71; American policy, 71-3; and the Korean War, 76-81; and Formosa, 81-2; and S.-E. Asia, 164, 188-9, 260; not a great power, 171-2; invades Tibet, 172; phases of diplomacy, 172-5; ideological rift with USSR, 174, 180, 208, 216-18, 220, 243-62, 302, 327-8; and African affairs, 204, 208, 213, 216-19; and Cuba, 237-41, 258; intellectual isolation, 297; concept of the 'just war', 299-300; indifferent

China—*cont.*
to colonies on her doorstep, 301; and revolution in capitalist countries, 303; outlook on war, 311
China Aid Act (USA), 72
Chinchow, Manchuria, 66
Chingwangtao, 65
Chou En-lai, 152, 173-4, 205, 217, 218, 249
Christian Democrat Party (CDU; Germany), 85, 104, 105, 124
Chu Teh, 64-5
Churchill, Winston, 91, 141, 142, 278; Fulton speech, 53; and Germany, 89
Clandestine Communist Organisation (Sarawak), 184, 185
Clay, General, 48, 96, 128
Colombia, 240
Comecon countries, 203
Cominform (Communist Information Bureau), 54, 55, 108, 109
Comintern, 169, 191, 294, 301, 302
Common Market, 197, 277, 278
Conakry, 201, 206; Afro-Asian Solidarity Conference (1960), 213
Congo, the, 286, 297, 324; and the USSR, 194, 203, 208-9
Copper Belt, 194
Cotonou Congress of (French) West African Trade Unions (1957), 201, 206
Council of Europe, 266
CPSU (Communist Party of the Soviet Union): Twentieth Congress (1956), 151, 194-5, 249, 250, 254, 315; Central Committee, 237, 238, 308; concept of its international duty, 314
Cuba, 137, 220, 258, 261, 270, 286, 294, 297, 315, 316, 326; and Zanzibar, 204; and the USA, 223-4, 226, 290; anti-American nationalism in, 228; and the cold war, 229; enters Socialist camp, 229-32; American invasion and miscalculation, 232-7; theories of revolution, and attitudes to USSR and China, 237-42; survival of revolutionary régime, 325
Cuban Independence Movement, 230
Cyprus, 159, 297

Czechoslovakia, 203; rejects Marshall Plan, 54; Soviet coup in, 54-6, 108; arms deal with Egypt, 149

Dairen, 65
Dakar, 206; conference of African foreign ministers (1963), 209
Dalton, Hugh, 96
Dar-es-Salaam, 205
DDR (German Democratic Republic, *q.v.*; *and see* East Germany)
de la Torre, Haya, 226
Denmark, 308
Dhahran, 146
Diem, Ngo Dinh, 82, 176, 177, 179, 186, 187
Dien Bien Phu, 80, 81, 83, 172, 173, 176
Dis-imperialism, Soviet concept of, 196, 203
Djakarta conference of Afro-Asian journalists (1963), 216
Dominican Republic, 225, 241
Douglas-Home, Sir Alec, 184
Dulles, J. F., 81, 115, 132, 246, 278; and the Middle East, 148-9, 152-3; differences with Eden, 152; and Vietnam, 176; attitude to neutrality, 323

East Africa, and the USSR, 194, 204, 205
East Germany, 89, 90, 103, 291; Soviet control of, 49-50; rising of 1953, 114, 132, 269; Communist party in, 122-6; refugees from, 136; and Berlin, 122 ff.
Eastern Europe, Soviet control of, 51-3, 59-60
Eden, Sir Anthony, 148; and Germany, 89, 115-17, 132; and the Middle East, 148-9, 152-3; differences with Dulles, 152
Egypt, 144, 147, 214, 286; foreign policy, 146; agreement with UK (1954), 148; arms deal with Czechoslovakia, 149; Soviet success in, 150; clash with Israel (1955), 151; Eden's resentment with, 152; the Suez crisis, 153, 291; British influence

The Cold War

Egypt—*cont.*
eliminated, 155; Communist party
in, 212
Eisenhower, President: and the Korean
War, 78-9; meets Khrushchev, 135,
252-3; and Vietnam, 176
Eisenhower doctrine, 154, 155
Escalante (Cuban politician), 236
Ethiopia, and the USSR, 198, 202, 216
European Advisory Commission, 89,
92, 102
European Coal and Steel Authority,
111
European Coal and Steel Community,
50
European Defence Community, 85,
111-16, 132
European Recovery Programme, 97,
108

Farouk, King, 144
Federal Republic of Germany: estab-
lished, 107, 131; and NATO, 85,
108, 110, 116, 117, 133; attitude to
German Democratic Republic, 264;
see also West Germany
Filipino Communist party, 166; *see also*
Philippines
Finland, 60
FLN (Algeria), 207
Foch, Marshal, 92
Foreign Ministers' conferences: Paris
(1946), 99, 100; London (January
1947), 99; Moscow (April 1947), 99,
101, 127; London (1953), 114;
Geneva (1959), 135
Formosa, 70, 75, 79, 81-3, 174; Geneva
conference on (1954), 81
Forrestal, James, 91, 142
France: and Germany, 47, 48, 92-3, 95,
98-9, 101-2; and the Schuman Plan,
50; Communist party in, 52, 101,
149; and Indo-China, 80-2, 171, 172;
idea of Franco-German condominium, 86; and West Germany,
110-11, 113; rejects EDC treaties,
116; and the Middle East, 146; and
Guinea, 200; objectives within
Atlantic Alliance, 277

Franco-German treaty (1963), 277
Frankfurt Charter (1948), 102
FRAP (Chile), 240, 242
Free Democrat Party (West Germany),
114
Frei, Eduardo, 228, 235
French West African Territories, 206
Friedensburg, Ferdinand, 127, 130
Friendship (later Lumumba) Univer-
sity, Moscow, 201, 208-9, 214
Front Demokrasi Rakjat (People's
Democratic Front; Indonesia), 168

Galiev, Sultan, 143
Gandhi, Mahatma, 144
Gaulle, General de, 92, 186-7, 242,
261, 270, 277
Gaza, 151
Geneva conferences: Far Eastern
(1954), 79, 81, 82, 173, 175; Summit
(1955), 84, 85, 117, 118, 132-3;
Foreign Ministers (1959), 135; fourteen-nation, on Laos (1961), 178
German Communist party, 87, 122-6
German Democratic Republic (DDR),
93, 264; established, 107; rising of
1953, 114, 132, 269; *see also* East
Germany
Germany: problem of, 45-7; economic
separation of, 48, 94-7; division of,
48-50, 58, 59, 107; the struggle for,
84-5; Soviet policy, 85-6; wartime
origin for struggle of, 86-93; the
settlement at Potsdam, 93-4; unified
in theory and separated in practice,
97-107; political parties, 104-5;
envelopment of the two Germanies
into East and West blocs, 107-12;
Soviet policy on the defensive,
112-16; end of the cold war, 116-19;
importance to the West, 272
Ghana, 211, 214, 217; and the USSR,
198-200, 202, 216
Gizenga, Mr, 209
Goa, 174, 286
Gold, Coast, 194, 199
Goldwater, Senator, 318
Gomulka, Mr, 139, 250, 251
Gouin, Felix, 111

Great Britain. *See* United Kingdom
Great Leap Forward (China), 252, 253
Greece, 51, 72, 145, 150, 286, 297, 316, 326
Grotewohl, Herr, 109
Guatemala, 229; Communism in, 226-8
Guerrillas, training and despatch of, by Communist countries, 210-11
Guevara, Ché, 238
Guinea, 214, 217; and the USSR, 200-1; trade agreement with China, 217
Gumede, J. T., 191

Hague Congress (1948), 266
Hammarskjoeld, Dag, 209
Hanga, Abdulla, 204
Hanoi, 181, 187
Harkins, General Paul, 180
Harriman, Averell, 91
Hentges, General, 178
Hiroshima, 268
Hiss, Alger, 73
History of Islamic Studies in the USSR, 148
Hitler, Adolf, 93, 101, 246
Ho Chi Minh, 166, 171, 179-81
Holden, Roberto, 209, 210
Honduras, 227, 229
Houphouet-Boigny, President, 211, 212
Hoxha, Enver, 256
Hukbalahap ('Huks'; People's Anti-Japanese Army in the Philippines), 167, 170, 185
Hulutao, 65, 67
Hungary, 50, 55, 297, 317; coalition government, 52; rising of 1956, 132, 134, 250, 269, 326
Hussein, King, 155
Hydrogen bomb, 148

Iceland, 109
India, 144, 174, 196, 253, 262; Communist party in, 217
Indo-China, 79, 80, 82, 165, 187, 286; Communist insurrection in, 171; American intervention, 175-6, 183, 275; *see also* Cambodia; Laos; Vietnam
Indonesia, 164, 260, 262, 287, 315; nominal independence under Japan, 165; party struggles in, 168, 180-2, 185; Dutch influence removed, 183; and Malaysia, 184; Sukarno's 'guided democracy', 186; debt to USSR, 187; conference of Afro-Asian trade unions in (1963), 217
International Confederation of Free Trade Unions (ICFTU), 205
International Federation of Journalists, 206-7
International Organisation of Journalists, 206-7, 216
International Union of Students, 170
Iraq, 147, 154; pact with UK (1955), 152-3
Israel, 147, 150, 151, 161, 200, 203; clash with Egypt (1955), 151; and USSR, 158, 216
Italy, 47, 61, 89; Communist party in, 52
Ivory Coast, 214
Izvestia, 193, 218

Jakarta, 182
Jamming of broadcasts, 296
Japan, 47, 56; war with China, 62-3; surrender in China and Korea, 64-7; sets up indigenous régimes, 165
Jiménez, Perez, 233
Jordan, 145, 154-6, 286

Kalinin, 200
Kardelj, Mr, 67
Kars, 141
Karume, Abeid, 204
Kasavubu, Mr, 208
Katanga, 287
Kennedy, President, 257; meets Khrushchev, 136, 187; and Cuba, 220, 237; on Western and Soviet outlooks, 328
Kenya, 204, 205
Kenya Federation of Labour, 205
Kenyatta, Jomo, 205, 213

Khrushchev, N., 151, 181, 183, 200, 217; and Berlin, 119, 133-7; and Germany, 132, 133; meets Eisenhower, 135, 252-3; meets Kennedy, 136, 187; in Egypt, 157-8; his 'troika' idea, 175; and Algeria, 207; and the Congo, 208-9; and Cuba, 220, 237-9, 290; and the rift with China, 243-4, 248-58, 260, 262, 327-8; on the 'just war', 300; opposes 'export of revolutions', 302, 316; on the cold war and coexistence, 308; on the class struggle, 313, 317; and aid to uncommitted countries, 324
Klingelhöfer, Herr, 127
Kolarz, Dr, 212
Kommunist, 314, 315
Kong Lae, Captain, 177, 178
Königsberg, 118
Korea: the war in, 55-8, 74-80, 110, 146, 172, 173, 175, 188, 225, 248; Geneva conference on (1954), 81; Cairo conference decision on, 73-4; military occupation of, 74
KPD (separate German Communist party), 88
Kuomintang party and régime, 62-3, 66-70, 80-2, 164, 247, 318
Kurdish uprising, 157

Labour Government (UK; 1945), 144, 166
LaGuma, J. A., 191
Lao Dong party (Vietnam), 179-81
Laos, 173, 179, 286, 287, 297, 301; 1961 conference on, 174-5; American intervention, 175, 177-8; breakdown of 'troika' system, 186
Lattre, General de, 172
Lava, Jesus, 167
Lava, Vincente, 166, 167
League of Nations, 267
Lebanon, 147, 156, 286, 297
Lee Kuan-yew, 187
Lenin, 121, 193, 194, 196, 217, 246, 249, 255-7
Leningrad, 192, 201
Liberals, German, 124
Libya, 51, 145

Liu Ning-yi, 216
Liu Shao Ch'i, President, 182
London conferences: Six-Power Western (1948), 103; Western Foreign Ministers (1953), 114; Malaya discussion (1961), 184; fifth pan-African congress (1945), 213
Lukman (Indonesian politician), 181
Lumumba, Patrice, 208, 209
Lumumba University, Moscow, 208-9

MacArthur, General, 64, 76-9
Machado (Cuban dictator), 223, 224
Macmillan, Harold, 134
McNamara, Mr, 180
Madagascar, 214
Madiun uprising (1948), 171, 182
Maevsky, V., 209
Magsaysay, President, 185
Maghreb countries, 214
Malaya, 165; party struggles in, 168-9; Communist insurrection, 171, 183, 185; and Malaysia, 184; independence granted to, 186
Malayan Communist Party (MCP), 168-9
Malayan People's Anti-British Army, 171
Malayan People's Anti-Japanese Army (MPAJA), 168
Malaysia, Federation of, 184, 187-8, 262, 278, 297
Malenkov, 147, 248
Mali, 214
Malinovsky, Marshal, 182
Malta Conference, 102
Manchuria, 51, 64-6, 76-7, 81; Communist occupation of, 65-8
Manila Treaty, 176, 178
Mansfield, Senator Mike, 176-7
Mao Tse-tung, 72, 166, 171, 172, 243; and the ideological rift with USSR, 243-4, 247, 251-3, 255
Marinello (Cuban Communist), 231
Marshall, General, 63, 68-9, 71-3, 102, 112, 152
Marshall Plan/Aid, 52, 54-5, 72, 103, 128, 145, 169, 263
Martí (Cuban political theorist), 230

Index

Marxist groups in West Africa, 212
Matos, Huber, 231
Matsu, 81
Mau Mau, 204
Mboya, Mr, 205
Mexico, 221, 224, 229, 233, 234
Mikolaczyk, S., 93
Mikoyan, Mr, 201
Military Assistance Advisory Group (MAAG) of USA, 175
Mir Tirzun Zade, 216, 218
Molotov, V., 49, 100
Mondlane, Dr, 209
Mongolia, Chinese People's Republic of, 83
Morgenthau, Hans, 91
Morocco, 214, 217
Moscow, 88, 198, 201; inter-Allied conference (1941), 87; Foreign Ministers' conference (1947), 101; meeting of Eastern bloc leaders (1961), 136; Institute of Middle Eastern Studies, 148; Twentieth Congress of CPSU (1956), 151, 194-5, 249, 250, 254, 315; Patrice Lumumba College, 160; African studies in, 192-3, 204; Friendship (later Lumumba) University, 201, 208-9, 214; Women's Conference (1963), 218; secret meeting of Communist parties (1960), 244-5; conference of Communist parties (1957), 250, 254; Chinese delegation in (1963), 259
Moscow Declaration, 250, 317
Moshi, Afro-Asian Solidarity Conference in (1963), 213, 216-17
Moumié, Mr, 207
Mountbatten, Admiral, 168
Mozambique, 203, 209-10
Mukden, 66
Mussadiq, Dr, 145, 147, 148
Musso (Indonesian politician), 170-1
Mussolini, 246
Mutual Security Act (USA), 150

Nadolny, Herr, 104, 107
Nagaland, 286
Nagasaki, 268

Nanking, 65, 71
Nasser, President, 149, 150, 153-5, 214; at Bandung, 151-2; and communism, 156
National Committee for Free Germany, 87
National democracies, Soviet concept of, 195-6
NATO, 105-6, 112, 115-16, 131-2, 159, 197, 209-10, 214, 262, 264, 266, 270-1; formation of, 58, 104; West Germany admitted, 85, 108, 110, 116-17, 133; USA threat, 110; purpose, and ambiguities, 264-5
Navarre, General, 172
Nazi-Soviet Pact, 120
Nehru, Mr, 174
Neo-colonialism, 183-5, 196
Netherlands, 109
Neumann, Franz, 125
Neutrality: neutralist group in Germany, 113; neutralism of Latin America, 229, 242; J. F. Dulles' attitude to, 323; question of Western defence of, 325
New Zealand: joins SEATO, 176; Communist party, 245
NeWin, General, 186
Ngo Dinh Diem. See Diem
Nhu, Ngo Dinh and Mrs, 179-80, 187
Nicaragua, 240; and USA, 223-5
Niemoller, Pastor, 113
Nigeria, 194, 211, 214, 282
Nkrumah, Dr, 191, 199-200, 213
Noack, Professor, 104, 107
North Atlantic Treaty, 54, 263
North Atlantic Treaty Organisation. See NATO
North Korea, 55, 64, 73-7, 83, 111; see also Korea
North Vietnam, 83, 176, 187, 189, 313; see also Vietnam
Norway, 272
Notgemeinschaft für den Frieden Europas, die, 113
Novy Vostock, 191
Nu, U, 174
Nuschke, Herr, 104, 107
Nyerere, President, 205, 216

OAS. *See* Alliance for Progress
Obote, Mr, 205
October Revolution (1917), 196
Oder-Neisse line, 85, 93-4, 114, 264
Odinga, Oginga, 216
OEEC, 108, 110
Office of Strategic Services (USA), 166
Okello, 'Field-Marshal', 204
Organisation of African Unity, 205
Osmena, Sergio, 167
Ostrowski, Otto, 126
Outer Mongolia, 62, 157

Padmore, G., 191
PAI party (Senegal), 212
Pajetta, Signor, 258
Pakistan, 109, 150, 262; joins Baghdad Pact, 153; joins SEATO, 176
Palestine, 142-3, 145, 150
Pan-Africanism, 203, 213-17
Panama, 241
Pan-Malayan Federation of Trade Unions, 168
Paraguay, 241
Pankow government, 133, 138
Paris Summit meeting (1960), 254
Partai Komunis Indonesia (PKI: Indonesian Communist party), 168, 181-2, 184
Partai Sosialis Indonesia (PSI; Indonesian Socialist party), 168
Pathet Lao, 177-9
People's Daily (China), 258
People's Democratic Front (Philippines), 170
People's Police (*Volkspolizei*), in East Germany, 101, 106, 110
Persia, 145, 150, 161; Soviet threat to, 51, 140-2; oil dispute with UK, 147-8; joins Baghdad Pact, 153; thrives on East-West discord, 158-9
Persian Gulf, 157
Peru, 221, 226
Petersberg agreements (1949), 107
Philippine Islands: nominal independence under Japan, 165; Communist schism in, 166-7; Communist insurrection in, 170-1, 185; join SEATO, 176; USA retain bases in, 183

Phoumi Nosavan, General, 177-8
Pieck, Wilhelm, 88
Pleven, M., 111
Poland, 50, 85, 90, 92, 109, 169, 326; Communist rule established, 51; fifth partition of, 93-4; revolt in, 250; and Chou En-lai, 251
Portugal, 210, 215
Portuguese Guinea, 203
Potekhin, Dr, 194, 199, 204, 212
Potsdam Conference, 48, 92-4, 96, 102, 112, 124, 141-2
Pravda: denounces the UAR, 157; African correspondent, 193; on national democracies, 195-6; on African liberation movements, 207-8, 215, 218; on the tasks of Communists, 218-19
Prussia, 93
Punta del Este meeting (1962), 233-4

Quemoy, 81
Quirino, President, 167

Radio Free Europe, 287
Railway Workers' Union (Sudan), 206
Renville (US Navy transport), 170
Reparations, 48, 84, 86, 94, 96, 97, 101, 103
Reuter, Ernst, 126, 130-2
Revolution of National Liberation, Castro's concept of, 234
Rhineland, 92, 100
Rio Treaty (1947), 233
Robertson, General, 110
Roca, Blas, 231
Rodriguez, Carlos Rafael, 231
Rome Congress of Italian Communist party (1962), 258
Roosevelt, F. D., 53, 91, 122, 141, 165, 223, 274, 278; 'good neighbour' policy, 223-4
Roosevelt, Theodore, 223
Roxas, Manuel, 167
Ruhr, the, 50, 92, 94-6, 100; proposed 'economic internationalisation' of, 111

Rumania, 50-1; Communist rule established, 52
Rusk, Dean, 86, 178

Saar, the, 50, 92
Saigon, 175, 176
San Martín, Grau, 224
Sarawak, 184; Sarawak United People's Party, 184
Saudi Arabia, 146, 154
Savannakhet, 177
Schroeder, Frau Louise, 127
Schumacher, Herr, 109
Schuman, Robert, 110-11
Schuman Plan, 50, 111
SEATO, 174, 176, 198, 214
SED (Socialist Unity Party; Germany), 50, 85, 88, 101, 103-5, 107, 109, 126, 129-30; defeat of, 99-100; equipped by Soviet Union, 106
Sekou Touré, President, 201, 211
Senegal, 212
Senghor, President, 219
Shanghai, 65
Shanhaikwan, 67, 68
Shanhaikwan Pass, 66
Sierra Leone, 214
Sihanouk, Prince, 174, 186, 188
Silesia, 93
Singapore, 168, 183-4, 187
Six-Power Western conference, London (1948), 103
Sjahrir, Dr Sutan, 168
Sjarifuddin (Indonesian Communist leader), 168, 170
Smith, Walter Bedell, 128, 176
Social Democrat Party. *See* SPD
Socialist Unity Party. *See* SED
Soe, Thakin, 167
Sokolovsky, Marshal, 103, 128, 129
Somalia, 204; and China and USSR, 217
Somoza, General, 223, 225
Souphannouvong, Prince, 177, 186
South Africa, Union of, 194, 203, 215, 286; Communist party in, 191, 212-13
South-East Asian Treaty Organisation. *See* SEATO

South Korea, 54-5, 64, 73-7, 79, 316, 326; *see also* Korea
South Vietnam, 176, 178, 186-7, 189, 326; *see also* Vietnam
Souvanna Phouma, Prince, 174, 177-8
Soviet Academy of Social Sciences, 148
Soviet Orientalism, 148
Soviet Union: pre-eminent position of, 46; and East Germany, 49-50, 291; control over Eastern Europe, 51-3, 59-60; Western reactions to, 53-5; responsibility for Czech coup, Berlin blockade, and Korean War, 55-8; treaty with China, 64-5, 72-3; and the occupation of Manchuria, 65-7; and Korea, 74-9, 111; and the German problem, 84-91, 93 ff., 131-2; and Poland, 93-4, 326; and Berlin, 122 ff., 291; and the Middle East, 140-1, 143, 147, 149-50, 152-62; and Turkey and Persia, 141-2, 158-9; and Asian nationalism, 147-8; and Egypt, 150, 153; and Syria, 151; and the UAR, 155-7; and Israel, 158; and S.-E. Asia, 163-4, 169-71, 180, 187, 189; ideological rift with China, 174, 180, 208, 216-18, 220, 243 ff., 302, 327-8; and African affairs, 191-8, 219; and Ethiopia, 198; and Ghana, 198-200, 202; and Guinea, 200-1; and African emergent nationalisms, 203-13; backs Afro-Asian grouping, 214; and pan-Africanism, 215; and Latin America, 220, 226, 228; and Cuba, 231-2, 236-41, 270-1, 290; and Hungary, 250, 326; and the UN, 267; concept of the 'just war', 299-300; and revolution in capitalist countries, 302-4; idea of 'cold war', 307-17; possible Western reactions to Soviet 'cold war', 317-28
Spain, 266, 286
Spanish Civil War, 246
SPD (Social Democratic Party; Germany), 85, 104-5, 109, 124; in Berlin, 125-7, 130
Sputnik, the, 155
Stalin, 54, 61, 91, 114, 124, 147, 158, 169, 191-4, 256, 314; and Germany,

Stalin—*cont.*
47, 49-50, 123, 131; and Eastern Europe, 51-3; and Czechoslovakia, 55-6; and Tito, 56; and the Berlin blockade, 56-7; and Korea, 57; and Finland, 60; and China, 65, 67, 246-9; and the Middle East, 141; and Asian nationalism, 144; on establishing communism in France and Italy, 311; and Communist régimes in remote areas, 316

Stettin, 93
Stilwell, General 'Vinegar Joe', 63
Stimson, Mr, 91, 223
Stuttgart, 100
Sudan, 194, 202; trade unionism in, 206
Suez Canal, 146, 153-5
Suez crisis, 153, 291
Sukarno, President, 174, 182, 184, 187
Syria, 147, 151, 154, 160; joins the UAR, and revolution of 1958, 155-6

Taipeh, 80, 82
Tanganyika, 202, 205
Taruc, Luis, 167, 170
Tashkent, Afro-Asian writers' conference in (1958), 214
Taylor, General Maxwell, 176, 179-80
Teheran Conference, 141
Test-ban treaty (1963), 239, 302
Thailand: joins SEATO, 176; forces sent to, 178
Tibet, 172, 173, 286
Tientsin, 65
Times, The, on Churchill's Fulton speech, 53-4
Tito, Marshal, 56-7, 72, 248
Togliatti, Signor, 251, 262
Tonking, 171
Trade unionism, 205-6
Tripolitania, 142
Troika system, 175, 186
Trujillo, General, 225
Truman, President, 57, 61, 142; and China, 68, 69, 73; dismisses MacArthur, 77; and Korea, 79-80; on the Soviet danger, 145; and Indo-China, 175

Truman doctrine, 51, 52, 72, 97, 127, 145
Truong Chinh, 181
Tsingtao, 65
Tudeh party (Persia), 141
Tun, Than, 167
Tunisia, 214; Communist party in, 212
Turkey, 72, 145-6, 150, 161; Soviet threat to, 51, 140-2; uncertainty of her outlook, 159

Ubico, General, 226
Uganda, 210
UGTAN (Union Générale des Travailleurs Afrique Noire), 206
Ulbricht, Herr, 87, 123, 135, 138-9
Ulbricht group, 123-4, 132
Umma party (Zanzibar), 204
Uncommitted countries, 324-5
United Arab Republic (UAR), 156-7, 217
United Fruit Company, 221
United Kingdom: and problem of Germany, 47-8; joins NATO, 58; recognises Communist China, 71; and Korea, 80; policy on Germany, 88 ff., 132; and Poland, 94-5; and Berlin, 137; and Egypt, 144, 148, 152-3; differences with USA, 145-6, 152; and Iraq, 152-3; and Israel, 161; and S.-E. Asia, 165-6, 178, 183-4, 186-9; and Malaysia, 184, 187; and East Africa, 204; and Zanzibar, 205; and Latin America, 221; and the Atlantic Alliance, 278-80; and Jordan and Lebanon, 325-6
United Nations, 82, 109, 122, 142, 143, 157, 173, 210, 213, 233, 263, 270, 288, 290, 298, 317, 327; and Korea, 55, 74-7; and Malaysia, 184; Economic Commission for Africa, 202; and the Congo, 209; a source of division to the West, 267; and the uncommitted countries, 324, 325
United States: pre-eminent position of, 46; and problem of Germany, 47-8; the Truman doctrine, 51-2, 72, 97, 127, 145; joins NATO, 58; and China, 63, 64; intervenes in Chinese